Tibet is my Country

Books by Heinrich Harrer

SEVEN YEARS IN TIBET
THE WHITE SPIDER

Heinrich Harrer and Thubten Jigme Norbu meet in Kitzbühel in 1959

TIBET
IS MY COUNTRY

The Autobiography of
THUBTEN JIGME NORBU
Brother of the Dalai Lama

as told to
HEINRICH HARRER

Translated from the German by
EDWARD FITZGERALD

E. P. DUTTON & CO., INC.
NEW YORK 1961

TO HIS HOLINESS THE

DALAI LAMA

IN RESPECT AND
FRATERNAL LOVE

The Tibetan Calendar

1927	Fire-Hare Year		1957	Fire-Bird Year
1928	Earth-Dragon Year		1958	Earth-Dog Year
1929	Earth-Snake Year		1959	Earth-Pig Year
1930	Iron-Horse Year		1960	Iron-Mouse Year
1931	Iron-Sheep Year		1961	Iron-Bull Year
1932	Water-Ape Year		1962	Water-Tiger Year
1933	Water-Bird Year		1963	Water-Hare Year
1934	Wood-Dog Year		1964	Wood-Dragon Year
1935	Wood-Pig Year		1965	Wood-Snake Year
1936	Fire-Mouse Year		1966	Fire-Horse Year
1937	Fire-Bull Year		1967	Fire-Sheep Year
1938	Earth-Tiger Year		1968	Earth-Ape Year
1939	Earth-Hare Year		1969	Earth-Bird Year
1940	Iron-Dragon Year		1970	Iron-Dog Year
1941	Iron-Snake Year		1971	Iron-Pig Year
1942	Water-Horse Year		1972	Water-Mouse Year
1943	Water-Sheep Year		1973	Water-Bull Year
1944	Wood-Ape Year		1974	Wood-Tiger Year
1945	Wood-Bird Year		1975	Wood-Hare Year
1946	Fire-Dog Year		1976	Fire-Dragon Year
1947	Fire-Pig Year		1977	Fire-Snake Year
1948	Earth-Mouse Year		1978	Earth-Horse Year
1949	Earth-Bull Year		1979	Earth-Sheep Year
1950	Iron-Tiger Year		1980	Iron-Ape Year
1951	Iron-Hare Year		1981	Iron-Bird Year
1952	Water-Dragon Year		1982	Water-Dog Year
1953	Water-Snake Year		1983	Water-Pig Year
1954	Wood-Horse Year		1984	Wood-Mouse Year
1955	Wood-Sheep Year		1985	Wood-Bull Year
1956	Fire-Ape Year		1986	Fire-Tiger Year

The element which is the first part of the name of each year, counts as "male" the first time, and "female" the second. Thus 1960 is the "male" Iron-Mouse Year. Apart from these divisions into elements and animals there is also a cycle of sixty years. At the moment, according to the Tibetan Calendar, we are living in the sixteenth cycle, which began in 1927 with the "female Fire-Hare year."

Contents

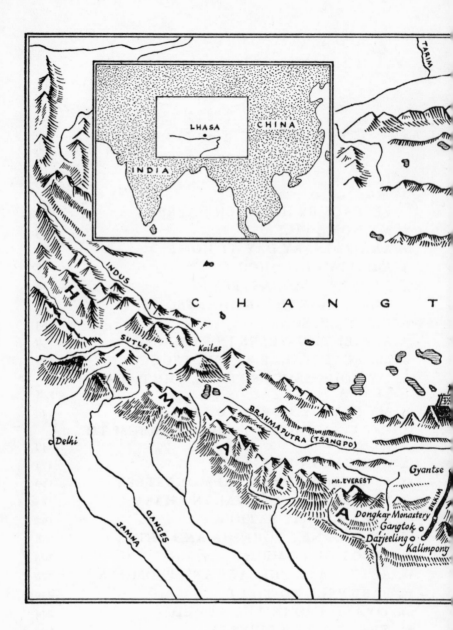

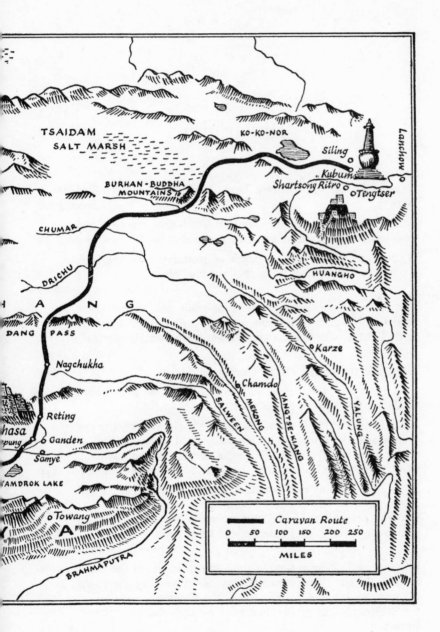

TSAIDAM
SALT MARSH

KO-KO-NOR

Siling

Lanchow

Kubum
Shartsong Ritro

Tengtser

BURHAN-BUDDHA
MOUNTAINS

CHUMAR

HUANGHO

DRICHU

H A N G

DANG PASS

Karze

Nagchukha

Chamdo

SALWEEN

MEKONG

YANGTSE-KIANG

YALUNG

hasa

Reting

pung

Ganden

Samye

KAMDROK LAKE

Towang

A

BRAHMAPUTRA

Caravan Route

0   50   100 150 200 250
MILES

Illustrations

Chronology

1919 Birth of Tsering Dröma in Tengtser.
1922 Sixteenth Day of the Eighth Month: Birth of Thubten Jigme Norbu in Tengtser.
1928 Summer: Birth of Gyalo Döndrub in Tengtser.
1931 Second Month: Norbu leaves Tengtser for Shartsong Ritrö.
1931 Eighth Day of the Fifth Month: Norbu leaves Shartsong Ritrö for Kumbum.
        Eighth Month: Norbu becomes a monk in Kumbum
1932 Summer: Norbu's first trip to Chukhar Ritrö.
1933 Spring: Lhagsam becomes Norbu's teacher.
        Fifteenth Day of the First Month: Tsering Dröma comes with her affianced, Püntso Trashi, and her parents to visit Norbu in Kumbum.
        Autumn: Birth of Lobsang Samten in Tengtser.
        December 17: Death of the Thirteenth Dalai Lama in Lhasa. Tibetan date: Thirtieth Day of the Tenth Month.
1935 January: Norbu's trip to Ditsa Ritrö.
        May: Norbu's trip to Shartsong Ritrö.
        June 6: Birth of the Fourteenth Dalai Lama in Tengtser.
1936 Second Month: Ohön Yongdzin becomes Norbu's professor in logic.
1936 Spring: Norbu takes his first examination: admission to the general assembly of monks.
        Seventh Month: Norbu and a friend cheat at an examination.
1937 Fifteenth Day of the First Month: Lobsang Samten begins his life as a monk in Kumbum.
        Early Summer: Death of the Panchen Lama in Kantze.
        Late Summer: Arrival of the Official Commission from Lhasa in Kumbum to conduct the search for the new Dalai Lama.
1938 Autumn: Death of Norbu's first teacher, Püntso.
1938-39 Winter: Norbu's youngest brother, the Dalai Lama, comes to Kumbum.

1939 Fifteenth Day of the First Month: Norbu takes part in the Butter-Lamp Celebration in Kumbum.

Fifth Month: Norbu's parents leave for Lhasa with the Dalai Lama.

1940 Fifth Month: Tsering Dröma and her husband Püntso Trashi leave for Lhasa.

Seventh Month: Norbu sits for the examination of the first five classes.

1941 Fifth Month: Norbu leaves Kumbum for Lhasa.

Summer: Norbu's younger sister Jetsün Pema born in Lhasa.

Ninth Month: Norbu's arrival in Lhasa.

Eleventh Month: Norbu enters Drepung Monastery near Lhasa.

1943 Summer: Building of "Changtseshar," the palace of the Dalai Lama's parents in Lhasa.

1944 Autumn: Gyalo Döndrub and Püntso Trashi leave for India. India.

1945 Summer: Lobsang Samten joins Norbu in Drepung Monastery.

1946 First Month: Norbu's youngest brother Tenzing Chögyel, later to be Ngari Rimpoche, born in Lhasa.

Seventh Month: Norbu sits for his Parchin examination in Drepung.

1947 First Day of the First Month: Death of Norbu's father in Lhasa.

Summer: Dalai Lama visits the monasteries of Drepung and Sera.

Autumn: Norbu leaves for India and China.

1948 Summer: Norbu returns to Kumbum.

1949 Ninth Day of the Third Month: Norbu becomes Abbot of Kumbum.

Autumn: Chinese communist forces enter Amdo.

1950 Ninth Day of the Third Month: Norbu resigns the Abbotship of Kumbum.

Sixth Month: Norbu leaves Kumbum for Lhasa.

Tenth Day of the Tenth Month: Dalai Lama takes full powers.

Tenth Month: Arrival of Norbu in Lhasa.

Eleventh Month: Norbu leaves southward with his mother and brothers and sisters for the Chumbi Valley.

1950 Twelfth Month: Flight of the Dalai Lama to the Chumbi Valley; residence in Dungkar Monastery.

1951 Spring: Norbu flies from India to the United States.

Summer: Norbu in Fairfax, West Virginia, for convalesence.

1952 October: Norbu leaves for the World Buddhist Congress in Japan, where he remains for three years.

1955 Summer: Norbu goes via Hongkong to India where he meets Gyalo Döndrub and Tsering Dröma.

Autumn: Norbu flies via Europe back to the United States.

1955–56 Winter: Norbu studies English at the University of Columbia.

1956 Autumn: Norbu goes via Europe to India where he meets his mother and his brothers again.

November: Arrival of the Dalai Lama in India.

1957 January: Discussion between Norbu and Chou En-lai.

February: Return of the Dalai Lama to Tibet.

Autumn: Norbu goes back to the United States via Japan.

November 16: Lobsang Samten arrives in the United States.

December 15: Norbu leaves the United States on a pilgrimage to India, Ceylon and Burma.

1958 May: Return to New York.

1958 Autumn: Norbu invited to the World Buddhist Congress in Bangkok.

1959 May: Norbu goes via Tokio to India where he meets his mother, the Dalai Lama and his other brothers, and his sisters.

Summer: Norbu working on this book. Refugee problems.

Preface

MORE than one reason has impelled me to write the biography of Thubten Jigme Norbu, the eldest brother of the Dalai Lama. I was, and still am, deeply impressed by his life; in particular because it is a very typical reflection of the fate of the Tibetan people in our day, and because I love Tibet. And then, though at my original suggestion, Norbu himself ultimately asked me to write this book for him. In doing so I have carefully refrained from expressing any opinions of my own; in fact it almost seemed better to me that I should not mention our personal relationships at all.

Without adding anything, and without suppressing anything, the book contains just what Norbu himself told me in many days and nights of conversation. If, nevertheless, the reader should feel my own emotion between the lines I must ask him to forgive me. My aim was to make myself an objective chronicler, and I hope that I may have succeeded as well as possible.

It was in January 1946 that Peter Aufschnaiter and I arrived in Lhasa, sick and exhausted after a flight across the Himalayas which had taken us almost two years. It was in Lhasa, in the house of Mr Thangme, the "Master of Electricity," that I first met Norbu. The quiet and yet humorous young man made a deep impression on me immediately. At that time he was living in the Drepung Monastery not far from Lhasa as the incarnation of Tagtser Rimpoche; and it was there that I met him again soon afterwards when I went on a visit to the monastery, which is probably the biggest of its kind in the world. We spent a beautiful summer's day on the banks of a nearby arm of the river

Kyichu, and Norbu sat watching me with all the delight of a
youngster as I dived again and again into the water. Later I met
him once more, but in the following year he went off on a pilgrimage, returning after many adventures only in 1950.

The story of Norbu's life traces the development of the situation in Tibet in those years, showing how it gradually became
more and more serious and finally hopeless. It was in the autumn
of 1950 that the Dalai Lama first had to flee from Lhasa. For
six months after that he resided in Chumbi not far from the
frontier of India. Norbu and I were amongst those who accompanied him. I shall never forget those days, because they were
the last we spent on Tibetan soil. The anxious problems raised
by the immediate future left none of us any peace. I was busy
with my own plans and I did not know that Norbu had already
made up his mind to leave his country. One morning he was just
not there. I was very surprised at the time to find that a man who
was within a few days of a difficult and decisive decision affecting
his whole life could remain so calm and self-possessed, for there
had been nothing in that otherwise so expressive face to indicate
the existence of a problem which must nevertheless have occupied
him day and night. Today I realise that this rare capacity which
allowed him to remain silent even towards his friend saved us
from a good deal of misunderstanding.

It was only when we met again in New York in 1954 that we
could talk freely and without embarrassment once more. We
spent many hours together in his small hotel-room on Lexington
Avenue. They were hours which took us back again to Lhasa, a
city which meant a great deal to me too. Norbu would play one
or other of his records of Tibetan music, and, moved by the
familiar sounds from his own country, he would talk to me—of
his childhood, of his mother, and of his brothers and sisters, and of
the Tibetan people, who are so much misunderstood in the West,
where anyone who has grotesque stories to tell can be sure of
eager listeners. Perhaps it was during these quiet and pleasant
hours that the idea first came to me that Norbu's life was a story
that ought to be written, but I can't really say for certain.

But when I did get the idea I cautiously tried to familiarise
him with it. At first, out of modesty, he opposed the idea. He
who, until comparatively recently, had been the Abbot of one of
the biggest and most important monasteries in Tibet, now
regarded himself as just another Tibetan refugee; and one who
was better off than most only because he happened to belong to
the family of the Dalai Lama. It was only when I pointed out to
him that with such a book he could help his country and his
people that he began to look at the proposal with greater interest.
But I did not over-persuade him. I wanted to force nothing. If
he decided to agree, then his decision must be carefully considered and arrived at gradually.

In the following years we heard little of each other. In 1957 I
went on my African expedition to the Ruwenzori Mountains in
the Belgian Congo, and by that time I had practically forgotten
the tentative proposal I had made to Norbu in New York. My
intention then was to write a book on Lhasa, the capital of Tibet;
an idea which had been in my mind for a long time. Then one
December morning—it was in 1958, and my diaries were lying
ready on the desk before me—the telephone bell rang. I lifted
the receiver and said my name, and a familiar voice answered
in Tibetan: "Henrig, I'm in Vienna."

"I'll be right along to see you, Norbu," was my answer as
soon as he had told me where he was staying. That same
evening we were together once more.

He now told me that in the meantime he had decided that I
should write his life as I had proposed, and we both agreed to
make a start within the next few months. Neither of us realised
then just how movingly topical our plan would become in a very
short space of time. In the following spring the world Press gave
big headlines to the insurrection in Tibet, and with that both
Norbu and I had something more important to do than spend
our time in a peaceable country house writing a book. Norbu
hurried off to his brother in India, and I took a plane to Dehra-
Dun with a commission from a British newspaper to interview
the refugees from a country which had become my own second

Fatherland. By a strange coincidence the Dalai Lama himself
had found asylum there, in the very place from which, fifteen
years earlier to the day, I had dared the flight from imprisonment
which had ended under the protection of the Dalai Lama himself and been crowned with the inestimable gift of his personal
friendship.

After that I acted for quite a long time as adviser and interpreter to Norbu, who was travelling around at the instructions
of the Dalai Lama to mobilise aid for the Tibetan refugees. In
those weeks I had every opportunity of seeing how seriously
and with what determination he carried out his tasks. His own
harsh fate, the loss of his country, the flight of his brother and of
his family, had all combined to hurt him deeply, and he now
looked for consolation and relief by devoting himself with heart
and soul to the great international relief action for the Tibetan
refugees. Although this new activity was very different from the
life of isolation and contemplation he had been used to in a
Buddhist monastery, he found no difficulty in regarding and
accepting it as the continuation of his old monastic life. Whether
as silent monk or busy organiser, he was serving the cause in
which he believed.

It was not until the autumn of 1959, when we were both in
Europe again, that we were at last able to turn our attention to
our long-cherished plan. I bought a sound-recorder and took
down Norbu's story on about twenty recording tapes. Tibetans
like to talk, and they talk well, and yet at first Norbu was hesi-
tant. He was reluctant to plunge into the story of his life. But
then he was quickly overwhelmed by all the memories that
came flooding up; and thanks to an astonishingly good memory,
which had been well trained by intensive study from childhood
on, he was soon able to recall the slightest detail. At first I had
frequently to beg him to go into greater detail, because for
reasons of diffidence he was inclined to omit too many important
points. Many things never before recorded in our literature on
Tibet were incorporated at my request in our recording tapes.
However, I was unable to alter his decision to talk as little

as possible about the religion of his people. He explained that as
so far he had passed only two out of his five examinations as a
monk, he was not yet a fit and proper person to deal with such
matters in any detail; and I had to be content with that.

The hours in which Norbu spoke for the tape-recorder are
unforgettable for me. His expressive features reflected every
mood of the story he was telling. He laughed heartily when he
was talking of amusing incidents. But how often during his story
was he near to tears! When he talked of his mother his voice
would become gentle, and there was a strange charm about him
which was all the more effective for me because I had had the
privilege of getting to know that remarkable woman.

And how seriously he took his responsibilities once he had
accepted them! It was only after great inner wrestling that he
had finally decided to give his story to the world, but now that
he had done so in order to help his country and his people
nothing was too much trouble and no amount of care too great.
He was determined to set down the truth, and nothing but the
truth. If he were in some doubt as to a date, he took care to stress
that he was unsure. And this, incidentally, is the explanation for
one or two more arid patches here and there in the book.

Our further work on the story recorded in Tibetan proceeded
by my translating the original text into German on fresh tapes,
which then served as the basis for the written version. I know a
great deal of the literature which has been written about Tibet,
and during the seven years I spent in that country I kept my eyes
and ears open very thoroughly. But during the course of my work
with Norbu on this book I realised that even the most conscien-
tious and intelligent traveller and explorer can never hope to
produce more than patchwork. Almost all books, except perhaps
those which confine themselves to some very specialised subject, contain errors which are very often not the fault of their
authors. Sometimes, for example, they have been deliberately
misled by their Tibetan informants. Very often this has been
due to nothing more than the childish pleasure simple people
experience in pulling other people's legs, particularly learned

ones. But very often too, of course, it was due to the fear of
giving away some secret. For example, no outsider has ever seen
the sacred tree in Serdong Temple in Kumbum. Nevertheless,
quite a number of books on Tibet contain detailed descriptions
of this tree. In reality, however, the tree described is always some
other tree, also remarkable because of its great age, and at the
same time more readily accessible to the outsider, and which
the monks have presented to the stranger as the sacred tree
itself.

When I had completed my German manuscript I translated it
back word for word into Tibetan for Norbu, and he corrected
minor errors and inaccuracies which had managed to creep in.
It was in this connection that he told me once again why he had
decided to exercise the greatest possible reserve where religious
matters were concerned. He declared that he regarded faith and
meditation as the innate and fundamental treasure of each individual, and therefore something about which it was impossible to
generalise. Thus as a result of this attitude only those things
he knew and experienced personally appear in the following
pages.

During the past few years in particular a wretchedly irrespon-
sible pseudo-literature about Tibet has spread, once more causing
a great deal of regrettable confusion. Just because it is so widespread we are unable to smile contemptuously and dismiss it as
summarily as it deserves. The Tibetan monk, or lama, makes do
with two eyes just like any other man, and when he wants to fly
in the air he uses an ordinary aeroplane for the purpose. That is
the sober truth, and in consequence those who prefer fairy tales
will probably be disappointed by what Norbu has to say, although
it represents the first authentic autobiography of a Tibetan which
has ever appeared in the outside world. Because of the unusual
circumstances of his life Norbu has been privileged to see things
that only a small group of specially chosen people ever see or
know anything about. Even so, monks flying through the air
without the aid of human inventions, third eyes, and so on, were
not amongst them.

All that remains for me is to recommend this book of my friend Norbu to readers with the wishes expressed in conclusion on our tape-recordings:

Trashi deleg! May much good fortune be yours!
Lha gyal lo! May the gods be victorious!

HEINRICH HARRER

1. My Home Village

THE Tibetan calendar has both good and bad days. I was fortunate enough to be born on a good day. My mother has often told me that my appearance was greeted with great joy, because I was the first male child, and it was hoped that I would be the first of a long line of healthy sons.

As a matter of fact I couldn't really have been born on a bad day anyway, because a very sensible Tibetan custom allows us just to strike any such bad day out of the calendar altogether; so that, for example, instead of counting the ominous thirteenth we just count the fourteenth twice. I came into this world on the sixteenth day of the eighth month of the Water-Dog year. My mother gave birth to me in the byre of our small peasant farmstead in the village of Tengtser in the province of Amdo. The meaning of "Tengtser" is "place on the heights"; that is to say, something like "mountain village," or "upper village," and, in fact, our village was perched on a hill surrounded by still higher mountains, all of which were dominated by the great glacier mountain Kyeri.

Tengtser was a small and poor village on the caravan route which leads from Siling, the seat of our Chinese government administration, to Labrang Trashi Khyi, the second largest monastery in the province. There were only thirty cottages in the village all told, and it was surrounded by many fields which were wonderfully green in summer and deep in snow in winter. The gentle slopes and the distant mountainsides were covered with aromatic conifer trees, and in those woods grew certain very tasty berries which made a pleasant change on our menu.

Our village lay higher than the other villages in the neighbourhood and it had therefore only a very small brook. If we ever
wanted to see a larger one, or perhaps even a river, we had to
walk for a good hour. These brooks, which were fed by the nearby glaciers, were usually crystal clear. We children loved playing
with and in the water, in which we caught more than one little
goldfish. But during the rains these gentle brooks, even the
smallest of them, would swell into dangerous reddish-brown
masses of rushing water which carried away the top soil of the
fields. In the fifth and the sixth months of the year it often rained
for several days on end, and then, because our soil was of loess,
you could hardly leave the house because the ground was so
swampy. But the rain was good for our fields, and it meant that
we always had enough water. Like those of all country people,
our lives were determined by the sun and the rain; and in times
of both drought and flood the monks would be called in to intercede with the gods on our behalf.

Tengtser was actually pasture land for the bigger village of
Balangtsa, which lay about two hours' distance away, and in
summer the peasants would bring their herds of cattle to us
to pasture. Our fields were rich with herbs and flowers and the
cows did well there and gave wonderfully rich milk. At one time
only herdsmen had stayed on the spot, living in their black tents
made of yak hair. But when the population in the valley increased
some families moved to our hilltop. They soon noticed that oats,
barley and wheat—and potatoes, too, and various kinds of
vegetable—did well in the soil on the higher ground, and so they
built themselves permanent houses so that they could stay there
through the hard winters too. Our house, like all the others, was
built at ground-level and it had a broad, flat roof. It happened
to be built against two other houses, and the small group thus
formed stood a little higher than the other houses of the village.
From our roof you could see far into the fruitful countryside
below. It was dominated by the great "house-mountain" Kyeri.
The sight of this majestic glacier mountain, which was the throne
of our protective deity Kye, always made our hearts beat higher.

Our house was rectangular in shape, and it had a big inner courtyard. When at dusk the one great door was closed, we felt very safe and well protected as though in a small fortress. There were no windows or other openings in the outside walls, though in the roof there were two chimneys and three air-holes. The rain in summer and the mountain thaw in spring brought us a great deal of water, and therefore around the roof were small gutters with spouts giving out into the courtyard. They were made of gnarled juniper wood and they had the oddest shapes. We children used to take pleasure in seeing flowers or animals in them, just as we saw things in clouds; and we were always delighted when we thought of something new and amusing to compare them with. Whenever I recall my home village I always see the forest of white, weather-worn prayer-flags fluttering in the constant breeze from the mountains. I shall never forget the eerie noise they used to make when they whipped and cracked against the flagpoles when a storm was approaching from Kyeri.

Sometimes we children were allowed to help with the building of a new house in the village. The laying of the foundation walls was always a great joy for us, and with a good deal of singing and laughter we would stamp the clay down into the wooden forms to become after a while the air-dried clay bricks. And finally came the roof with its boles of wood, over which brushwood was laid to provide a firm basis for the layer of terra-cotta-like earth, laced with oil and then trodden firm, which served the inhabitants as a protection against the wet. When it was quite finished the house would be whitewashed. As all the houses were whitewashed freshly every year, in the autumn our village invariably looked as clean and shining as a new pin. When the building work was complete came the erection of the prayer-flag. Exactly over the entrance to our house there was a socket fixed in the roof to take a flagpole perhaps ten feet high. The flag itself was a large length of white cotton material on which innumerable prayers were inscribed.

You could enter our homestead only from the east or lee side, which gave us protection from the weather. Over the large, handsome door there was a coloured cover hanging from a small ledge. The great door itself pivoted on strong wooden hinges, and it opened and closed noiselessly because its wooden pivots were bound in sheepskin. You went through a wide corridor into the yard, and to the right along the side, and at the back, was a covered way. The first room to the right was the kitchen, and it took up almost the whole of the eastern wing of the house. In the north wing there was the best room, the altar-room and the khanchung, or the bedroom of our parents; and these were all connected with each other. The byre, the guest-room and the storeroom were in the western wing, whilst the stable, the kennel and the sheep-pen were in the southern wing. The yard, the covered-in way and the stalls were laid out with large flat stones, whose irregular interstices were filled with tightly packed clay. The rooms themselves had neatly laid wooden floors.

The greater part of the family life was lived in the kitchen, which was divided into two unequal halves by a stove-oven and a wooden partition with a hatch. You entered the larger part from the yard. Its ceiling was supported by a wooden post against which stood our great water tub, an earthenware container with a beautiful green glaze and a wooden cover. The long stove-oven made of clay bricks had four fireplaces. Behind the oven you went up three steps to a wooden platform which covered the floor in the smaller part of the kitchen. We would spend more than half the winter there, but it was a favourite place of ours at any time. The chimney pipes from the fireplaces went under this wooden platform and gave off a very agreeable warmth. The kitchen walls were covered with wooden panelling. The other part of the kitchen had only a stamped-earth floor, and our fuel was stacked in one corner. There were wood, yak and cow dung, brushwood and dry straw for roasting barley, which needs a quick intense fire. The oven was lighted from the side through four openings, and the fire-holes were covered by big kettles. The first kettle was for tea-making, and it was refilled several times a day. Apart from utensils of copper and brass there were also a number of earthenware pots. But milk was always kept in wooden containers.

My mother, who was an excellent cook and knew how to prepare the most tasty dishes, did almost all the work in the kitchen herself. There was a small table against one wall and on this table she used to make the pastry and the delicious rolls which are amongst my favourite food even today. She was renowned for her pastry throughout the village. She also used to make the best yeast, so much so that the other peasant women would come round and beg for some of it—always to the accompaniment of great praise. We used to have rolls both with and without yeast, but the ones we liked best were those that were baked in oil, or even butter. As a baking oven my mother used an iron tin in which she scattered glowing coals.

We had to have our grain ground in the mill by the village stream in Balangtsa. At exactly fixed times my father would turn up there pulling the mule behind him with the grain sacks on its back. In payment, one-tenth of the flour ground from the grain was left with the miller.

We ate potatoes at nearly every meal, and meat when it was available, but we didn't much care for pork, preferring beef; best of all we liked mutton. Fresh meat was really more or less confined to the autumn when the sheep were fattest and we had slaughtered. If fresh meat came on the table in summer it was because an emergency slaughtering had been carried out for some reason or other. Sometimes, too, wolves would pull down one of our animals, and then we would eat the rest, if any. The favourite cut from the sheep was the ribs, where the layer of fat was as thick as your finger. It was eaten boiled or roasted, but also raw and as dried meat.

When a sheep was slaughtered every single part of it was used, from the skull to the trotters. The intestines were drawn, carefully washed and then used as casing for blood, sausage, tsampa flour and pieces of fat. The lungs were regarded as a special delicacy. And the trotters, once the outer horny substance was peeled off, tasted excellent. We children used to love to look on when the intestines were filled and turned into sausages which, boiled or roasted, made excellent eating. We liked to roast them ourselves. The kidneys, embedded in sheaths of fat, also went into the glowing embers. Tripe was another highly prized delicacy, and it was carefully washed and prepared with herbs and spices like salad. Some tripes which were left over after the autumn slaughtering were used for storing butter in. Otherwise for the rest of the year there was only dried meat. It was easy to dry in the open, because our village was so high that there were only a few weeks in the summer when there was any danger of things going bad. In summer we lived chiefly on vegetables and salads. A favourite salad delicacy was a kind of radish which mother pickled in a wooden tub with sour gherkins. We usually used wooden spoons to eat with, but sometimes chopsticks. After use all these table utensils would be tucked into the interstices between the wall panelling.

But our staple food was tsampa flour. All flour obtained from roast grain or roast leguminous fruits was called tsampa. There are wheat tsampas, pea tsampas and maize tsampas, but the usual variety is barley tsampa. The barley is roasted in the kitchen. Sand is put into an iron frying-pan and heated over a fierce fire, and the grains are then poured onto it. As soon as they touch the hot sand they split open and a wonderful smell pervades the room. The contents of the frying-pan are then poured into a sieve through which the sand runs away. The first crisp, golden-brown grains are always eaten by the family straight away. This barley roasting is carried out only at long intervals, but then usually a whole day is devoted to it. The roasted grains are afterwards shovelled into sacks and taken to the miller to be ground into tsampa flour, which is then eaten with tea, milk or beer, or just on its own.

The preparation of the dough demands a certain skill. For example, you sprinkle tea into a wooden dish and then pour tsampa flour on top of it, then you turn the dish with the left hand in a clockwise direction whilst at the same time you stir the mixture in the opposite direction with the middle finger until it has reached the desired consistency. As children we were not adroit enough for this performance, so in order that none of the precious mixture should be lost, mother taught us to prepare the dough in a leather bag held closed with one hand whilst its contents were thoroughly kneaded with the free hand. For the big ones at table there was a dish with three compartments containing butter, tsampa flour and pieces of dried cheese respectively. This dish was then passed round in a circle. When each of us had sufficiently kneaded the dough in his own wooden bowl, he would make little balls of it and put them in his lap or line them up on the table in front of him. Tea or soup was then poured into the empty bowl, and the meal could begin. Our eating-bowls for daily use were made of birchwood, and of such a size that they could easily be held in one hand. For the children, of course, there were smaller bowls. Each bowl differed a little from its neighbour, and the most sought after were those made from gnarled knots. When the wood was being turned the most astonishing patterns would come to light, and it was the beauty and clarity of the graining which made a bowl highly prized.

Bowls intended for fermented liquor were lined with brass and even silver, and for guests the finest porcelain bowls were taken out of the cupboard under the altar. When mother visited this cupboard I would keep close to her side, because it contained other very interesting things too; for example, my favourite pastries were kept there. I knew from experience that in the presence of guests I should be able to wheedle one or two of those rolls made with milk, sugar and currants out of her. The yeast recipe for these dainties she kept a closely guarded secret.

2. An Ordinary Day at Home

NOWADAYS, when I rely almost completely on my wristwatch, it seems almost unbelievable to me how punctually our days were regulated then without a watch or clock of any kind. Of course, nature helped us quite a bit. Just before dawn the cock crowed for the first time. That woke up mother, and before long you would hear her busy in the kitchen where the fire in the oven began to crackle. Although we already had matches we still mastered the art of making fire by means of a flint. The first thing in the morning was to heat up water for mother and father. When the first grey light of dawn was visible father led the horses to water. Then was the time to wake us children. I didn't always find it easy to get up, but if I wanted to ride with my father when he took the unsaddled horses to the watering place then I had to be washed and dressed by tse-shar, which was the moment when the rays of the sun lit up the first peak. The prospect of being allowed to ride with my father to the watering place made the disagreeable duty of washing in the big copper basin not quite so onerous.

A little later mother would go into our small house chapel in order to perform the daily sacrifice. The accompanying trimming of the butter-lamps was a solemn act. First of all mother would carefully wash her hands, then she would twist a new wick out of cotton and insert it into the wick-holder, after which she would fill up the container with butter which was already standing ready melted on the stove. The lighting of the lamps was the privilege of our parents. One lamp went before the big altar in the house chapel, and the other stood in the small room of our parents before a statue of Buddha. We always accompanied them, and like them, we prostrated ourselves three times before the gods and said our prayers. Then came a further religious ceremony: the visit to the incense vase in the middle of the courtyard. This was an earthenware container in a permanent clay socket, which had openings at the sides and on top. Father or mother shovelled glowing coals through one of the side holes and then scattered herbs, usually dried alp roses, into the top. When the fragrant smoke rose up into the air, the distant Kyeri was already glowing pink, and the warm rays of the sun were already falling across our flat roof into the yard.

The working day began only after these religious ceremonies had been performed. Our first tea of the day was drunk at breakfast. It was always mildly exciting to watch the water beginning to boil in the copper kettle, and then see mother break a piece off from the tea brick, rub it between her palms and then throw the curling leaves into the bubbling water. After that she would add a little salt and then let the tea boil for a moment or two. In our province of Amdo people used dried tea leaves pressed into bricks which were imported from China through the province of Kham. It was a rather coarse kind of tea, and these bricks often contained whole leaves, and sometimes even stalks. Our salt came from Changthang in the northern plateaux of Tibet where it was obtained from the salt lakes there and sent by yak or similar transport to other parts.

A figure which keeps popping up in my earliest recollections is that of the village herdsman. I was just five years old when he first became the hero of my boyish dreams. Every morning when we were at breakfast he would pass our house with the village flocks and herds. Small groups of cows and sheep joined him from every yard as he passed on his way, and soon there was a many-headed, pushing, lowing, bleating mass of animals with him; all making their way to the rich grass of the mountain pastures. Our sheep and cows would all be waiting impatiently in the yard to surge out and join him and go off with the others. This herdsman was a great fount of country lore, and he also had the physique and the strength necessary to control such large herds and flocks. To keep the animals together at all was something of an art; but he also had to protect them from wolves, which were dangerous not only to the flocks but also to the herds. In order to defend himself and his charges from the four-legged robbers he was armed with a sling and a double-edged sword. We village boys were, of course, all very anxious to be on friendly terms with so fascinating a person, and I for one succeeded. He was my aider and abettor when I used to steal off secretly into the mountains with the herds, a thing I was really forbidden to do.

A day spent like that with the herdsman and one or two other village lads in the mountain woods and meadows went all too quickly. The secrets and treasures of the mountains seemed inexhaustible to us. And we could play our wildest games without interference; though when we got too riotous even for the herdsman he would call us together to play a quieter but nevertheless very popular game: we all had to go off in various directions and gather as many different flowers as we could in the woods and the meadows and then bring our bunches back for him to decide which was the best. The fortunate victor was then given a sugary dried apricot. If we felt hungry we would eat the raspberries, strawberries and bilberries which could be found in the woods in large quantities at the right time of the year. But in the afternoon, as the time approached for going home, I would begin to think apprehensively of the inevitable punishment that awaited me when I got back. The exciting games had helped me to forget that I had gone on this expedition without permission. Then I would go back into the woods and pick a hatful of ripe berries of some sort as a propitiatory offering for my parents.

The herdsman would often sit silently on a stone and look dreamily up into the sky. And I would sometimes think I saw his lips move as though he were talking to the clouds, the trees, the birds and the water. By the time we returned tired out to the village the shadows would already be lengthening. Those were the days when I used to dream of one day becoming the herdsman of Tengtser.

After breakfast my father usually went out to the fields with a labourer, perhaps taking a mule or an ox along. Normally we children were not expected to help with the field work, though in the spring when father did the ploughing we used to go with him to collect the sweet white tubers the ploughshare turned up. The plough was a long piece of hardened wood tipped with metal, and it ripped up the soil to a depth of about two handbreadths. It was drawn by an ox, and my father would encourage the beast and shout strange-sounding orders in such a loud voice that we could often hear him where we were playing quite far away. My father grew barley, wheat and oats, and planted potatoes and sowed large quantities of peas, but these latter were used solely as fodder for the horses. When the young seedlings began to show over the ground we children had to help with the weeding. At first we always found this occupation quite interesting, but it soon got boring and then we would long to get back to our games. A day's work in the fields was hard, and on such occasions we would go out at sunrise and come home only when the sun was setting.

As soon as the men were out of the house my mother would take her brushes and brooms and sweep up the kitchen and the house generally and then go on to clean up the byre. Only after that would she start the cooking, which wasn't, in fact, very complicated because all she had to do was to prepare one or two accompaniments to our staff of life, the tsampa flour.

At midday mother would take food out to the fields for my father and the labourer, and sometimes also for one or two neighbours who happened to be helping him in the fields. She would carry the basket in a shoulder sling, or on her back with the help of a rope. In one hand she would hold the end of the cord or the sling, and in the other she would carry an earthenware container of tea. We used to like going with her on these journeys into the fields, dancing and playing around her on the way. Our small farm was made up of separate strips of land situated in different places. This came about by ancient custom, because as the soil was not all good many generations of peasants had divided it up so that each family should till both good and less good patches, always sowing and planting various crops in a settled sequence. The hard work would naturally make the men hungry, and they would devour their food eagerly. Their obvious hunger would make us hungry too, and we would join happily in the meal. When the men were finished we would go back to the house again with mother, who still had a lot of work to do.

On arriving home she would exchange the food basket for the ordinary water-carrier in which she fetched our daily supplies from the well, which was about ten minutes' distance away from our farmstead at the other end of the village. During the summer my mother would have to make this journey at least four times a day, and in winter perhaps three times. So long as my sister Tsering Dröma had to look after me and carry me around on her back she would welcome any change in the routine and she would often beg my mother to let us go with her to the well. Mother would then strap me to Tsering Dröma's back, and the water-carrier to her own, and we would all set off together.

It was lively and jolly there. The women gossiped and told each other the latest news, and they were so occupied with each other's tales that they would leave the children to do as they liked—and the wet clay was a wonderful plaything. We would make it into the most fantastic shapes, and, of course, get ourselves smothered with it at the same time. The "well" was really only a depression, not more than a couple of handbreadths deep and perhaps four or five feet across. Mother would stoop down and scoop up the water with a large dipper used for the purpose, taking great care not to stir up the mud at the bottom, and transfer it to her own container, which had a wooden cover to prevent the water from slopping over on the way home. If she happened to forget the wooden cover, as she sometimes did, she would just pluck a few branches from nearby bushes, and they would have to serve the purpose. This excursion would usually make us children hungry again, but as it would not be time to eat, mother would give us a couple of stone-hard rolls, which we would then soak in a basin of hot water and devour with great appetite.

As it began to grow dusk mother would prepare the main meal of the day. Usually there was a nourishing soup with meat and vegetables in it, and still further thickened with tsampa. And, of course, there was tea. If we were still hungry when we had finished our share of this we could always fall back on our tsampa dish with its three compartments.

Every evening Tsering Dröma and I would wait impatiently at the door for father to come home, and we also kept our eye open for our animals when the herds and the flocks went by. Not that this was really necessary, because all the animals knew their own farms, and they would branch off into the various courtyards without the herdsman or their owners having to bother about them. Only after the animals had been attended to did we ever sit down to our own meal. Whilst father led the horses and the mules to drink, mother would milk the cows in the byre. This byre was paved with stone flags. It had no windows, but there was a hole in the roof which could be closed in very cold weather. The fodder troughs were made of mud bricks lined with wood. At milking time each cow had her own fodder tub containing softened oil-cake and chopped chaff. If mother happened to be a little late the cows would hurry her up by lowing loudly. Our cattle were sent out into the pastures every day except when the weather really was too inclement; with violent snow-storms for example. The herds and the flocks could normally be taken to the pastures even in winter, because the winds were strong enough to sweep the snow from the meadows so that cattle and sheep could usually find sufficient roots and herbs to feed on.

When it grew dark our lamps would be lit. They consisted of shallow saucers filled with oil of mustard with one or more wicks of cotton half in them and half over the edges, and they stood on slate shelves which jutted out from the walls. There was one of these lamps in the byre too. This was the only form of domestic artificial light we ever knew.

When she had finished the milking mother would bring the milk into the kitchen in wooden pails. These pails were made of juniper wood brought by my father from the mountains. At regular intervals a handicraftsman would come in from Balangtsa to make it into tubs and bowls. He was also a general handyman who could do any necessary repairs. The best bowls were reserved for the curdled milk. These were particularly strong and they were decorated with carvings on the outside. But the greater part of the fresh milk would be poured into a large copper container and then boiled. A small amount was put to one side to be used with the tea. Always, before the milk boiled, mother would put a large scoopful to one side to thicken. The next day the cream would be taken off and put into a special wooden tub. After a few days this tub would be filled to the brim, and then its contents went into the butter churn—though we could sometimes wheedle mother into letting us have a spoonful of it with our tea. Before it had completely mixed with the tea we would take a delight in pushing it below the surface with our hard rusk-like pieces of bread. Fresh cream was a treat, but we were allowed to drink as much as we liked of the buttermilk, which always had fascinating little globules floating around in it. If mother wanted to make cheese she would boil up the sour milk once more, after which she would pour the white mass into a sieve and keep it in a cool, dark room for a while, where it slowly dried into the crumbly cheese we ate for breakfast with our tsampa. The greenish whey that dripped through the sieve was given to the animals.

Our stock of cattle and sheep increased in the usual natural fashion, and as a rule we had at least four cows in the byre. The cows calved without any attention at all. My parents didn't even think it necessary to go into the byre at all when the cows' time had come. I used to jump up at once on mornings when mother told me that a cow had calved in the night, and I would rush off into the byre without even washing to watch the awkward long-legged little calf making its first wobbly attempts to walk. The way in which the newborn calf would push and nuzzle impatiently at its mother's udder never ceased to astonish me; and the mother would stand there, still exhausted, gently licking her calf. It was in those early days that I first realised that nature had her own laws which were different from and harsher than our laws, which have been worked out only after mature consideration. I used to regard a newborn calf as my special plaything, and I would often wrap it up in a blanket and carry it out into the yard to enjoy the sunshine. A calf was altogether a pleasure, because now the mother would give rich, dark-yellow milk which we children particularly loved. But mother always kept careful watch on the milk. She would never take more than about half of it, and the rest was left for the newborn calf. Apart from the cows we also kept oxen in the byre, and the young steers were soon castrated. Only bigger villages kept a bull for breeding purposes, and the cows were taken to him. The oxen were called yak and the cows di. A yak is used exclusively as a draught beast or a beast of burden.

There was a lot to do in the evenings and my parents were both kept fully occupied. At such times we children were left to our own devices, and usually we were in the way, so we would look forward impatiently to supper-time. This was always a very pleasant meal: the work of the day was done, the animals were all safely locked up, and the door of the farm was closed. When father finished his supper and got up to go into the back-kitchen that was the signal for us children that the time had come for us to go to bed.

3. A Happy Childhood

THE nights were often icy, and in winter it was usually bitterly cold. I can still clearly see the great brass firepot with its three iron feet, in which the wood or coal glowed. We usually heated with juniper or firwood, but on particularly cold days we would use coal, which was brought to a red-hot glow in the furnace and then put into the brass firepot. This coal was precious because it had to be fetched on yak or muleback from a distance, and its transport required several days. When the work in the fields was over for the year my father would take a horse and set off for the coalmines, leading a number of mules carrying butter or flour to be exchanged for coal. About two weeks later the little caravan would return. In this way we always had enough coal to keep us warm on the long winter evenings. We would sit cosily round the glowing warmth and drink tea, whilst the adults drank perhaps beer, and sometimes spirits. On the broad rim of the brass firepot would be food or table utensils. An earthenware pot with tea would stand in the glowing coals, and by its side perhaps a sizzling piece of meat, or a kidney still in its sheath of fat. The grown-ups would often sit there together over their drinks until midnight.

The beer, of which a good deal was drunk in summer, was brewed by my mother herself. She simply boiled up barley in a big pot, and before it was cool she tossed in a piece of yeast. After a few days the brew looked rather like a watery milk soup. But on account of its alcoholic content and its stimulating effect it was very popular. When this beer was distilled it very quickly produced a crystal-clear spirit.

There were many places to sleep in the house, and we children chose our sleeping-quarters in the pleasantest spot according to the weather. When it was particularly cold we all flocked into the "kang" in the best room. This stove built of clay took up the whole of the wall which separated the best room from the kitchen. It was about two feet high and it was heated from the kitchen. Lying on the kang it didn't matter to the sleeper how cold the night might be outside. Yak or horse dung glowed under this resting-place often for days on end, and a quilted covering filled with wool, and one or two sheepskins, contributed to making the kang a very agreeable bed in the cold weather.

The north wall of the best room was one large cupboard which reached from the floor to the ceiling and contained not only the clothes of the whole family, but also the woollen cloth made on the farm and the huge balls of wool spun by my father by hand. Opposite this cupboard there was a small table on a raised platform, and there we would sit around cross-legged to play games or chat. Above this platform was a long window divided into several squares and looking out into the yard. The wooden frames were covered from the inside with stretched material, and the richly-carved wooden shutters were artistically painted, as indeed all our woodwork was. They could be lifted up and kept open by means of a cord attached to the ceiling. Below this window, in the covered-in gangway, there was a sort of couch. Surreptitiously we children often used this forbidden short cut when we were playing hide-and-seek.

When mother had put us to bed and we lay there under the clothes in the dim light of the flickering oil-lamp I would often beg my sister Tsering Dröma to tell me some of the many fairy stories she had learnt from mother or grandmother. Tsering Dröma could tell a good tale and keep you interested and thrilled, and I would listen happily until my eyes closed of their own accord and I went to sleep. When grandmother, or one of our aunts, was on a visit it would be her job to go on telling us fairy stories until we fell asleep. One of my favourite stories was about the donkey and the tiger. When the donkey was taking a bath in the river he hee-hawed so loudly in his delight that a friendly tiger came running up, thinking that someone was calling for help. The donkey thought this great fun, and kept on doing it until finally the tiger stopped coming. But one day the donkey did get out of his depth and had to cry out for help in real earnest, but this time the tiger ignored his cries, no one came near him, and he was drowned.

Amongst our many visitors, my favourite ones were my mother's parents. They were peasants too, and as they lived only a day's journey away from Tengtser, which wasn't so very far, they came to see us quite often. They must have been very pleased with the happy family life they found in our home. In Tibet it is the custom for marriages to be arranged between the parents of the bridal pair, and this creates a close bond between the generations. When my grandparents came to visit us we had to squeeze together a bit because my parents always gave them their room. This room, which was entered through a double door from the altar room, also had a raised bed but no kang. There was a cupboard in which more cloth was stored, and also my mother's ornaments, which she wore only on high days and holidays: there were, for example, three red ribbons on which silver coins, shells, corals and turquoise stones were sewn to make very colourful finery.

The woollen cloth was woven by craftsmen who went from farm to farm and set their looms up in the yards. They would weave pieces about eight inches wide and many feet in length; these pieces were then sewn together edgewise. The thread used to sew them was spun by my father during the long winter evenings. Wherever he was, standing or sitting, his hands were always occupied making something or other. The Tibetan peasant is never idle, and if just for the moment his hands do not happen to be making anything, the rosary is slipping bead by bead through his fingers. My mother made all the clothes for the children, and a proper tailor was called into the house only to make the gala clothes of my mother and father. I can remember watching him with wide-open eyes and marvelling at his skill with the needle. In cutting out shirts he would always fold the stuff and then press the fold in by sticking forward his dirty neck and pulling the fold across it. I always used to laugh when after that a dirty mark appeared on the light material.

Along the edges of our fields my father grew enough jute to supply thread for our boots. When the jute had been dried out on the roof of our house my father would dampen it again, beat it with a stick, then remove the outer husk and spin the fibres into thread or yarn. The cow leather for the soles of our boots was bought in Balangtsa. We had no leather of our own because we never slaughtered cattle in our own yard, but always sold them. In summer of course we went around bare-footed, but in winter we used to wear out so many boots that the cobbler had to come to our house several times during the winter and attach new leather soles to the stuff tops of our boots. My father always had the leather ready soaked so that all the cobbler had to do when he arrived was to cut out the soles and sew them onto the old ones.

In addition to the cobbler, the tailor and the weaver, other tradesmen also came into the house to work; for instance, the carpenter and the carpet-maker. These artisans, and also passing caravan drivers, would live in the guest-room next to the cow byre, sleeping on a broad bench which took up the whole of one wall. And if they had animals with them then these were provided for too. In the yard there was a round base made of cemented stones to take our big prayer-mast, which was over thirty feet high. Round this base were large irregular stone slabs which served as feeding troughs. There were also holes worked in these stones to which halters could be fastened.

The prayer-flag itself was a long white piece of cotton material about a foot wide, covered over and over with prayers. It reached from the top of the mast right down to the stone base below, and occasionally it had to be renewed. Before certain feast days we would take a suitable piece of cotton material to a neighbour who possessed the wooden blocks for printing prayers on the flag, and have it covered with prayers like the old one. We brought our own printer's ink along—father had previously scraped soot from the kitchen ceiling, and from the bottom of the cooking-pots, and mixed with it with size.

We bought the glue from itinerant vendors who made it themselves from cow hooves, bones and skins. There were many itinerant pedlars of this kind who went from village to village and from house to house offering all sorts of goods for sale. I think the jolliest visitor for us children was the potter, whose donkey was almost hidden by the many pots, some of them many feet high, hanging round him. In our house we had three of these great green-glazed earthenware pots, and as a rule they didn't have a very long life. During the winter one or other of them would probably burst from the cold, despite the fact that it was carefully swathed in sheepskins. In summer, when we needed more water, two other water containers stood outside the kitchen. They were attached with yak-hair cords to the first pillar of the covered way.

One unforgettable childhood memory is connected for me with one of those green-glazed water jars. We were strictly forbidden to play near the big ones, and if I wanted to clamber up on a stool and get a dipper of water I had to have special permission from my mother. But sometimes I ignored the stern prohibition, and on one such occasion fate overtook me.

One warm summer's day I was playing by the much-reduced stream when, in a tributary which had almost no water any more, I noticed a number of goldfish desperately striving to make their way to deeper water. Now from early on every Tibetan is imbued with a great veneration for life in all its forms, whether human, animal or insect. Since Buddha taught us to hold life in awe we Tibetans have been a peaceable folk, trying to avoid disputes, and, where they arise, to settle them peacefully. It was therefore a matter of course for me that these small goldfish had to be saved from the certain death which threatened them when the shallow water finally dried up. I therefore collected the floundering little beasts in an earthenware fragment and took them home, taking great care that none of the water was spilled on the way.

Cautiously I crept round the house to make quite certain that no undesired observer was in the neighbourhood. In my mind I had already decided that the big water jar in the kitchen, which was fastened to the kitchen pillar, was to be their temporary refuge. My plan succeeded and after that I would stand from time to time on a stool and watch them swimming around happily in our drinking water.

Naturally I eagerly informed my playmates of what I had done, and after that hardly an hour passed without my climbing onto the stool to take another look at them. But on one occasion I was in too great a hurry; my friends were impatiently calling out for me, so I couldn't be bothered to take the stool to stand on; instead I got hold of the rim of the jar and pulled myself up. But a large piece broke away in my hands and I fell on my back on the kitchen floor with water pouring all over me and fragments of the broken jar all around me. And there I lay gasping as though I were myself a fish out of water.

It was a terrible shock. Not only were the fish I had taken such pains to rescue now in great danger again, since they were writhing and jumping all over the kitchen floor, but I was wet to the skin—and the precious water jar was in fragments. And then a dark shadow appeared in the doorway. It was my mother. She stood there for a moment or two as though rooted to the ground, staring at the disaster I had caused; and for the moment I didn't know whether to be pleased that she had appeared on the scene so quickly to help me or frightened at the idea of the stern but just punishment I should receive for my disobedience. I couldn't find a word to say in my excuse but I pointed silently to the jumping goldfish on the kitchen floor.

With swift movements my mother now bustled around cleaning up the mess and putting her kitchen in order. The biggest trouble was baling the water out of the flooded floor recess where she kept various foods to cool. First the kitchen, and then me; and I was hurriedly undressed, dried and put into fresh clothes. Very depressed and a bundle of misery, I sat in the courtyard holding in my fingers a bowl of water containing the once-more rescued goldfish, and awaiting with a heavy heart the return of my father. Actually I got away with the fright, because on consideration my parents recognised that I had acted with the best of intentions, and they therefore remitted the punishment due to me for having broken the water jug. Much relieved, but still very depressed, I carried the goldfish back to the stream and let them loose in it.

The consequences of my first experience with another element —fire—might have been much more serious. Secretly I had got hold of a fine large potato, and I carried it around with me in my jacket pocket looking for an opportunity to creep unobserved into the altar-room and roast it at the butter-lamp there. The mere idea of this titbit made my mouth water. As soon as I thought myself unobserved I crept into our house chapel and started to cook the potato. It was already beginning to bake on one side and a wonderful smell tickled my nostrils, when suddenly I heard footsteps in the covered way outside, and in a panic at the thought of being caught I made a sudden grab at the potato, knocking both it and the butter-lamp to the floor where lay the open matchbox which my parents used to light the lamp. The matches caught fire, and in an instant a big sheet of flame leapt up, and the spilled butter on the wooden floor began to burn too. I shrieked in my fright, and there was my mother to the rescue again. She had been about to hang cloths out to dry in the yard and instead she now used them to beat out the fire. But this time when the job was done she turned on me with a face far more angry than I usually saw and gave me a couple of stinging clouts.

I loved both my parents dearly, but it was to my mother I always turned when I had done anything wrong, because she would often intercede for me with my father, who could sometimes be very short-tempered. But this time there was no mercy to be expected at my mother's hands either, and she threatened to tell my father about my impious behaviour. Very much ashamed, and afraid too, I crept away from the scene of my naughtiness and sought refuge in the neighbouring wood. It was only after what had happened that I began to realise how wrong my behaviour had been; I had desecrated the sacred flame by trying to roast a potato on it. And because I was frightened of what was likely to happen to me when my father came home, I stayed in the woods until it became quite dark, and the owls began to hoot. I knew that melancholy tone very well indeed, because there were a lot of owls in our neighbourhood, but now in the darkness their hooting frightened me out of my life. I therefore preferred to run home now and face what was coming to me—but reluctantly, and with the hooting of the owls still ringing in my ears.

When I got to the farmstead door I stood there for a while hesitating. I was afraid to knock. And then it suddenly opened, and there was my father on his way to search for his missing son. My distress didn't save me this time. My father put me across his knee, bared my bottom, and with his hard and heavy hand he gave me a thorough drubbing. If I had set the house on fire as a result of my naughtiness I could hardly have been thrashed more thoroughly than I was because I had desecrated the sacred butter-lamp and the picture of Buddha before which it burned.

In his heart my father was a kind and good-natured man, and he didn't like it at all when he had to punish me. Soon afterwards he would always find some opportunity for surreptitiously giving me an apricot, or he would ask me casually if I would like to go with him to the fields. Or if he happened to be in a great hurry I would hear him from the corner where I was sulking whispering to mother to give me a sweet later on. But this time it had really hurt, and I wasn't prepared to forgive him so quickly.

My mother kept the sweetmeats in the store-room, which was next to the guest-room and had a small window giving onto the courtyard. Pieces of meat hung from the ceiling to dry, and sometimes whole sheep carcases. And hanging from pegs in the wooden walls were rolls of butter sewn into skins or tripes. There were also rows of barrels with various sorts of grain. The oil of mustard was also kept here in earthenware jars. But the finest thing of all was the pastries and rolls in their box. Wooden covers and sacking protected the foodstuffs from the many mice, which were a real nuisance. But the window also had to be covered with particularly strong cloth because our cat was very fond of prowling around the storeroom.

That cat was much spoilt by my parents, though none of us ever called it anything but Shimi, which is just "cat." I haven't any very pleasant memories of it, because on one occasion it caused me real sorrow. A friend of my father's, a passionate trapper, caught a baby musk-deer in the woods and gave it to me as a present. I quickly became very much attached to it, and I used to carry it about with me everywhere. My grandmother told us that she had once had a musk-deer and that she had brought it up on bread, milk, leaves and flowers. It had become completely tame, she said, and the children had played with it. So I fed my little animal several times a day and hoped that it would grow up into a good playmate. Musk-deer are small animals without antlers but with particularly long hind legs, and a three-cornered tail that ends in a sort of bobble. They get their name from a gland in the navel area which secretes musk, a product which is greatly sought after for the making of scent. The musk-deer is very shy and extraordinarily helpless when attacked, and is therefore of no danger to man.

I loved my little musk-deer very much and I even took it to bed with me under the warm covering. In the morning it would wake me up by licking my cheek with its gentle tongue. But one morning it didn't wake me up; I woke up on my own and found I was cuddling its lifeless body. And then I saw that there was blood around. In the night that wretched cat had bitten through my poor musk-deer's throat. Once again I learnt how harsh and cruel nature could be. The loss of my beloved musk-deer caused bitter and resentful tears, and for the first time in my life I felt a desire for vengeance and would have liked to see that cat suffer a similarly bloody end. But by a piece of good fortune our domestic sow was delivered of no fewer than twelve piglets on that very day. In addition, there were a couple of newborn lambs which needed attention, so we had our hands full for a while, and this helped me to get over the loss of my pet more quickly than I would otherwise have done.

Our sow was completely black. She liked to stay outside all day and was usually to be found rooting around the refuse heap, as this was, of course, the spot where she was most likely to find scraps to gobble up. In the evening when she returned to her place behind the door next to the sheep-pen, she was given a swill of tsampa flour in a hollowed-out stone. If mother was late bringing this thick swill, as she sometimes was of course, then the sow would come to the kitchen door grunting indignantly and demanding her food.

Above the sow's sleeping-place there was a board for the hens to roost on. The cock would roost on his own high up in the beams. It was he who woke my mother up every morning with his crowing and started her off on the day's work. But a few of the hens preferred to roost on the ledge above the holes which allowed a certain amount of light to penetrate into the sheep-pen during the day.

We always had about seventy white and one or two black sheep. We preferred the wool of the white sheep, though the skin of a black sheep which had not lived long after its birth was the most valuable pelt. In early summer the sheep were shorn, and we children had to help in earnest, holding the feet of the sheep, which kicked out wildly in a panic when they were being shorn. But we liked shearing time, when the wool piled up in the yard into white mountains waiting to be packed into jute sacks, work which was invariably accompanied by a good deal of shouting and jollity.

It was not until there was no longer so much work to be done in the fields that the sacks were again brought out, emptied, and the wool soaked in great wooden tubs before being washed, teased and hung up to dry. When a large quantity of wool had been spun my mother would colour the thick ropes with dyes made from the bark of trees, earth and plants. Our favourite colour was the warm reddish brown we obtained from the wild rhubarb which grew in the mountains and represented an extra source of income to the mountain peasant women. But it was not only its colour which was highly prized, but also the acid it contained, which would be mixed with other colours.

Certain colours could be obtained only by buying them in Balangtsa or Chakhyung. When my father went in to town to make such purchases he would usually take advantage of his journey to visit the horse-fair, for he was not only an expert on horses but a great lover of them too. Races were run in connection with the horse-fair, to give the horses on sale a chance of showing their paces. Horses were also taken in part exchange, the difference being made up in sheepskins, wool or barley. Argument would often run high during these transactions, and crowds would gather round the chafferers; some taking sides with the seller, others with the buyer. Often the noise would become so tremendous that the disputants could no longer make themselves heard above it, and then they would go on with their bargaining in finger language. Hidden under the long arms of their jackets, hands would touch and the bargain would be settled silently.

A journey to the market usually meant an absence of several days, and when my father returned he would be greeted with loud shouts of welcome from us all, including excited barking from Kyimo our dog, who would rush out from the kennel between the sheep-pen and the stable, yelping with delight and straining at his chain, which was fastened to a leather collar round his neck. Kyimo was a huge black beast with shaggy matted hair that hung down to the ground. Incidentally Kyimo just means bitch, which our dog was. As she was powerful and rather savage she had to stay chained up during the day and was allowed to roam around the courtyard only at nights when the great door was closed. She was usually fed on the remainder of our soup and tsampa, but occasionally there was meat for her, because, as we never ate veal, when one of the calves died Kyimo had the meat.

The horses were also known only according to their size or their colour. In the stables each horse was attached to its own particular place by a halter passed through a ring. The fodder

Young couple in Tibetan ceremonial clothing. Both woman and girl wear characteristic and often quite costly necklaces

It took this monk many months of plodding over the high plateaux of Tibet
before he reached the holy places

The magnificent colours (made from plant and animal dyes) on the rock murals of Buddha are kept constantly renewed by pious Tibetans who live from the alms given to them by pilgrims

troughs were the same as those for the cows except that the
bottom of them was laid out with stone slabs. The roof of the
stable, which was open to the yard, was supported by three posts,
and the saddles, harness and so on hung from pegs on these posts.
Straw and chopped chaff were piled up in a protected corner.

In autumn the grain harvest would be brought in. The sheaves
were spread out in front of the house, and moving around in
circles the horses pulled a six- or eight-sided stone roller over
it. The barley obtained in this way was shovelled into baskets
which were then held high and gradually emptied in order
to let the wind do the work of winnowing, and carry away
the chaff. The straw would then be piled up in the nearest fields,
often higher than the houses; and these heaps were wonderful
places for us to play in during the winter months. For example,
we would scoop ourselves out comfortable holes in them, and
then pay each other visits.

But our favourite place to play was always the bumkhang.
This was a conical hollow tower made of clay topped by a large
piece of quartz. It was just large enough for three children to
embrace with their arms outstretched round it, and it stood in
front of the big entrance gate behind the six-foot-high wall which
bordered the caravan route for some distance from the south-
east corner of the house. This bumkhang was the centre of certain sacrificial ceremonies, and it was intended to protect the
house and the farm from all harm.

Inside there were innumerable small figures of gods called
tsa-tsa embedded in the clay. In a niche opposite the door there
was a representation of Buddha painted in colours. In the course
of time cracks appeared in the walls of this bumkhang, and we
could look through them and see the tsa-tsa. Mother felt we were
safe when we were playing in that wind-protected spot, and we
enjoyed ourselves there enormously, though perhaps just because
it was the bumkhang, we never misbehaved ourselves.

Neighbours' children used to come and play games with us
there, and we would have trials of skill with the help of coins,
coloured stones and sheep's osselets such as every Tibetan child

carried around with him like an amulet. And like all children all over the world we would scratch squares on the ground and then throw small stones into them, after which we would hop on one foot and propel them forward with the toe—without ever treading on the lines. Hopscotch! We also had a ball of wool into which we stuck hen's feathers, and this had to be kept in the air as long as possible by kicking it up with the instep. A kind of football we played with a leather ball stuffed with wool was by no means so difficult. The ball was supposed to be round, but it never really was.

I liked playing with the neighbours' children, but I was happiest of all with my sister Tsering Dröma. When I was very small she used to carry me around on her back, and later on she would always take my part against other children when there were quarrels. But there weren't many quarrels, and usually we were able to sit down together happily and eat the cakes and drink the tea our mothers brought us after hours of happy playing— by which time, of course, we were all very hungry. Literally translated bumkhang means "a hundred thousand houses," and for me the word always summons up a hundred thousand pleasures. I only wish all other children all over the world had a wonderful bumkhang too!

During the winter when there was snow on the ground for five months we would build huge snowmen, making their eyes with pieces of burnt wood. And we slid down the slopes so often that in the end we had slides as highly polished as mirrors. But our greatest fun was to shoot down steep inclines on a short plank, shouting at the tops of our voices.

At the age of six I discovered another place to play: on our flat roof, to which we would climb by means of a ladder. It wasn't easy for me to clamber up the rungs, because they were very wide apart, being, of course, intended for adults. On the outside the roof had a protective wall, and I could just about look over it. Herbs for incense, yak dung and wood were piled up there to dry. But on the courtyard side there was no such protective wall, and, in addition, the roof sloped slightly inwards towards the yard. Now I was very fond of flowers and I discovered to my delight that all sorts of lovely flowers were growing in the protection of the warm chimneys, and with the help of my sister I now planted many others. My parents didn't much care for these roof expeditions of mine. My mother was afraid I might fall down, and my father was afraid that the many flowers might make the roof leak. From my expeditions into the pastures with the herdsman I brought back small onion plants from the mountains, and Tsering Dröma and I planted them on the roof. As mother could make good use of them in the kitchen she ended up by tolerating my clambering around above her head.

From up there you could see Kyeri in all its majesty. In summer there was only a small ice cap on top, but in winter it was completely covered with a thick mantle of snow and ice. Kyeri showed itself to us in many guises, and my father in particular knew how to interpret its moods. If you could see it very clearly in the mornings, with perhaps just a light pinkish hue on it, then you could expect a fine, sunny day. But if a large cloud happened to be settled like a hood over its peak then you had to expect rain. And if at sundown there was a bank of cloud before Kyeri then we carefully closed up all the holes over the kitchen and the stables and prepared ourselves for the approaching storm. Kyeri means something like "Mountain of Happiness," and for me it has certainly become the embodiment of a happy childhood. It was under Kyeri that I experienced the love of my parents and my brother and sister, that I rode on our horses over the flower-dotted pastures, and accompanied the herdsman and his beasts. It was towards Kyeri that our prayers were directed, because Kyeri was the throne of our protective deity and bore his name. Throughout life the idea of terrestrial and heavenly happiness will always be connected with Kyeri. For me Kyeri has become the symbol of a full life.

The temple which stood surrounded by shady trees on the outskirts of our village was dedicated to Kyeri out of a feeling of mingled love and gratitude. The temple precincts were quite roomy and offered plenty of space for the approximately one hundred and fifty inhabitants of our village, though the temple proper was quite small; and inside, because ours was not a rich village, it was a trifle austere. In the centre was a statue of our protective deity in the guise of a horseman. Like the other statues this equestrian one was made of clay. I can well remember the small black pointed beard which covered the god-rider's chin.

Behind the temple was a small eminence on which a stone altar had been erected, and here the inhabitants of Tengtser would burn incense in honour of our protective deity and to beg him to grant peace and prosperity to our village. Before going to the altar you first entered the temple and placed a few flowers before the effigies of the gods, or fixed a prayer-flag. There was no monastery in Tengtser and therefore there was no monk to look after the temple and supervise the ceremonies, and this was done by one of the men of the village who was appointed caretaker.

The temple was surrounded by a covered way in which we children sometimes played hide-and-seek—until the caretaker angrily drove us away. But the wonderful green sward and the fine old trees of the temple grounds were too tempting to us, and we would always return.

For special feast days monks would be invited from the neighbouring monasteries of Shartsong and Kumbum to officiate at the ceremonies. On such occasions the whole population of the village would assemble in the inner courtyard to take part in the service. I can still see these special occasions very clearly in my mind, with the new prayer-flags fluttering in the wind and the festively-dressed villagers listening devoutly to the drums and gongs of the visiting monks.

The fifth and sixth days of the sixth month were both devoted to Kyeri. The villagers would start off on their way a few days beforehand, well prepared to pay their respects to the mountain and make the customary offerings. By this time the snow on its flanks was all melted away, and only the topmost pinnacle still glistened with its covering of eternal ice. The ride to the foot of the mountain lasted three days and went through a completely uninhabited area, so the villagers had to take everything they needed along with them. When they arrived at the end of their journey we children would be left behind in tents whilst the adults went on up to the ice limit, there solemnly to burn incense. During their absence we would spend the time picking flowers, collecting attractive stones, and playing hide-and-seek around the old workings left behind by the gold seekers. There wasn't a great deal of gold in our neighbourhood, and it required hard work and a good deal of preparation to get at it. Prospectors would provide tents, provisions, spades and sieves, and gold-diggers would set off for the mountains. They were paid a fixed wage, but any gold found outside the normal working hours belonged to the men.

On a small hill not far from Tengtser there was a labtse, that is to say, a heap of stones dedicated to the protective deity of the village. Our labtse was surrounded by a high wooden fence which kept the stones together. Here you offered up white quartz, coins, turquoises and corals, and prayed for rain, or for sun, or for a good harvest, or for protection from bad weather. Once a year, on the twelfth day of the sixth month, all the inhabitants of Tengtser would march in a long procession to the labtse, where they solemnly burnt incense and erected prayer-flags. Monks from neighbouring monasteries would be invited to conduct the ceremonies on this auspicious day, and the beating of their gongs and the sound of their bells would help to heighten the solemnity of the occasion. But, the religious observances upheld, a joyful feast would follow, with tents erected in the meadows, and dancing and plenty to eat and drink.

But the most popular feast of all was that of New Year's Day, when people not only visited each other from house to house but also from village to village; and on such occasions each housewife would do her best to entertain her guests as magnificently as possible. No pains or expense were spared; and meat, which was normally scarce, was generously provided, whilst constantly refilled beer glasses helped to maintain the general good spirits, which reached their peak with the dancing on the snow-covered village square. On the fifteenth day of the first month the butter-lamp celebration was held in the nearby monastery of Kumbum, and many people from the neighbourhood would come in to attend it. For example, those inhabitants of Tengtser who could afford it did not hesitate to make the twenty-five-mile journey to take part in the splendid celebration organised by the biggest monastery in the neighbourhood, whilst those who remained behind celebrated in their own fashion by lighting great piles of straw in the fields and leaping through the dancing flames both singly and in groups.

We led a happy and contented life in our remote little village, and we found it strange when the occasional travellers who passed through sometimes felt it necessary to express their sympathy with us on account of what they conceived to be our hard lot. In fact we felt that we had everything we needed for life and enjoyment. We certainly would not have changed places with any of those travellers. We lived peaceably; and on feast days even gaily; and the gods listened to our prayers. As far as I can remember, the peace of our village was seriously disturbed on only one occasion. I was very small at the time and it was not until later that I realised that we really had been in terrible danger.

I was woken up one night by unusual noises, and when I ran to my mother to find out what was happening I was astonished to find my parents hastily packing up our belongings. To my questions they replied briefly that the Hu-hus were on the way and that I should go back and dress. I was used to the customary and not very serious threats that the evil spirits would get me if I misbehaved, but these Hu-hus were obviously different, even my parents seemed to be afraid of them; from which I concluded that they must be much worse than the evil spirits. It was certainly not the moment to explain to me at any length that these Hu-hus were armed Mohammedan bands who scoured the land plundering, with Chinese troops on their heels.

The Hu-hus did come that night, but the men of our village—and the women too—defended themselves so vigorously with a few ancient firearms, pitchforks and other improvised weapons that the Hu-hus preferred to go on their way and give our village a wide berth. The success of our people in driving off the well-armed Hu-hus was regarded as a piece of great heroism by the inhabitants of the surrounding villages and the affair redounded greatly to the credit of Tengtser and its headman, Pasang, who had organised and led the resistance.

This Pasang was an intelligent, cheerful fellow, and a man of many parts. He could make up doggerel as he went along to pull the legs of his neighbours, guy their little weaknesses, and make everyone laugh. And his advice was thought a lot of too; for example, if anyone had an important letter to write, or had to go to Siling to interview the officials there about anything, he would invite Pasang to a good meal and then see what he had to say about it. His sound common sense and his long experience would find some solution to every problem. But once he had listened to the trouble, considered it seriously and given his advice, he would be jolly and light-hearted again at once, singing his songs or playing with the children. He also happened to be the best hunter for miles around. And when the wolves had once again got out of hand and caused grievous losses amongst the flocks then it was always Pasang who organised the wolf hunt. The only firearms the village possessed were a few ancient muzzle-loaders, and they weren't much good because it was such a complicated business to load and fire them. First the powder had to be thrust in with a ramrod, and made tight with a wad, and then came the bullet. The gun was supported on a fork attached to the barrel and the contraption had to be fired with a quick-match. Pasang used to arrange practice shooting outside the village, but my father for one, who was none too patient a man, much preferred his tried and trusty sling, with which he could obtain much better results. Altogether, hunting played quite a role in our lives, because there was plenty of game in the neighbourhood. Above the tree-line there were wild sheep and mountain goats, and in the woods there were deer, lynx and foxes; and the latter often penetrated right into the village itself. But the really dangerous beasts were the wolves. They did not confine their attacks to our sheep, but would on occasion pull down cattle and even horses. Whoever managed to kill a wolf had not only the satisfaction of having destroyed a dangerous beast, but also the much-desired skin.

The village headman was re-elected every year, though this election was not a very formal affair. The men of the village would just come together and discuss amongst themselves who should be elected. It always had to be a farmer who was sufficiently well off to have someone to carry on the work in his fields during his period of office, as he would sometimes have to go off on horseback to negotiate with the authorities on behalf of the village. In connection with the taxes and imposts he would even have to travel into Siling, the seat of the Chinese authorities for the province of Amdo. Amdo was a beautiful province; there were snow-capped mountains in the background, lush green pasture land, conifer forests, masses of rhododendron bushes, and innumerable salt lakes; and it was a fair size too, for a caravan would take about a month to pass through it from one end to the other. Tibetans formed the great majority of its population, but in the market-places and along the caravan routes you could hear Chinese and Mongolian spoken, and even the tongue of the Hu-hus. We had to pay our taxes to Mapufang, the Governor appointed by the Chinese Government. Altogether the tax system was rather arbitrary. At irregular intervals we would be told to deliver certain quantities of grain, or to make certain payments in kind. And if Mapufang happened to feel that his forces needed strengthening then he would increase our taxes. Now and again officials came to visit us, and occasionally even recruiting sergeants, intent on enrolling any strong, powerful young fellows who could be so persuaded.

The nearest fair-sized town was Balangtsa, where the school was. Eight years old was school-starting age, and I often stood at the door of our house and looked enviously at the older children gathering cheerfully for the march to school. I had never seen Balangtsa, and I greatly wanted to do so; and then one fine summer's day my parents at last fulfilled my wish and took me with them on a journey there. The circumstantial preparations in themselves were enough to put me in a holiday spirit. Excitedly I strutted around the courtyard in my new coat of sheep's wool, my artistically embroidered top boots and a fur cap specially made for the journey out of pieces of sheepskin, waiting impatiently for the long-desired journey to start.

The way went through deep and twisting gorges and over rickety bridges, but we passed safely through and over them all, and finally found ourselves in the busy market-place of Balangtsa. I stood there overwhelmed by all the new impressions and comparing them with my dreams. At first I was quite confused by the tremendous number of strange treasures spread out before my eyes. Wherever you looked there were wonderful things to see. Here was a smith shoeing a horse; there was a great display of glazed earthenware pots in all shapes and sizes, and piles of colourful necklaces and rings all glistening in the sun. And over there was an enticing heap of carefully arranged brown sugar-cakes. I could have stayed there and looked at it all for hours, but my parents urged me on. They had not come to Balangtsa to buy in the market, but to visit relatives of my father.

To my delight it turned out that there were children of my age in the family so I was immediately provided with suitable companions and we got on splendidly together. For the first time in my life I saw a really wide river with a great bridge spanning it, and my new cousins showed me their favourite spots along the banks of the river and taught me new games we didn't know in Tengtser. Together we built a dam and very quickly they constructed a water-mill which actually worked. The time passed like lightning, and then in the afternoon we had to say goodbye to Balangtsa and my new friends. And we had to hurry too if we wanted to be home before dark. I was a bit scared at the thought of travelling in the dark because of the evil spirits who lie in wait, so on the way home I held my parents' hands and stepped out willingly with them up the hill.

And, in fact, the way from Balangtsa to Tengtser was not without its dangers at night. Travellers could be attacked by wolves, for example. And there was the alarming story of the poor pilgrim who had been gobbled up so completely by them that nothing was left at all. Generally speaking the Tibetan regards both birth and death with philosophic resignation. And when a little brother died in our family we were consoled by our deep-rooted and unshakeable belief in the inscrutable wisdom of divine providence. My memory of that sad day is no longer very clear, but I can, for example, very clearly remember another morning when we were woken up by the vigorous crying of another newborn brother. When we tiptoed into the room of our parents my happily smiling mother held him up for us to see. She had borne the kicking, wriggling little bundle during the night in the cow byre. He was given the name of Gyalo Döndrub. In all she gave birth to five children in that gloomy byre lit only by a feeble wick. Just that one lamp shed a flickering light on the birth of my other brother, the Dalai Lama, who came into the world amongst the cows and their calves, the world in which he was to play such an important role.

4. I Enter a Monastery

WHEN I was born my parents named me Tashi Tsering, but I can't remember that I was ever called by that name. Many Tibetan children receive their names only later on in connection with some important occasion; for example, the recovery from serious illness, or the visit of some high prelate, who would then be, so to speak, the child's patron and choose a suitable name for his protégé. Until they are named they are addressed as "Boy," "Girl," or just "Child." I was three years old when a high lama visited our house and spent the night there. On that occasion he named me Thubten Jigme Norbu. After that my parents usually called me Jigme, which means "Fear Not," often using the honorific form "Jigmela." But my brothers and sister called me "Jola." That means "oldest," and it is a compliment, because in Tibet the eldest son enjoys precedence.

For a good many years my parents had known that I was the reincarnation of the famous monk Tagtser, and that therefore when I was eight I would not go to school in Balangtsa with the other children, but enter the monastery of Kumbum and take over the benefice of Tagtser Labrang. They frequently referred to the fact that I was destined to live the life of a monk when I grew older, but there was really nothing so very extraordinary about this because there were other children in Tengtser who were similarly destined to become monks. However, I gradually noticed that I enjoyed certain privileges by comparison with those other children. For one thing I had the title of Rimpoche, and I learned that every reincarnated person, or Trülku, was addressed by this highest titular honour in Tibet, though in the

ordinary way it is granted only for specially meritorious services
in the sphere of religious knowledge.

I was naturally proud of my privileged position, and in my
mind I would paint my future in rosy though very vague colours.
I therefore longed for the day when I would enter the monastery;
and the closer the day came the more impatient I was. It happened
sometimes that in childish ignorance and petulance I would
sometimes threaten to go off to the monastery at once. Once or
twice in my obstinacy I even ran away and hid myself. But my
parents were wise, and on such occasions they would let me stew
in my self-imposed exile for a while before sending out my sister
Tsering Dröma to bring me home again.

Now and again monks came to our farm and they always
chatted with me at length; but I was still small, and the sweets
and the nice clothes they brought for me didn't prevent me
from running off to the bumkhang at first opportunity to play
with the other children. However, as I grew older I entered
into their conversation and did my best to show them every
consideration.

I was already of school age when one bright spring morning
in the fourth month of the year the mission arrived which was to
take me away to the monastery. I happened to be in the back
kitchen when the monks arrived, and I could hear my mother
and father talking with them. I already had an idea why they had
come, and silently I went to one of the small windows which
looked out into the courtyard. In order to get a glimpse of the
arrivals I made a hole in the thick rice-paper which served us
instead of glass, using spittle to soften it up, and one finger to
make the spy-hole. We were strictly forbidden to do anything
of the sort, but at the moment my curiosity and impatience
were stronger than any fear of punishment. However, in the
meantime my mother and father had led the visitors to the
kitchen. I now tiptoed over to the wooden partition which
divided the kitchen and stood close to the wooden hatch through
which the food was passed, and through which we children had
often stolen titbits from the pots on the stove.

Through the hatch I now heard the leader of the mission announce formally to my mother and father that he had come in order to take their son to the monastery of Shartsong Ritrö in order that he should begin his schooling there. At the same time he introduced himself as the Steward of Tagtser Labrang, the rich and splendid monasterial household of the far-famed Tagtser in Kumbum, which was the superior monastery of Shartsong Ritrö. As the reincarnation of this Tagtser I was now to go into residence in Kumbum, but only after a short preparatory period in the smaller monastery of Shartsong Ritrö which, together with four other monasteries, also belonged to Tagtser Labrang.

The monks stayed with us for four days, and, of course, they occupied the best room, which was the only one with a kang. They had brought large cases with them containing the clothing I was henceforth to wear. It was not greatly different from the clothing I was already accustomed to wearing, except that it was of better cut and material. The woollen cloth was also dark brown, but the weave was much finer, and the boots were of better leather and the shafts were more richly embroidered. But at first I was not greatly impressed with all this, and I continued to play with the other children, much enjoying the new respect they suddenly paid me. Everything in the house now revolved around me, little whipper-snapper though I was. So far I had not properly realised that this journey to the monastery I was about to make was at the same time a final farewell to my childhood, to my much-loved parents, to my brother and sister, to the familiar courtyard with its animals, and to all the things which had such a big place in my heart.

On the morning of the fifth day I was dressed from head to foot in new things. I was not supposed to take even the smallest of all the things which had belonged to me up to then, though at the last moment I succeeded in smuggling the small bag with my much-worn and polished sheep's osselets and the coloured pebbles into the folds of my new clothes. Apart from that I was completely taken up with eagerness and curiosity about all the things that lay ahead: the monastery, the school, the journey. At last our small caravan of nine horses assembled in front of the house. My parents and my brother and sister were to accompany me to the monastery, and Gyalo Döndrub sat before my father in the saddle. I mounted the horse that the monks had brought for me. It had a high wooden saddle, which was to prevent my falling off. But I was used to riding bare-backed, and my new horse, the handsomest I had ever seen, turned out to be very gentle.

Shartsong Ritrö, the Shartsong Hermitage, was only about a couple of hours' distance from Tengtser, and our path led down to a river which was spanned by a bridge. When we had crossed this bridge and followed the course of the river round several bends we saw the monastery perched above us like an enormous eyrie clinging to the rockface. I had never seen anything like it in my life before. The white houses contrasted brilliantly with the brown rock, most of which was covered with lush green conifer trees. A deep blue sky was like a dome over the spectacular scene. In astonishment I wondered how we were ever going to get up that five-hundred-foot-high cliff. First of all we rode along narrow serpentine paths through aromatic cedar woods, gradually rising higher and higher until we came to a tunnel-like door before which twenty monks carrying incense sticks were lined up. They all bowed low as we arrived.

As a greeting they handed me a white good-luck scarf, the kata, which is a symbol of good fortune, divine blessing, gratitude and intercession, peace and hospitality. There are many kinds of kata, ranging from the long, broad scarves of costly silk to small, stiffened strips of tulle. As I was the reincarnation of Tagtser, the highest prelate of this monasterial community, I was naturally presented with particularly beautiful silk ribbons, which I accepted without dismounting. Naturally, I much enjoyed being received in this solemn fashion, and in particular I appreciated being treated as though I were an adult.

My horse was now led by the bridle through the doorway up

to a large house where I was then helped from the saddle and solemnly welcomed by the Abbot of Shartsong Ritrö himself. He invited us into the great assembly hall of the monks and offered me and my parents tea, curdled milk and rice, the foods customarily offered in welcome. But although the buttered rice with sugar and raisins looked very attractive I was hardly allowed even to taste it because they are merely part of a short symbolic act of greeting. We then took our leave of the Abbot and the monks of my retinue, and were taken by my Steward to the Tagtser Labrang. It was a large building whose one-storeyed front had two courtyards through which one passed to reach the main two-storeyed building. The upper part of the main house was to be my quarters. When we got there we took off our outer clothing and drank tea.

After that we went in the company of the Abbot to offer a sacrifice in the monastery proper. This solemn act of sacrifice is called Chöjal. At all the altars we passed we had to set up butter-lamps, light incense sticks, and lay down white good-luck scarves. The path to the monastery skirted a steep rock-face and passed over a wooden bridge that was so narrow that we could cross only in single file. This dangerous-looking structure was held in place by posts embedded in the rockface. The sight of it scared me and I would have liked to turn about, but I pulled myself together and courageously went forward step by step. To my left trees growing from fissures in the rockface stretched out crippled branches towards me, obviously much buffeted by the wind, whilst to the right was a dark abyss that made me giddy to look at. My father, who noticed that I was scared, took my right hand, and with the left I groped my way along the rockface looking straight ahead all the time. Finally we came to a small chapel. With a sigh of relief I looked round once more at the narrow bridge. The monastery porter could easily remove the planks if it ever became necessary to prevent the entrance of undesirables. But us he received with deep respect. I immediately said a prayer of thanksgiving in the little chapel with its tiny flower garden.

We were now in the secluded area of the monastery, and I found myself strangely excited as we made our way up steps hewn out of the solid rock. These steps were so high that now and again my father had to help me, or let me clamber up on all fours. Before long we reached the house of the porter, which was beside another chapel, which was dedicated to the god Jampa and was therefore called the Jamkhang. It was no more than a large cave hewn in the solid rock, and the stone steps led into it through a small door. As well as a statue of Jampa it contained many small figures of gods. For the first time in my life I saw walls painted with coloured frescoes.

About thirty steps higher up we came to another such cave. Hundreds of years before, pious hermits had decorated the walls with scenes from the life of Buddha. Some of the paintings were so faded as to be unrecognisable, but others had since been restored. We went up another fifteen steps and then we stood before the biggest temple in the monastery, the Karmapa Lhakhang. It was also hewn out of the solid rock and twice as high as the others. In the lower storey there were three statues of Buddha, and in the flickering light of the butter-lamps they gave an impression of being alive. In the upper storey there was a Chörten, a reliquary shrine of one of the reincarnations of the founder of the sect, Karmapa. This was the most valued possession of the Shartsong Monastery. It was a tomb about eight feet high, containing, amongst other things, one of Karmapa's bones. I was told that the Karmapa who was honoured here had initiated the great reformer of our church, Tsong Khapa, into the mysteries of the Tibetan script almost six hundred years ago when Tsong Khapa was a small monk at the tender age of three. Although I found it difficult, and sometimes impossible, to follow the explanations of the Abbot, I was very conscious of the privilege of being allowed to go to school here.

The window in the upper storey attracted me so much that finally I went up to it and leant out. Down below I could see a narrow bed in which hollyhocks and asters were blooming. But already my mother had caught hold of my coat and pulled me back. The dangerous climb had scared her too and now she was anxious for the safety of the child who was to spend the immediate future up here. Many pilgrims were too giddy to dare the climb and went no farther than the lower part of the monastery. Whilst a few of those who braved the steep climb had grown dizzy and fallen.

From Karmapa Lhakhang it was not much farther to the highest point of the monastery, on which four houses were built: a one-storeyed dwelling, a chapel and two four-storeyed buildings. The path ended there, though experienced climbers would go on higher in order to burn incense beyond the last buildings, or perhaps to set up a prayer-flag. These houses were astonishingly perched on the solid rocks; and with their white walls against the ochreous background, in which here and there a gnarled and twisted juniper bush had managed to fix its roots, they made an impressive picture. From up here you had a splendid view down into the deep gorge with its tossing, tumbling river, ~nd over to the snow- and ice-covered mountains in the distance. Clearest of all you could see Chöchungla and Chakhyungri, which are named after the villages at their foot. Incidentally, almost all our mountains are named either after gods or villages.

Each of the twenty or so monks who lived up here had a room of his own in one or other of the two big houses. These rooms were very modestly furnished, and the only decoration was a picture roll with scenes from the lives of Buddhist saints. Apart from certain books each monk had a bell and a thunderbolt. During the day their bed served as a seat. A curtain cut off the small kitchen in which there was nothing but a stove, a water pail and a store cupboard. In accordance with the general solemn atmosphere which prevailed you kept as quiet as possible and moved always with measured tread. You had to be particularly careful when using the few stone steps because they were very steep. In addition many rungs of the age-old wooden ladders were broken, and the ropes that served as a hand-rail were dark and greasy from long years of use.

The monks led a very frugal life. They lived on the alms given to them by pious pilgrims, and from barley-meal and butter sent up to them by relatives from the surrounding villages, whilst now and again a load of provisions would arrive from the Tagtser Labrang in Kumbum. But at least there was no shortage of fuel, and when going down to the stream to fetch water, each monk would always bring back with him the brushwood he needed to boil the water for his daily tea. As there was no well or other source of water in the monastery the monks had to go down to the river. This they would do with wooden barrels strapped to their backs, and it took them about an hour to clamber up the steep way back carrying their water. To obtain even a modest supply of water in such circumstances was very hard work indeed, and it was therefore all the more touching to observe that each monk had a small plant in a pot before his window, which he kept carefully watered.

The two big houses were dependencies of the Kumbum monastery. The one had been founded by my Tagtser Labrang, and the other by Marang Labrang. The most beautiful building was the small one-storeyed house, which was also occupied by monks. It stood on a rocky prominence which jutted out over the abyss, and it had a veranda on which I was often to sit in the sun and enjoy the marvellous view. The particular situation of the monastery allowed a very simple solution of the problem of sanitation. By the side of the small house a latrine had been erected which jutted out over the abyss.

The fourth building, the Rigsumgön Lhakhang chapel, contained the sixteen-foot-high statues of Chenresi, Jambaiyang and Chagtor, which were the biggest the monastery possessed. These three divinities together represented the threefold nature of Buddha, Chenresi, the God of Mercy, is reincarnated in the Dalai Lama. Jambaiyang is Wisdom Become God, and he is also the patron of astronomy. In his right he holds the sword of science, and in his left, bedded on a lotus leaf, is the Book of Wisdom. Chagtor is the Defender of the Faith. There are small tables before the effigies of the gods in this chapel too and on them are butter-lamps, incense sticks, little figures of gods, flowers and many katas or good-luck scarves. Pieces of jewellery, coins and other small gifts, precious to those who offered them, had been brought here by pilgrims to fortify their prayers to the gods. The monastery is a holy place, and pilgrims visit it from all the surrounding areas, for Tsong Khapa, the great monastery founder of the fourteenth century, received his first lessons here; and the monastery was built many, many years before that with the help of the inhabitants of Balangtsa, Tengtser, Chakhyung, Chöchung and Gyatsa Mani.

Deeply impressed by all I had seen, I returned from my sacrificial errand to my house. I was quite overwhelmed by the thought that Tagtser Labrang belonged to me, that I was the most important person in this whole wonderful place, and that in the future I was to live here with these monks, who had all received me so amiably and considerately. I was shown the stables in the first courtyard, and then the quarters of the cooks and other servants round the second courtyard. A beautifully furnished room had been prepared for me in the two-storeyed house. The mattresses were covered with choice rugs and valuable coloured thankas decorated the walls. I even had my own house altar. But for me the greatest advantage of the place was that I could go through a door out onto the roof of the lower house and there enjoy a marvellous view over the valley to the distant mountain peak.

The ceremonies in connection with my induction lasted three days, and during that time I became acquainted almost exclusively with the agreeable aspects of my new life. My parents and my brother and sister took part in the ceremonies and spent their free time with me, but I certainly was beginning to feel that my new position was separating me from them more and more, and this made me surreptitiously feel the little sack with my sheep's osselets and my coloured pebbles, which was round my neck, as practically the last tie with my old life. And then the moment came when we had to part. When I saw my parents preparing to leave, a terrible regret invaded my heart and I wept bitterly, and not all the loving encouragement and persuasions of my parents and the monks could console me. I felt a stranger in the new surroundings, I wanted to go home with my parents, and I was moved by a deep longing for my playmates and for all the things I had left behind.

The monks did their best to distract me; they brought me toys and sweetmeats, and they tried to entertain me with stories, but I rejected the toys and even the lovely titbits they offered me, and I was deaf to their stories. Finally they decided on a subterfuge. I was persuaded that my mother had to go home for a short while in order to see that everything was in order on the farm, whilst my father would stay with me here in the monastery. That did deceive me, and I was quite cheerful when I said good-bye to her as she set off for home with Gyalo Döndrub and Tsering Dröma. Quite reassured I went to bed that evening firmly convinced that my father would be sleeping in the next room as he had done on all the preceding nights since our arrival.

But the next day there was no sign of him, and when I made anxious inquiries as to his whereabouts I was told that he had gone to the nearest village in order to buy a sheep's head for me. As I regarded the soft and gelatinous parts of this dish, and in particular the tongue, as a great delicacy, they succeeded in fobbing me off for a while with this yarn. But it was not long before I became mistrustful again; and, on the point of tears, I impatiently demanded to see my father. The monks did their level best to turn my attention to other matters. They made me the most wonderful wood and paper dolls and they kneaded the most laughable figures out of tsampa dough. And one monk, who had a gift for making the funniest faces, even did make me laugh. But not for long, and the next moment I was in tears. And even when the fat, good-natured cook appeared with a dish of roast mutton which smelt wonderful I couldn't get a mouthful down. Disconcerted he carried it off again, and I was left behind staring out into the dusk and shaken from time to time by violent sobs. The only one with me now was Püntso, the monk who was to be my teacher and servant. He prepared my bed for the night and spoke to me in a soothing sing-song. But I didn't want to listen to what he said, my grief was too deep. However, in the end my tiredness got the better of me and I sank into a deep and dreamless sleep.

5. Three Months in Shartsong and the Journey to Kumbum

THE worthy Püntso finally succeeded in dissipating my sadness; and time, which heals all wounds, did the rest. Every morning he came into my room, woke me gently, and then saw to it that I washed properly. He brought a brass bowl with warm water, and also a small piece of wood, with which, after biting one end into a sort of brush, I learned to clean my teeth. At home we had always cleaned our teeth with a wet finger. After that Püntso would hand me a wooden bowl with hot fragrant tea. With it there were rolls or tsampa, and usually a dish with vegetables or meat. Püntso was a kind and considerate major-domo, and before long I trusted him completely. He was forty years old, rather small and very thin, and he wore a pointed beard such as I had never seen previously except on the equestrian statue of the protective deity Kyeri in the temple of my native village.

During the first days of my stay in Shartsong, Püntso didn't leave me alone at all, and he always did his best to dissipate any fears, even the most trifling, from which I suffered on account of my new environment. And very gently he introduced me to my few duties. One morning he appeared with a wooden tablet and explained that I must now begin to learn to write. The wooden board was fairly solid and it had a convenient handle with which you could hold it on your knees. The upper surface had been darkened by being rubbed with some sort of fat or oil, and it was then strewn with chalky powder. You wrote with a diagonally sharpened piece of bamboo stick, which, used skilfully, allowed you to make strokes of varying thickness by scraping away the chalk powder to reveal the dark wood beneath.

Püntso told me to copy a letter which was already inscribed for me as a model. The task appealed to me, and I set to work with a will. Of course, I didn't succeed straight away, and my first attempts were more like the scratchings of our cock when he dug up the ground for worms. When it was obviously proving too difficult for me Püntso would guide my hand. After this morning handwriting lesson I was allowed to play. Usually Püntso himself went out with me into the woods, but sometimes it was one of the older monks. This was the time when I missed my playmates very keenly. There were one or two young fellows in the monastery, but they were all quite a good bit older, and they all wore the red monastic habit already, whereas I still went around in my brown chuba or woollen coat.

However, on the whole, my day was so filled with lessons, games and instruction that I had no time to give myself up to sad thoughts. But at night when I lay on my mattress and the flickering light of the butter-lamp cast eerie shadows on the walls I was overcome by homesickness and very painfully conscious of the separation from everyone and everything I had loved. In particular I missed my mother, who would lovingly stroke my forehead when I felt upset or unwell; and the next day I would once again ask Püntso the same constantly repeated question: When would my parents be coming to visit me?

In the woods there was a large bumkhang which I visited frequently, and I soon felt myself at home there even without company. Before I started to pick flowers or look for berries I would walk round the bumkhang several times in a clockwise direction as prescribed by long-standing religious tradition. Sometimes I was allowed to go down to the river and play on its banks, but then I was always accompanied by one or other of the monks who happened to be going down to fetch water. Perhaps they were afraid that I might run away, and I really think I might have done had I been left unguarded, and, above all, had I known which of the roads that met at the bridge led back to Tengtser.

However, as time passed I gradually settled down to my new life in the monastery. My circle of duties extended too, and after only a few weeks I began to receive the first pilgrims from the neighbourhood in my house, where they presented me with the usual white good-luck ribbons together with various gifts, including butter and flour. They would bow reverently before me and I was taught to bless them by the laying-on of hands.

One fine summer's evening after my lessons I was sitting on my roof veranda and looking longingly in the direction in which I thought Tengtser must lie, when I heard the sound of horse's hooves in the yard below. I leapt to my feet and let out a shout of joy: my father had unexpectedly come to visit me! I rushed headlong down the steps and out into the yard and embraced him eagerly. Tears of joy and happiness rolled down my cheeks and for a moment or two I was speechless. My normally so unemotional father had to pull himself together too, and with suspiciously bright eyes he handed me a basket of my favourite pastries mother had sent me. We kissed each other on forehead and cheeks, and I made no attempt to stop my tears, forgetting the well-meant exhortations of the Abbot and of Püntso that a Rimpoche must behave like a man and not cry like a child. I squeezed my father's hand repeatedly, as though I never wanted to be parted from him again. He stayed for two days, and when he went back it was with the solemn promise that he would come again soon and bring my mother and my brother and sister.

I now had something to look forward to, and it made me quite cheerful. Suddenly I found it twice as easy to learn, because I was anxious to show my parents that I was a good scholar; and after a month I knew so many letters that under Püntso's guidance I began to read the first words in the prayer books for beginners. We also began to learn certain prayers by heart, and thanks to an excellent memory I made rapid progress. Püntso was a good teacher, and he never made the mistake of driving me too hard. If my attention began to wander during lessons he would take me by the hand and go for a walk with me, whilst at the same time, but almost unnoticeably, continuing the lesson.

I knew my way around in the monastery very well now. The long connecting bridge between the two parts had long lost its terrors for me and I could go over it without assistance, as I often did when I went on my own to visit the monks in their cells. They always made me very welcome, and they usually had some little surprise for me: wonderfully complicated paper dragons, or funny little figures kneaded from dough; or they would give me sweets.

And at last one day my parents did appear with Tsering Dröma and Gyalo Döndrub on a three-day visit. Full of pride I showed my brother and sister round my little kingdom. They were particularly impressed when I took them on to my little veranda and fed the birds, which came flying up as soon as I had scattered the first grains for them. My special favourites were the thrushes, because they sang so beautifully, but I had to watch out for the cheeky choughs, who would always try to snatch away the food of the other birds with their big yellow beaks. In particular I was proud of being able to tell my brother and sister the names of all my feathered guests. From my veranda you could also occasionally see a musk-deer or two scampering over the rocks. They are usually very shy animals, but here, where no one ever killed anything, they seemed to know that they were safe, and they would therefore come up quite close. Of course I presented my brother and sister to the other monks too, and we spent happy hours with white-haired Thubten, who would perform his tricks with paper and stones to the great delight of Tsering Dröma and Gyalo Döndrub. He had already taught me the "Pick up sticks" game, and my sister showed herself to be very skilful at it. But the three days passed very quickly, and then with a heavy heart I had to say goodbye to them again, but this time I suffered the parting with greater composure.

I had been three months under Püntso's experienced guidance when one day the Abbot and the Steward came to inform me that now I must leave Shartsong and go on to the head monastery of Kumbum. I had quite quickly got used to life in the monastery and I had made satisfactory progress. And, of course, I had known all along that my stay in Shartsong Ritrö was to be temporary and to serve merely as a preparation for my formal inauguration in Kumbum. It was therefore not all too painful to leave Shartsong Ritrö, and I eagerly joined in the preparations for my departure. A tailor and a boot-maker had been sent from Kumbum and they now fitted me out with even better quality clothing and boots than before. I still had to wear brown lay-clothing, but this time it was of the finest silk, and the shafts of my boots were even more sumptuously decorated. As head covering I was now given a shallow broad-brimmed hat made of gilt papier mâché such as only rimpoches and abbots wear when they go out riding in summer. These two artisans were both monks themselves, and with them had come a third monk who was a saddler. It was his duty to equip my horse for my entry into the main monastery. He decorated my wooden saddle with small chased-metal plates, and with his awl he made me a new set of harness from yak leather. The headdress for the horse of a man of my rank had a gilt buttonlike top, and from the neck harness sprang a bushy yak-tail dyed scarlet.

To my great delight I learnt that the way to Kumbum went through Tengtser, so I now had something else exciting to look forward to: the day when I could present myself to my old friends in my new state. In the meantime we had been joined by one or two dignitaries from my labrang in Kumbum, and early one very beautiful morning our little caravan finally started on its way. The bridge below the monastery was still in shadow and it was actually covered with a thin layer of ice, so the good Püntso carefully led my horse by the bridle over the dangerous part, whilst I cast a last look at Shartsong Ritrö where I had shed so many tears and nevertheless had spent so many happy days. I was still too young to realise just how much I owed this old rock-perched monastery, and I was only too anxious to leave it now and get to Tengtser. My expectations were screwed high, but in the event they were not disappointed.

The first to greet me was my old friend the herdsman. I wondered whether he had deliberately set out late that morning

in order to be still there when my little procession made its way
into Tengtser. Even from a distance I could see that the villagers
had made preparations for my reception. For example, new
prayer-flags waved a cheerful welcome from all the roofs. And
over the doors there were freshly-washed colourful sun-blinds.
At the same time the incense fumes of burning mountain-rose
petals climbed straight up into the sky. The small community
was anxious to express its gratitude that a Tagtser Rimpoche
had been chosen from its ranks.

The whole village was assembled to welcome me, and as I
slowly rode through the crowds I could see the women furtively
wiping their eyes with the backs of their hands. My mother
received me at the door of our farmstead, and I dismounted and
took the kata and a bowl of sweet cream from her hands. Then
we joyfully embraced. After which, accompanied by Püntso
and the other monks, I went through the courtyard, where the
incense rose vertically into the sky, into the best room of my
parents' house, which had once been my home too. To my surprise there were new carpets and silk covers, all more colourful
and obviously more valuable than any I had ever seen in our
modest home before. They all came from Kumbum and they
had been brought to the house by the monks to embellish my
reception. Before long there was a joyful crowd in the courtyard, where the twenty horses of our company were tethered.
There was plenty to eat and drink for everyone, and our neighbours were obviously enjoying the unique occasion enormously.

After we had offered sacrifice to the gods I sat down with my
parents and the monks to have our own meal. We drank the
steaming tea in silence. My mother had once again baked the
most wonderful currant pastry for me and she put a large
quantity of fresh cream into every cup of tea I drank, whilst I
sat there on a silk cushion and was treated as a rimpoche by
everyone. I took food and drink even before the Abbot and the
Steward. It was a strangely exalting feeling to play the chief role
amongst all those adults, but at the same time it imposed an
obligation and so I did my best to show myself worthy of my

privileged position. The good Püntso was in his element, and he was here, there and everywhere, making quite certain that the formal protocol of such ceremonies was strictly observed.

Despite all my good resolutions I was soon longing for the end of the extended meal, and I could hardly wait until it was ended and I was allowed to go into the kitchen to my mother. Püntso's thoughtful warning to take good care of my silk clothes was soon forgotten of course, and from the kitchen I ran into the byre where I pressed a newborn calf in my arms. Kyimo, the yard dog, came jumping up and licking my hand, but the cat, who seemed to know that I hadn't forgiven her for killing my little musk-deer, kept out of my way. When Püntso finally ran me to earth in the kitchen again, where my mother had prepared one or two dainties for me, my beautiful silk clothes were covered with spots and stains. But he seemed to have reckoned with this, because he immediately produced a new coat for me, and I was a neat and tidy child again.

I was thoroughly tired when I was brought to bed that evening, but my father and mother sat beside me for a while and gave me good advice, saying that if I behaved myself well in Kumbum and did my very best then that would be to their advantage too, and in gratitude they would soon visit me again. And with the firm intention of giving my parents nothing but joy and satisfaction, I finally fell asleep.

I didn't stay in bed long the next day, and after breakfast I would have liked above all to go out to the bumkhang with my old playmates, but it was pointed out that I was now a rimpoche, and that it was therefore not right and proper for me to play in the dirt and dust. Regretfully, I admitted the truth of this; but although I couldn't do exactly as I liked, the three days I spent in my old home went all too quickly. The further preparations for my journey to Kumbum took up some time. Once again my parents and my brother and sister were to accompany me, and in order that they should be suitably garbed they were presented with splendid silken garments from Tagtser Labrang.

When we finally set out on the fourth day the whole village

gathered once more to see us off. I was already mounted on my horse and I acknowledged the good wishes and blessings of our neighbours as they stood there with folded hands lining the caravan route. Then the village headman, shrewd old Pasang, came up to me and urged me in his jocular way to be a credit to the village in Kumbum. But behind his jocularity it was easy for me to see that he too was deeply moved, and I, of course, was very near to tears. However, I was getting used to partings now, and I was looking forward with excitement to my entry into Kumbum.

The journey took two days. We stayed the one night in Churkha, where my mother's parents had a large farm, much larger than our small property in Tengtser. Churkha was also a bigger village and had twice as many inhabitants. Here too the whole village turned out to greet me warmly. In the house of my grandparents I met a nine-year-old cousin named Gyantsen, the son of my mother's brother. We quickly became friends and we spent the rest of the afternoon playing merrily. Gyantsen told me about life in Churkha, and asked me about my stay in Shartsong Ritrö. That evening when I was lying under costly coverings in the best room in the house it was a long time before I could sleep; the idea that in Kumbum I should be still farther away from my parents disturbed me, whilst the certainty that in the future I was to occupy a high and honourable position did not altogether console me.

The next day was the eighth of the fifth month of the Iron-Sheep year. A Tsipa, a highly respected astrologer of the monastery, had calculated that my arrival on this day would be particularly auspicious. In my country we use the lunar calendar, and the first day of the New Moon is the first day of the month, and Full Moon is the fifteenth day of the month. The years fall into various cycles. In each cycle there are twelve constantly recurring years, and each bears the name of an animal: Mouse, Bull, Tiger, Hare, Dragon, Snake, Horse, Sheep, Monkey, Bird, Dog and Pig. Parallel with this cycle there is a further cycle of five pairs of years, and these five couples bear the names of elements: Wood, Fire, Earth, Iron and Water, whereby the individual element is used in its male aspect in the first year, and in its female aspect in the second. Such double cycles are completed once every sixty years. According to Tibetan reckoning, we are now living in the sixteenth cycle of our modern era, which lasts from 1927 to 1986.

As a lunar year is quite considerably shorter than a solar year, which coincides with the seasons, the difference has to be made up frequently, and the Tibetan calendar does this by adding a full month every three years. The months themselves have no particular names and they are merely counted. The days of the week are called after stars or their symbols. Every Tibetan can tell you what animal the year he was born in was named after, but very few Tibetans can tell you anything more detailed than that. The innumerable combinations made possible by the Tibetan calendar offer a promising field to astrologers, who are held in high respect in Tibet. If they distinguish themselves they can rise to the rank of Tsipa, and each fair-sized monastery has at least one Tsipa.

At dawn we started off again, moving still farther northwards. About halfway between Kumbum and Churkha we were met by five monks on horseback, who had been sent out to meet us and to accompany me into Kumbum with due solemnity. There were bells on the collars of their horses, and you could hear the gay jingle at a great distance. As they came up to us they sprang from their saddles, bowed deeply, and offered me magnificent good-luck scarves with long silk fringes.

Our way now passed through tilled fields bordered by silver poplars, and after a while we reached the first foothills of the mountains. Beneath us was a wide valley into which we had to descend, and before doing so I gave a last farewell glance at the mountain Kyeri, deeply affected, yet certainly in no mood for sad thoughts. Püntso now trotted his horse alongside mine and gave me detailed instructions as to how I was to behave during the coming ceremonies. Ahead of us I could already see an enormous snow-white cotton tent decorated with the eight Tibetan good-luck signs, and standing in a vast meadow of blossoming flowers. Püntso informed me that the name of this meadow was Trashithang.

A great number of monks were gathered round the tent and as we came up they greeted me with deep bows. I was now the only one to remain mounted, and, taking the bridle, Püntso led my horse up to the tent entrance, where he assisted me to dismount and then accompanied me inside. Large cushions had been placed on the ground inside the tent, and in the middle was one which was higher than the others, and had been covered with a rich cloth of silk. It was on this one that I now sat down. Tea and rice were offered to me, and afterwards white katas. As he presented his gift each giver always opened his mouth wide, drawing in his breath in a deep sigh and showing the tip of his tongue, which is the traditional way of expressing loyalty and devotion. The widespread belief that the tongue is thrust out is erroneous.

After this ceremony of welcome we mounted our horses again and continued our journey for perhaps an hour through gently undulating country, until suddenly from the brow of one of the hills we negotiated we saw Kumbum below us. It was a fascinating sight. The monastery lay within brown hills whose slopes were dotted with juniper bushes and cedars, whilst in the valley itself the lush fields were bordered by poplars and willows. To complete a wonderful picture white clouds sailed slowly over a deep-blue sky. I was deeply impressed by the size and beauty of Kumbum, and I felt that I could already sense the spirit of orthodox piety and ancient wisdom for which this monastery with all its rimpoches was renowned. I reined in my horse and remained there for some time lost in wonder, until after a while Püntso gently nudged me.

It was then that I noticed very many red dots at the foot of the monastery. They seemed to be moving like corn in the wind. And then I could hear, at first softly, and afterwards more and more clearly, the sound of oboes and trumpets, followed a little later by the sound of the monks chanting. Was this really all for me, the incarnation of Tagtser? I sent my horse forward again and before long we reached the beginning of the long double line of monks in red gowns who were there to welcome me. We passed the temple flags Pen and Gyeltsen, and made our way through the bowing, murmuring monks up to the monastery itself. Followed by a monk who held an umbrella of yellow silk over me as a further sign of my dignity, I rode slowly through the narrow streets of the monastery, and through further lines of monks murmuring prayers and bowing. The silken umbrella is, by the way, one of the traditional Tibetan good-luck symbols.

I saw the Chörtens, or tombs of dead and gone lamas, and once again I was keenly conscious of the great honour which was being shown to Tagtser in my person. At the great gate of the labrang I was greeted by a white-haired monk with a kata and a bowl of fresh cream. This was the moment at which I was able to dismount; and Püntso and the chief steward of the labrang accompanied me into a large hall, where a throne about six feet high had been erected for me. A number of steps led up to it and many hands were now outstretched to assist me to my seat. But I rejected them all and called upon Püntso and my father to render me that service. Then, sitting cross-legged on my throne, I waited silently and expectantly to see what was going to happen next.

I was already very tired by this time, but I still had the real ceremony of welcome to go through. From outside could still be heard the gradually diminishing chant of the monks, and from time to time the sound of drums and the clash of cymbals. Tea, rice and curdled milk were handed to me, and bareheaded I received the chief dignitaries of the monastery, led by the Abbot himself, a dignified but obviously very agreeable personality to whom I immediately felt myself drawn. He was followed by the Shengo, the highest dispenser of justice in the monastery, who also takes second place in the monastic hierarchy. He was a very big, broad-shouldered man, and as a symbol of his office he carried a long four-edged metal sceptre. Dark-brown pock-marked features ended in a small white beard, and altogether his appearance was quite formidable, and I shivered and looked first to my father and then to Püntso for reassurance, who both immediately soothed my fears with un-obtrusive gestures. Later on I was to learn that the Shengo was by no means as frightening as he looked, and that, in addition, he was well-disposed towards me.

Behind the Shengo came about thirty rimpoches, who represent the aristocracy of the monastery, with their stewards. They all ceremoniously handed me good-luck scarves. This solemn greeting by the inmates of the cloister lasted about an hour, and it cost me a great deal of effort to receive the greetings of the monks quietly and not to fidget. But now and again I did chance a swift glance at the many sacred pictures grouped around an enthroned Buddha on the walls. As I already knew from the temple in Shartsong Ritrö, the figures by his side were those of Chenresi and Jampa.

Most of the monks who filed past me were old and dignified men, and they all smiled at me in a very friendly fashion. I did my best to return their smiles, and to suppress my increasing inclination to slide around on my seat. But finally the ceremony was over, and then I lost no time in getting down from my throne— once again refusing all assistance but that of my father and Püntso. Then at last I found myself alone with my parents, my brother and sister, Püntso and just those who actually belonged to my household. We withdrew to the rooms which had been set aside to serve as my living-quarters, and there I was able to rest for the first time after a very busy day. There were two large and beautiful rooms, and a huge window of real glass through which you could look out into a courtyard with beds of red and yellow flowers. My labrang had four such yards, and they all had neatly kept flower-beds.

Püntso now helped me out of my stiff silk clothes and gave me a more comfortable coat of soft brown wool to wear. It was the one I had worn in Shartsong on informal occasions. When we had all refreshed ourselves and rested a little I received a number of young monks I already knew from their visits to me in Tengtser, and, to my great delight, amongst them was Dön-drub, the son of a well-to-do peasant in Tengtser, who was a friend of mine. He had been one of my favourite companions when we used to play around the bumkhang in front of our house. He was already a monk and he was thus able to answer all my eager questions about the life in Kumbum. Although Döndrub was already a monk, and I was not yet a monk, he took great care to see to it that whilst we were sitting there eagerly talking together and eating the dried apricots which he had brought with him, he respectfully sat a little lower than I did.

Whilst we were together, the door opened and a number of my servants came in bearing a large copper dish decorated with silver which contained almost a whole stewed sheep, which they set down before me. It was difficult to believe that this enormous portion of stewed meat was intended for me alone. However, I took a knife which was offered me and cut myself a particularly succulent piece out of the ribs. There were large portions for the other guests too, though served up to them on rather smaller dishes. Noodle soup and various other meat and vegetable dishes completed the meal. We were offered further helpings again and again, and our tea-cups were kept constantly replenished.

After this meal I was left alone with my parents, my brother and sister, and my old friend Döndrub; and we sat there chatting in the flickering light of the mustard-oil lamps—a further reminder of home for me—until it was time to go to bed. Püntso then spread out the blanket and the sheepskin we had brought with us from Shartsong; and with that what had been the greatest day in my life so far finally came to an end. I was so very tired and worn out by the long day that I fell asleep at once, and I hardly heard the loud gong strokes which warned the monks that their night's rest was at hand.

6. First Lessons

THE next morning I carried out my first important duty. Accompanied by my parents, the Steward of Labrang and Püntso, I had to make the Chöjal, or great sacrificial way, throughout the whole monastery, setting up butter-lamps in each one of the thirty temples, burning incense and laying down white good-luck scarves. For hours on end we went up hill and down dale, climbing steep steps and traversing stony paths. On this errand we also came to the most famous part of the monastery, the Temple of Serdong; where, legend has it, our great reformer, Tsong Khapa, first saw the light of day. But even after the strenuous Chömche there was no rest for me, and I had to make inaugural visits to the Abbot and to the many rimpoches of Kumbum; and to each of them I had to present a white good-luck scarf. They all received me amiably and even affectionately, and offered me sweets or made me presents of toys.

In Kumbum they had had a good deal of experience with little boys, and they knew that the first days were the worst. In addition to Döndrub they therefore sent me two other youngsters, Tentsing and Jangchub Nyendra, to me in my labrang; and with these three companions I spent many happy hours, and settled down very quickly in Kumbum; though despite this the renewed parting from my parents and from my brother and sister, who left for Tengtser after six days at Kumbum, was still not easy. But Püntso, who supervised the course of my day, saw to it that a variety of lessons gave me no time to indulge in sad thoughts.

My day was now regulated down to the minute, for in Kumbum the time did not rely on cock-crow or even on the sun. For the first time in my life I saw watches and clocks. In fact, it appeared, I owned no fewer than fifteen cuckoo clocks, many of which hung on the walls in my room. My labrang was one of the largest, and I was passably rich, because my predecessor had accumulated many treasures. However, I was still too small to bother much about my possessions and my real interest was directed to the cases with toys, which, like the clocks, had been brought from Tsarist Russia by my predecessor. I think perhaps that I got most pleasure out of the musical-boxes, which played both gay and sad little tunes. When one of them, perhaps the most beautiful of all, was played, the little figure of a girl appeared, and that always moved me deeply. She pirouetted gaily round and round, and in her hands she carried a box from which, to my great delight, an even smaller figure emerged. I loved this particular toy, and played it again and again, and I used to imagine that the tiny figure which came out of the box carried a still tinier box from which a still tinier figure emerged—and so on, and so on. Perhaps this was my first meeting with the puzzling conception of eternity. Already I had a vague idea of many of the great secrets which were still a closed book to me.

Naturally, it wasn't long before I wanted to learn more details about the life of the man to whom I owed all these wonderful things. One or two of the older monks were able to tell me extraordinary things about him. He had lived to be an old man, and he had escaped with his life during the terrible insurrection of the Hu-hus in the previous century when Kumbum was burnt to the ground. His butcher, who, like all butchers in Tibet, was a Mohammedan, hid him and his teacher from the marauding hordes. But when things became so dangerous that he could offer them asylum no longer he gave them a tent, and they fled from the Hu-hus as beggars, making their way to Mongolia. They suffered great privations, losing even their tent, but in time my predecessor developed a natural gift for healing, and before long it brought him fame and, ultimately, fortune. After a while he was called to Russia where he also met with great success. Finally, as a mature man, he returned to Kumbum with a caravan full of treasures, including the cuckoo clocks and the musical-boxes, and at Kumbum he caused the Tagtser Labrang to be rebuilt. On his death he left the next reincarnation, in other words me, a very rich living indeed.

Thus as a little boy I was already installed as master over my kingdom, the Tagtser Labrang, with about seventy souls under me. I lived in the biggest and most beautiful rooms in the administrative buildings. Püntso, to whose care I was entrusted, had a small apartment not far from my own, whilst the monks of the labrang lived in a number of smaller buildings. The stables were in the biggest of the courtyards, and there were never fewer than a score of them. During the course of centuries wise stewards had increased the wealth of the labrang, which had passed from one Rimpoche to another. In addition to the revenues from the farms and lands of the labrang there had been rich gifts from pious princes and prosperous merchants of the immediate and even the more distant neighbourhood. The fields and the farms were leased to peasants and farmers who had to deliver up a certain agreed percentage of their yield as an annual impost; and from this the labrang paid taxes to the Chinese Resident in Siling.

Tagtser Labrang had enormous storehouses in which the contributions of the various tenant farmers and so on were put by, though it was only unwillingly that I ever entered them, for they were enormous and gloomy, and as yet I could not find my way around in them alone. The granary was intimidating enough, but the buttery made me quite frightened. It was dark and dank, and the walls were so cold that to go in there made me shiver. It was here that the large quantities of butter we required were stored away. In Tengtser we had always put milk in our tea, and a little butter only at the main meals, but here in Kumbum, as also in Lhasa and throughout Central Tibet, they drank exclusively what we call butter-tea. Very often two or three hundred monks would come to our temple to pray, and as we had to provide them with butter-tea and tsampa, we certainly needed large supplies.

In the first weeks in Kumbum, Püntso was again the only one to give me my lessons, just as he had done before; and after a while he expressed himself as satisfied with the progress I was making in reading and writing. Then one day he told me that I had made such good progress that it was now time for me to have another teacher; and he took me to Minyag Rimpoche, whose profound knowledge did credit to the monastery. It was to this very learned and highly intelligent man that I owe the greater part of my education, though Püntso continued to give me lessons in grammar and orthography. Every morning at nine o'clock, together with my two friends Jangchub Nyendra and Tentsing, I presented myself to Minyag Rimpoche for lessons; in which, incidentally, about fifty other lads of more or less our age also took part. To our great regret, we three friends were never allowed to sit together, and from the very first lesson Minyag Rimpoche wisely gave us places away from each other. I learned to read certain prayers and to recite them by heart. My ambition was aroused now, because I had to compete with other boys.

By midday the lessons were over, and after a meal together my two friends and I used to play until four o'clock. Tentsing and Jangchub Nyendra were not rimpoches, but they both came from rich and highly respected families. During our games it naturally happened that we sometimes squabbled. Püntso, who always kept an eye on us, would then talk very seriously to me, pointing out that as a rimpoche it was my duty to control myself. I and my companions must never quarrel about a sweet or a toy. At four o'clock we had to be in our rooms and then we would go once more through the material we had dealt with during our morning lesson; a sort of homework session.

After our evening meal at six o'clock came prayers and religious exercises in the nearby temple. We said our prayers very conscientiously and painstakingly, adopting exactly the prescribed attitudes; which were, in fact, familiar to me from prayers in our house chapel in Tengtser and from prayers in Shartsong. But here in Kumbum we had to repeat our prayers many times.

First of all we folded our hands, then we put them to our foreheads, lips and chests. Kneeling, we would then touch the ground again and again with our foreheads, at the same time murmuring prayers, usually the best-known *Om mani padme hum*, which, roughly translated, means: "Oh, thou treasure in the lotus." It was not unusual for particularly pious monks to develop a permanent horny nodule from constantly pressing the forehead against the hard wood or stone of the floor, a sort of excrescence covered by very hard skin. Apart from this form of prayer we also had to practise a sort of proskynesis, prostrating ourselves three times before each of the seven statues of the gods, of which Jampa's was the most important. This full prostration is even more difficult and arduous than praying on bended knees. Just now and again we small boys did not show the appropriate solemnity required by these involved religious exercises. But hardly had we allowed ourselves a little latitude than we were called to order by Püntso, or one of the other older monks. When we had performed these complicated devotions before all seven statues we were always anxious to run off and play, but Püntso usually headed us off by taking us through whatever we had already learnt by heart that day. Whoever had not mastered his lesson had to keep at it until he could repeat it fluently.

After three months I had learnt so much that I was ready to be ordained a monk. The Steward of Tagtser Labrang now went to visit one of the most respected of the lamas of the monastery, Cheshö Rimpoche—taking a good-luck scarf with him as a present—to ask him to ordain me and hear my vows. One of the many common errors and misunderstandings about Tibet which I have met with since leaving my country is that the name lama applies to every Tibetan monk. This is not so; lama is a title, and means "superior." And, for example, a layman who has distinguished himself in the sphere of religious knowledge may properly be addressed as lama. It is therefore also wrong to refer to the Tibetan religion as Lamaism. If it is to be given a special name of its own at all then it would be much more accurate to call it "Tibetan Buddhism."

In Tibet we refer to our religion just as "the" religion, and at the utmost perhaps as "the religion of Buddha." A Tibetan who does not by chance belong to one of the religious minorities will, if you ask him what his religion is, tell you that he is a "Nangpa," which means "one who belongs." Actually anyone, provided that he belongs to some confession or other, can call himself a Nangpa, since Buddhism knows no religious fanaticism. Outside Tibet the word "Chipa," which we use to describe someone who is not a Buddhist—actually the word means someone who does not belong—is wrongly translated "foreigner" or "stranger." The correct word for foreigner or stranger is "Chilingpa."

The Lama Cheshö Rimpoche granted my steward's request, and it was arranged that on a certain day of the eighth month which was considered particularly propitious for the ceremony, the lama would hear my vows together with those of a sixteen-year-old named Kesang. At the agreed time, in the cool early hours of a radiantly clear summer's day, Cheshö Rimpoche appeared in my rooms together with four other high lama priests. My father, who had hurried to the monastery from Tengtser on hearing that this great event was to take place, awaited them in my company together with Püntso and Kesang.

The five lamas sat down on costly cushions prepared for them, and immediately became deeply absorbed in prayer. The solemn event had a very strange effect on me. I was suddenly seized with terrible fear; I wanted to flee and renounce the monastic life. I was afraid of the monk's habit, which was already lying ready on a small table. According to the strictly prescribed ritual I was now asked whether I wished to become a monk, and to the astonishment of everyone present I remained silent. Both Püntso and my father urged me to answer, but I found it impossible to get a word over my lips. Even their repeated urgings had no effect, and I remained silent. Even the tears which finally came did not relieve my tension. However, as I was already a rimpoche the ceremony went on nevertheless. Kesang, who was not a rimpoche, answered all the questions in the affirmative with firm "La-les, la-les."

Then our heads were shaven and all our clothes were removed, after which we were washed from head to foot in holy water. This latter was a symbolic action by which the whole of our past life as laymen was washed away. After that we were given our religious names as monks, the names by which we should henceforth be recorded in the monasterial roll. The name Tenpa Rabgye had been chosen for me. We then stood in our new habits before the priest who explained to us in solemn words that henceforth our lives would be devoted exclusively to religion. The ceremony was now over, and Püntso handed each of the lamas the usual thanksgiving present, the kukel, consisting of a kata and a sum of money in an envelope. After which they retired and left us alone.

I was a prey to strange and confused feelings. Deep inside me I was profoundly gratified that I had been accepted as a monk of the Order of the Gelugpa sect, which had been founded by Tsong Khapa almost six hundred years previously; and I was filled with pride to think that I, a nine-year-old boy, was entitled to wear the same type of simple, maroon woollen garment that the great reformer himself had worn. But I was still not able to talk about the reasons which had caused my strange silence during the ceremony. My father and Püntso were both deeply disturbed, and they questioned me urgently. But I could only shake my head. I wasn't even prepared to admit how deeply ashamed of myself I was.

The next morning Püntso ordered me to present myself every day at the same time to Cheshö Rimpoche and prostrate myself before him three times in succession whilst saying my prayers. I regarded this as a kind of penance for my behaviour and, in my childish shame, I at first inwardly resented it. But before long this daily penitential act became the most beautiful hour of my day. In order to present myself to Cheshö Rimpoche in his quarters I had to walk for a good quarter of an hour through the monastery grounds, and, keenly interested in everything as I was, I missed no opportunity of looking around me on the way. So many things went on in the streets and byways of the great monastery. You could meet and talk to so many strangers who came up to inquire the way. I found these penitential journeys so interesting that I was truly sorry when the seventh day came and I set off to Cheshö Rimpoche for the last time—without any idea of the wonderful surprise which was awaiting me on my arrival.

When I had concluded my prayers, prostrate before him on the floor, and was about to leave he asked me to wait a moment. Then he went to his altar and took a small brown effigy of a god in his fine, slim hands and gave it to me as a present. I joyfully accepted the ancient clay Buddha statuette in its brocade dress. Sangye Chömden De, who had protected so many in the past, was henceforth to protect me and go with me everywhere. But as I pressed the statuette to my breast in the room of Cheshö Rimpoche I certainly had no idea where my future fate would take us both.

My acceptance into the monastic order brought a number of changes with it. For example, Püntso now woke me at four o'clock in the morning; and particularly in winter I did not find it easy to fulfil my religious duties at such an early hour. After I had quickly washed my face, Püntso would hear the prayers which I had already learnt; and I was allowed to have my breakfast only after I had learnt another one from him. Our timetable remained unchanged, but the lessons themselves required greater effort as they became more difficult; at the same time the prayers I had to learn by heart became longer. In consequence the everyday life of the monastery now occupied my time completely. Week followed week, and month followed month, though now and again the strictly regulated course of the day was interrupted by a short visit from my father, who would bring me a basket of sweet currant buns with their exciting and familiar smell.

The beautiful summer gave way to a cool autumn, and then came winter and covered the black mountain and the monastery building with dazzling white snow. The surrounding landscape was frequently shrouded in thick mist, and I often felt as though

I were on an island. It is in this period that the Festival of Light falls—the Ganden Namchö, with which we celebrate the anniversary of the death of our founder Tsong Khapa, who died on the twenty-fifth of the tenth Tibetan month, that is to say, some time in December, in Ganden, the third largest monastery in Tibet, and then rose amongst the saints. In his honour his followers light thousands of lamps, and during the feast Kumbum was turned into a sea of light. The snow-covered temple and the other monastic buildings shone brightly in the light of innumerable butter-lamps and candles, whose flickering made the ice crystals give back a golden light. I remember that it snowed several times as the great torchlight procession wound its way through the monasterial precincts. It was as though the Heavens themselves wanted to enhance the solemnity of our celebration. It would be difficult to imagine a more beautiful and dramatic picture than that offered by the endless procession of red-garbed monks each holding a flaring resin torch. Many people had come from the neighbouring village of Lussar to join the end of the great procession in honour of Tsong Khapa, and it was regarded as a good omen if the lights burnt steadily and strongly in the frosty air.

Kumbum also celebrated the New Year's Feast with great magnificence. Everyone in the monastery got up just before midnight on the eve of the first day of the first month and entered the house chapel dressed in new and costly garments, there to light new butter-lamps, burn incense, lay new good-luck scarves on the altar, and make offerings of grain, rice, cakes and butter. The most important offering however was the Torma, a conical cake made with tsampa flour and butter, intended to appease the gods. When the ceremonies were over these tormas were destroyed; the smaller cakes were thrown to the dogs and the birds, and the bigger ones were burned in a fire started specially for the purpose in front of the monastery walls. The biggest torma, which was many feet high, was consigned to the flames as part of the Torgya, a very noisy ceremony indeed. When all the offerings had been made on New Year's Day, the inhabitants of a labrang would come together for a joint breakfast. And immediately after that came the great tour of congratulation from labrang to labrang, whereby the younger monks always visited the older ones. There were mutual wishes of good luck and an exchange of katas; and very often, too, money wrapped in paper was presented as a gift, in order to convey that the giver wished the other riches.

As one of the youngest amongst the approximately two hundred rimpoches living in the monastery of Kumbum I had to make a great many such visits. This was not only very exhausting but also very expensive. However, Tagtser Labrang was one of the richer monastic households, and I was one of the richer rimpoches, though not one of the richest by any means; not, for example, so rich as Cheshö Rimpoche and my teacher Minyag Rimpoche. Later on both of them were to become very good friends of mine. Seto Rimpoche and Akya Rimpoche were also amongst the very rich. Each rimpoche that I visited offered me tea and kabse, a pastry which is prepared in large quantities and baked in many different forms and according to a great variety of recipes for the New Year's celebrations. In its basic form it is dough made of wheaten flour and kneaded into strange forms and fried in seething butter.

The tour of congratulations went on for three days, and after that came a long series of banquets, to which all the rimpoches invited each other. Very often one would have liked to refuse, but that was impossible: one had to turn up unless one was prepared to risk grossly offending one's would-be host. The atmosphere at some of these banquets was very lively, particularly when young monks were present, though when older rimpoches were guests great formality was observed. For fear of making a gaffe we younger ones would then confine ourselves to giving brief answers to any questions addressed to us; and, for the rest, remaining silent throughout the whole banquet. When a particularly feared master was to be present the news would spread like the wind, and then more than one of the invited guests would try to excuse himself with this, that or the other pretext—often very feeble. However, as a general rule the older rimpoches would go back to their own quarters early leaving the younger monks to enjoy themselves on their own.

The rest of the day would be spent in playing games; and we were particularly fond of dice games. We used a large wooden die with six sides, each of which was marked with one syllable of the prayer *om mani padme hum*. Together with this game there was a large map on which favourable and unfavourable places were marked. You arrived on these spots or avoided them according to the particular syllable you threw. Amongst the favourable spots was Lhasa, various pilgrimage centres in India, and a number of mythical centres such as Devachen and Shambala. Amongst the unfavourable spots were various hells in which the unfortunate who landed there was subjected to appropriate torments. For example, in one it would be intolerably hot, in the other intolerably cold, and so on. The winner was rewarded with a prize of sweets. Sometimes such a game would last for hours, and occasionally it would get very noisy. Particularly fortunate or unfortunate throws were greeted with a chorus of congratulations or groans as the case might be. Now and again we also played dice with small rectangular sheep osselets, just as we had done as children in Tengtser. Almost every young monk carried a bag of such dice bones under his habit. Even in the snow and cold, provided that the weather was otherwise good, we would hold races and jumping competitions in the court-yards. I was always very eager to take part in these competitions although I was not a very good athlete.

A monk named Payenpa was a highly valued guest everywhere. He was about thirty years old, and he possessed a concertina. In addition, he was regarded as the best raconteur and entertainer in the monastery. He also possessed great histrionic abilities, and he always had the laugh on his side. I can see him before me very clearly even at this distance, helping us to pass the long winter evenings. Red-hot coals glowed in the large brass fire-pan, the tea steamed in our saucers, and kabses were ready on a little table as we sat there listening with interest to the stories Payenpa told us. And sometimes he would have us roaring with laughter when he made up doggerel or sang little songs about people we knew, or imitated their amusing characteristics in mime.

At large parties we often played a kind of hunt-the-slipper game. We would sit round in a large circle and pass some object from one to the other under our habits whilst one of us stood in the centre of the circle and tried to guess who had the object and challenge him. But the most highly prized guests were perhaps those monks who possessed a gramophone. There were one or two old-fashioned machines with huge horns which had been brought from China or Mongolia along the great caravan route on which Tengtser lay. There was also a good collection of records, chiefly of Chinese and Mongolian songs. When I sat there and listened to the sound of strange instruments and songs emerging from the vast horn I was always astonished and impressed anew. My favourite pieces were the Mongolian songs.

At Kumbum I came into contact almost exclusively with those monks who had devoted themselves to study and contemplation, because my own education was wholly turned in that direction. For the same reason I had very little to do with those numerous other monks who were not pursuing scholarly aims, and who were known as Dopdops. It should certainly not be thought that they were in the least intimidated by their lack of scholarly training, because, of course, they performed functions whose importance could not be denied. For example, at procession times they acted as marshals, upholding law and order and ensuring the smooth running of the ceremonies. For this particular role they were armed with long wooden staves, which they often handled with great dexterity. This staff was the symbol of their office as custodians of law and order. They also formed a kind of monastic guard, and they would provide escorts to accompany important rimpoches and watch over their safety when they were travelling. They were usually strong and vigorous men whose presence as escorts on long journeys through the countryside was very welcome as a protection against both wild beasts and bandits. They were athletically trained, and at various festivals they would give gymnastic displays. As in general they attended no classes the menial tasks fell to their lot; for example, they acted as kitchen hands.

They made a point of being different from the rest of us in appearance too; letting their hair grow rather longer, hitching their habits rather higher, and quite generally bearing themselves with a somewhat martial air. Even in the depth of winter their right arms were always bare, and decorated with a piece of dark-red ribbon. As a protection from the cold they would rub their faces with butter, whilst thick black soot marks around their eyes helped to give them a rather awe-inspiring appearance. Now and again you would find a more scholarly monk amongst these Dopdops. Their rougher life having appealed to him, he had transferred himself to their ranks. It inevitably happened that sometimes these Dopdops would use their physical strength and prowess in a fashion not consonant with the dignity of monks, and now and again there were even ugly brawls and physical violence. Such incidents, which necessitated the intervention of the proctorial authorities, were naturally abhorred by the more scholarly monks. On the other hand, the physical strength and endurance of the Dopdops made it possible for them to go on much longer with the physical prayer exercises; for example, they would throw themselves down before the statues of the gods many, many times in succession, completely outdoing the ordinary monks.

For myself I rarely performed this arduous physical prostration more than three times in succession, and I never had any ambition to excel at it. Nevertheless, on two particular occasions, once in Kumbum and once again later on in Lhasa, I succeeded in prostrating myself in this fashion more than a thousand times in one day. Many monks preferred this particular religious exercise to any other, and they would often become extraordinarily adept at it. In the temple of Tsuglagkhang in Lhasa there were large flagstones which were not only highly polished like mirrors from the prostrations of so many monks, but even worn away into depressions. When you remember that many monks vow to prostrate themselves several hundred thousand times then it is not surprising that the thirteen-hundred-year-old stone flags are beginning to show signs of their zeal.

7. Apprentice Years in Kumbum

VIOLENT sandstorms announced the approach of spring. Deep-black clouds raced across the skies, and the wind howled day and night in and around the temples and the monastic buildings. But at last the power of winter was broken. The warm desert wind melted the ice from the roofs, and everywhere water from the thaw dripped, ran and gurgled. The first green blades of young grass were showing on meadows which only a little while before had been covered by deep snow. And then finally the snow thawed even on the northern slopes of the black hills.

Spring had actually arrived when on the tenth day of the fourth month we set out from the monastery to welcome it in due form. The trees were covered with young green leaves and the first flowers were giving off their scent into the air. Tents had been set up in the meadows, and inside them everything had already been prepared for a great banquet in celebration of the advent of spring. This fourth month was particularly sacred to us because its eighth day was celebrated as the anniversary of the Enlightenment of Buddha under the Tree of Wisdom, whilst on its fifteenth day came the anniversary of Buddha's death.

On these holy days everyone, novice, monk or lama, had to make a circular tour of the Lingkhor, a path which wound in a great circle right around Kumbum. However, it was not a question of walking; the pilgrim had to measure the whole way with the length of his body by repeatedly throwing himself to the ground. As a good nangpa eats no meat at this time of the year, this procedure represents a very great physical effort. For this reason we were allowed to divide the performance into parts, doing one stretch one day, and the next on the following day, and so on over a number of consecutive days. I always took advantage of this permissible alleviation, and at the end of one day I would mark the spot with branches or small stone so that I should know where to begin again the next day. In all I measured the Lingkhor four times in this way. On two or three such occasions I did it together with my father and mother and my sister who used to come to Kumbum to see me on such high feast days. But on other occasions I loved to stroll along the Lingkhor with friends. Usually we would walk through the forest clearings up to the top of a hill where we would lie down and enjoy the view over Kumbum and away to the distant glaciers. At dusk we would return hungry and pleasantly tired, and still deeply under the impression of a wonderful trip into the countryside.

In the warm months of the year we would often make trips lasting for several days. On my first expedition I was invited by my teacher Minyag Rimpoche to go with him. Püntso, my friend Chone Rimpoche, and my subsequent teacher, Lhagsam, were also members of the party. Our objective was the mountain monastery of Chukhar Ritrö, which was a day's ride away from Kumbum. I eagerly watched the preparations being made for our expedition, and when we set off in the first rays of the sun my heart was beating high with joy and expectation. That ride through the early spring with nature awakening on all sides has remained unforgettable for me. In my memory I still seem to be able to smell the aromatic scent of the fields and the meadows; to see the constantly changing landscape lit up by the rising sun; and to hear the great chorus of bird calls everywhere.

We erected our tents below the rock-perched monastery, and settled down for a stay of several days. They were the round Mongolian tents known as yurts, held up by poles and with an opening at the top. I slept in the same tent with the strict Minyag Rimpoche and my friend Chone Rimpoche. As I had never slept in a tent before it took me a long time to get to sleep that first night, partly because of the strangeness of the situation, and partly for fear of disturbing my teacher in his sleep, perhaps even pushing him. But despite my fears the trip was wonderful, and we were warmly and most hospitably welcomed in the monastery itself. Chone Rimpoche and I wandered through the surrounding countryside and found many beautiful plants and interesting stones. We all enjoyed our short stay in the monastery itself, and our teacher Minyag Rimpoche was so pleased with our behaviour that on the way back he promised us another trip.

I was eleven years old when Lhagsam, whose acquaintance I had made on that trip, became my third teacher. He was about forty years old, and he had a round, dark-skinned face with a large nose and clever, kindly eyes. I hadn't to go to him in his quarters as I had with Minyag Rimpoche; instead he moved into my labrang, where he was provided with a servant for his needs, and with horses from the stables whenever he wished to undertake a journey. Lhagsam was a good man and an understanding teacher, and before long I was completely under his influence, and our friendship became increasingly firm. Lhagsam came from a family of nomads, but even in his early years in the monastery he had so distinguished himself that he soon became one of the most respected monks in the community.

When he took over my education I already knew the Commandments, had mastered the most important forms of polite behaviour, and knew several smaller religious works and a number of proverbs by heart. Lhagsam, an outstanding teacher, whose nobility of character will always be a glowing example to me, now began to prepare me for the great examination whose successful termination would entitle me to take part in the Tsogchen, or general assembly of monks. To my shame I must confess that in the first few weeks I sometimes abused his good nature and confidence. Every morning, and in the afternoon from four o'clock until late in the evening, he had to be present at the general assembly for prayers, and whilst he was gone he relied on me to do the work he had set me. But when he left me in the early morning I would go back to bed again and have some more sleep. But by the time he returned, there I was virtuously poring over my books, the outward model of zeal and industry.

For a time I managed to deceive him by reciting prayers which I had already learnt from Püntso and Minyag Rimpoche, but one day he questioned me more thoroughly, and then it all came out. In holy anger he put me across his knee, raised my habit and administered a thorough slapping with the palm of his hand. I burst into loud howls of pain, with the result that the worthy man was deeply shocked at his own outburst of anger, suspended the punishment and rather clumsily took me into his arms and tried to console me. Taken completely by surprise at this sudden change in his attitude, and feeling deeply ashamed of myself, I pressed my head to his chest and sobbed as though my heart would break. When he saw that neither fair words nor even my favourite sweets could soothe me he gave me the whole afternoon free in which to play as I liked. But I didn't really enjoy this unexpected freedom, because my bad conscience over the whole affair pricked me too closely. When I returned from my playing still a little upset, Lhagsam was sitting in his favourite position on a cushion, his hands in his lap, and his rosary gliding through his fingers as he prayed. When I think of him now that is always the position I see him in.

If the weather were fine on the anniversary of Buddha's birth, which, as I have said, falls on the tenth day of the sixth month, all the monks would leave the monastery in a body and move out for a week to the great meadow at Trashithang, where I was first received on my entry into Kumbum. In the days before the exodus we youngsters were always greatly excited in anticipation, and we hardly talked about anything but the weather; because if it unexpectedly rained on that day then we should be condemned to stay in the labrang and pore over our books. However, as a rule it was fine on Buddha's birthday, and we would ride out and pitch the traditional white cotton tents embroidered with their good-luck symbols, and the cooks would set up their fire-places before them, and prepare the most wonderful meals. This great meadow of Trashithang extended for many miles, and the monastic community, large as it was, would quickly distribute itself along the three crystal-clear streams and over the specially beautiful and favoured spots. My friends and I were naturally attracted by the running water, and we would build dams, play ducks and drakes with stones, and Chone Rimpoche would proudly demonstrate how well he could swim.

On one of these expeditions I slept in a small tent with him. One night we went off to sleep tired and happy as usual, only to be awakened in the middle of the night by a terrible storm. The rain poured down, the thunder rolled and the wind shook our tent ominously. Before we were properly awake, the wind had ripped out the tent-pegs and the tent collapsed on top of us. Trembling with fright we shouted for help, but in the noise of the storm we were not heard for quite a while, and it was not until the storm was moving away that rescue arrived. We were then towelled down vigorously, given new clothes and taken to another and larger tent which had stood up to the worst the storm could do.

During the terrible moments when we were waiting, apparently in vain, to be rescued from our very disagreeable situation, it occurred to me that hell must be something like this; a hopeless situation with no way out. I had desperately called out for help to our old friend Tentsing, who was as strong as an ox. But I had completely forgotten that he was no longer with us. One day he was missing, and no one knew what had happened to him. We could hardly believe it when we were told that he had run away. Later on we learned that he had joined the nomads and then attached himself to a caravan going to Lhasa. From Lhasa he made his way to Drepung, the biggest monastery in Tibet. Many years later I was to meet him again.

Apart from that one alarming night, I spent only happy hours in the Trashithang meadow. When we were not playing by the water we were passing the time agreeably with rope jumping, racing and wrestling. If the weather happened to be inclement we would gather in the tent of my friend Seto Rimpoche, who was somewhat older than Chone and me. The three of us once spent a wonderful fortnight's holiday in the meadow when the steward of my labrang allowed us to stay there until our supplies were exhausted. It is hardly surprising I suppose that we found it very difficult to return to our books and our disciplined way of life after these short periods of freedom.

But whether we liked it or not, we were always once more taken firmly in hand after these welcome respites. All things considered, the monotonous days went by very quickly with many hours of study and prayer, broken by short pauses for play and talk. In consequence winter was practically on us again before we noticed its coming. My parents had let me know that they would visit me for the New Year's celebration, and now here it was quite close again. I looked forward with great longing to this visit, and I was particularly happy at the thought of seeing my mother again; because in this all-male community it was she I missed most. The exact date of their arrival had not been fixed and I almost fevered with impatience and uncertainty. I can still remember how I stood at the window one evening and stared out into a light flurry of snow. For a long time the landscape had become white and glistening, and thick icicles hung down from the roofs. A little nostalgically I thought back on the winter pleasures of my early childhood at home, recalling the playmates with whom I had made slides, tobogganed and built snowmen. And I could almost feel once again how carefully my mother tended my chapped hands with warm, oily butter, which she scooped from the ready-made tea.

I was so lost in my happy-sad memories that I did not immediately notice the little party which entered the courtyard below me. Thick white flakes were dancing around them now and they looked like snowmen on horseback. But then they looked up to my lighted window and waved, and I realised that it was my parents and my brother and sister. I rushed down to welcome them and our joy at being together again was great. My sister Tsering Dröma then presented a young man who had come along with the party this time. His name was Püntso Trashi, and she was to marry him in a year's time. He came from the village of Chungtsi, which was famous on account of its hot springs and was therefore visited by many people. The parents on both sides had discussed the proposed marriage and agreed to it some time before. Incidentally, marriages in Tibet are purely secular contracts, though afterwards the partners go to the temple to make offerings and beg the blessing of the gods on their union.

My brother Gyalo Döndrub was there again too. On account of his particularly large and beautiful eyes we often called him Mig Chenpo, or big eyes. He had a particularly beautiful voice and even as quite a youngster he knew a great many of our folk-songs by heart. He was altogether an agreeable child, and he was able to exploit his favoured position as the youngest to the full; which was just as well for him because in the following autumn he was to lose it, when my mother gave birth to another son, who was called Lobsang Samten. The party were guests of my labrang of course, and we spent a very happy New Year together; though, to the great regret of all of us, they could stay only for a few days this time.

After that the onerous everyday jogtrot began again, and the traditional banquets given by the rimpoches at the beginning of the year only made it seem more arduous. The Düra, as the examination for admission to the Tsogchen, or general assembly of monks, was called, extended over a very wide field of knowledge, and therefore the preparation for it was spread over several years. Lhagsam was an excellent teacher, and he always very effectively presented the material I had to master. I gave no further trouble now; in fact I learned zealously, because I was only too anxious to cut down as far as possible the long period of preparation by making particularly good progress.

In order that this long period should not seem too long to me, and in order to give me a refreshing change and at the same time broaden my horizon, Lhagsam organised a visit to the monastery of Detsa Ritrö, which lay about two days' journey away from Kumbum. We travelled in the company of Minyag Rimpoche, Chone Rimpoche, and a very old monk whom we boys never called anything but "toothless uncle." Püntso, several servants, and Lhagsam's personal cook completed the company. We proposed to spend a couple of months in the hermitage at Detsa

Ritrö, and continue our studies there, so we had chosen the inclement season of the year so that we should not be tempted to spend our time making pleasure trips into the surrounding countryside.

We made our way forward between high banks of snow, and an icy wind troubled both us and our horses. It also caused the long icicles which were hanging from the trees on either side of the way to clash together, so that we were accompanied all the time by their strange and rather eerie music. We spent the first night in the village of Khyungya, and the next day we set off to tackle the steep ascent to the Gomang Pass. The neighbourhood through which we were passing was notoriously bandit-infested, and travellers had often been attacked. These bandits were said to live in caves in the mountains, from which they would emerge to attack and plunder small caravans. Although we were armed to the teeth against the possibility I must say that my heart pounded in my chest at the thought of being attacked. My companions, who had done this same journey several times, seemed to like to talk about these bandit attacks, and they kept urging each other to keep a good look-out in case the bandits attacked us too. A biting wind swept through the pass, which was becoming increasingly narrow, with the result that before long I hardly knew whether I was shivering from fear or cold. I found my heart jumping into my throat each time a branch, too heavily laden with snow, suddenly cracked and collapsed; and I breathed again when one of the many tracks we came across in the snow turned out to be the spoor of a harmless stag or musk-deer, and not the track of bandits.

All those stories of bandits and their exploits excited my imagination and soon every strange-looking shape was an object of suspicion. I happened to know that Lhagsam had a brother who had at one time thrown in his lot with bandits for a number of years and had actually killed a man during one of their raids. But on that occasion he had been caught and sentenced to cede all his possessions to the family of the deceased as blood-money. But as though that were not enough, Lhagsam, who was, of course, quite innocent, had been called upon to surrender his few yaks and sheep as well. Thanks to Lhagsam's mediation this brother was exempted from all further reprisals, and in return he abandoned his evil life and became respectable again. When I met him later on I was quite astounded to find that he looked no different from any other Tibetan of my acquaintance.

But there was one story of robbers which was even a little heartening. It was about two monks on the way from Mongolia to Kumbum who were attacked in their tent whilst they were asleep. The robbers approached unperceived, pulled out the tent-pegs and let the yurt collapse on the sleepers. The two unfortunate monks, who at first did not know what had happened and were unable to free themselves from the clinging folds of their tent, were now subdued with threats and blows. Only a ruse succeeded in extricating them from their unenviable position: one of them called upon the other in a loud voice to cock the pistol and fire. At that the robbers, who obviously did not possess firearms, took to their heels, leaving the monks, who were not even armed with staves, to continue their journey unmolested.

Despite all my nervous fears we finally arrived safe and sound in Detsa Ritrö where we were warmly welcomed and consoled for the terrors of the journey by friendly hospitality.

There were about four hundred monks in Detsa Ritrö, and the rules of their order were particularly strict. They abjured all possessions and lived entirely from alms. As an outward sign of their poverty they were allowed to wear a yellow cloak instead of the red one worn by other monks. They were rightly proud of this privilege, because this colour was normally reserved for the Khenpo. They also enjoyed a high reputation as masters of Kachö, a discipline which Detsa Ritrö had practised and perfected for ages. Now Kachö is a particularly highly developed form of dialectics; and in fact one of the reasons why we had come to Detsa Ritrö was in order that Chone Rimpoche and I should meet a certain famous exponent of Kachö, Lakho Rimpoche of Labrang Trashi Khyi, and be initiated by him to the introductory stages of Kachö as part of our education.

As there were no guest-rooms in the monastery we shared cells with the monks. I lived with Nyingka, a monk of quite herculean proportions. Apart from this great physical presence he also possessed the deepest voice I have ever heard. Both these characteristics naturally made him an ideal prayer-leader in the assemblies of the monks. He was tremendously proud of his bass voice and he exercised it conscientiously in daily elocution and singing practice.

Chone Rimpoche and I regularly attended the lessons of Lakho Rimpoche, but neither of us took very kindly to the subject; in fact occasionally I used to find myself nodding off during his lectures and sermons, which often lasted for hours. Though he was not particularly attentive himself Chone Rimpoche would at least manage to stay awake, and when I dropped off he would wake me up again by tickling me behind the ear with a piece of paper, which would rouse me with a start. In the first week or so we were not greatly pleased by the very frugal and monotonous life in Detsa Ritrö, and it was only when the snow began to thaw and we were able to go out into the countryside that we felt happier. Not far from the monastery a stream ran through a conifer wood, and as soon as the weather became sufficiently clement the monks of Detsa Ritrö would take their debates on logic into the open air there. We were always invited to be present, but I must say that at the age of twelve I was unable to understand much. And every evening there was practice Kachö in the open amongst a smaller group of monks. These disputes were argued out very vigorously, and on occasion they even developed into downright squabbles. Quite a number of monasteries practised this Kachö discipline, and Labrang Trashi Khyi, the monastery from which Lakho Rimpoche came, was one of those which was known far and wide for the proficiency of its adepts at this particular form of disputation. It was a large monastery with about three thousand monks and it lay about seven days' journey from Detsa Ritrö.

In the early spring of this year I was surprised by the news that my father was coming to visit me in Detsa Ritrö. I was deeply moved at the news, but at the same time I began to fear for my father's life, because for an individual the journey through a neighbourhood made unsafe by so many bandits was quite a risk. But my parents took such a keen interest in my well-being that they never allowed more than a few weeks to pass before at least my father came to visit me, and thus even the onerous journey to Detsa Ritrö to see me was not too much for him. My pleasure at seeing him when he finally arrived safe and sound was all the greater, and it was only with great sadness that I let him go again the next day.

Soon after that the time came for us too to leave the austere but friendly hospitality of Detsa Ritrö behind us; and, as kindly as its monks had been to us, I can't say we were sorry to start on our way back to Kumbum again. This time we travelled through a green and blossoming countryside, and when we had climbed the pass, which I still had in unpleasant memory, and reached the top, we all shouted our "Chöshe" and "Lhasölo" from the depths of our hearts, which means "The gods have been victorious!" I was in the best of spirits now and I urged on my horse with all sorts of pet names, and I would have rivalled the birds in their carollings if I had been able. As a matter of fact I had very good reason for my high spirits, because Lhagsam and Püntso had proposed that on the return journey we should visit Shartsong Ritrö and spend an extended visit there. And the way to Shartsong Ritrö went through Tengtser.

I could hardly summon up sufficient patience to wait for the appearance of my native village ahead of us, and in the end my companions had mercy on me and quickened our pace in order to cut down the time of waiting. After passing through a deep valley with huge rhododendron bushes we reached the familiar caravan way which passed my parents' farmstead and I shouted aloud with joy when I spotted the first houses of Tengtser ahead.

To my great surprise I could see from a distance that something unusual was going on there. As a matter of fact, the news of our coming had gone on ahead of us and the inhabitants were now hurriedly making preparations to receive us appropriately. As soon as we came up, Pasang, our village orator, delivered a warm and humorous speech of welcome, and it made me feel at home immediately. My parents and my brother and sister then led me over the threshold of our house. My mother was already engaged in preparing my favourite meal and she was hardly able to contain her excitement at this unexpected visit of her son. At first we certainly did not have much time for confidential talk because people came from all the houses in the village with good-luck scarves and presents of sour milk, butter and pastries to meet me and have me lay my hands upon them in blessing. In consequence it was quite late before I was able to go to bed. Even as I lay there in the best room and although I was very tired I could not sleep at all at first. The unexpected visit to the scenes of my childhood had stirred me deeply. I lay there listening to the familiar noises in the courtyard and the stables, and breathing in the aromatic air of the mountain meadows with full lungs. But finally with a great feeling of happiness in my heart, I dropped off.

We spent only one day in Tengtser, because the day after that both Lhagsam and Püntso insisted on continuing our journey, so we set off for Shartsong Ritrö, leaving Tengtser behind us once again. But this time the parting was not so difficult because I knew that in a couple of months when we left Shartsong Ritrö to return finally to Kumbum our way would once again take us through Tengtser.

When we arrived in Shartsong Ritrö I could see no obvious change since my departure four years previously. Time seemed to have stood still here. On entering my old rooms a strange feeling came over me when I found everything still in the same place as before. But once I had got used to the place again the weeks I spent there represented a wonderful holiday for me because Püntso left me a good deal of freedom, whilst Lhagsam took advantage of our stay there to fulfil an ancient vow. He practically took up his quarters in the temple where the reliquary of Karmapa was kept, and spent the whole day there in prayer, speaking to no one, and allowing no one to speak to him. Only when it grew dark would he take a little of the food which was brought to him. But the time passed quickly and enjoyably for me, and almost before I realised it the moment had come for us to set off for Kumbum again.

This time we stayed only a very short while in Tengtser. We descended at the house of my parents one radiant morning in early summer, and we did not know that in the meantime my mother had given birth to another son, who had been named Lhamo Döndrub. When we arrived she presented me with the most delightful baby I had ever seen. But which of us at that moment could have had the slightest idea that we were in the presence of the fourteenth incarnation of the Dalai Lama, a being who before long would be recognised by all Tibetans both inside and outside Tibet as their spiritual and temporal leader? I should have liked to play with the little fellow for much longer than I did, but Püntso was urging us to be on our way, and the horses, which we had not even unsaddled, were pawing their hooves with impatience to be started.

That we should have met the future Dalai Lama at that time without knowing it was not altogether so very improbable, because in principle any Tibetan baby of the male sex could be chosen for this supreme distinction. The Thirteenth Dalai Lama had died in the tenth month of the Water-Bird year, and I can well remember the day the news arrived at Kumbum. The deep gloom that immediately descended on the monastery and the subsequent mourning celebrations made a deep impression on me. For the first time in my life I was affected and deeply moved by the news of a death, and when the red-cloaked monks streamed together for common prayers they all had solemn faces. Tens of thousands of butter-lamps were burning on the roofs of the monastery buildings. There were, for example, three hundred on my labrang alone. I mourned with the other monks, and together we sorrowed for the death of a great ruler who had been highly respected during his lifetime both as a great churchman and a great prince. The period of mourning lasted forty-nine days, and during that time any form of amusement was strictly prohibited. Throughout those seven weeks all the men wore their old clothes, and the women wore no article of jewellery or any adornment of any kind. I was so carried away by my sorrow that I couldn't conceive that things would ever be the same again, and that in time our ordinary everyday life would start up once more. I was even angry at the tattered prayer-flags because they fluttered in the wind just as they had always done, and at the cheeky magpies who continued to chatter in the high trees as though nothing whatever had happened. Amidst my tears I directed my dearest wish to heaven: that we should soon be granted the return of the Dalai Lama; and in that I was like the great majority of Tibetans in those sad days.

8. My Acceptance by the Tsogchen

MY preparation for the first great monastic examination, the Düra, was now approaching its end. We had entered into the Fire-Mouse year, and I was now a novice of fourteen who no longer took pleasure in childish games, but who instead devoted himself to his studies with industry and determination. Although I was by no means a model pupil, at least I had made sufficient progress to please my very exacting teachers, who were greatly interested in my progress. I had been introduced into the deeper mysteries of the Buddhist faith, and under careful guidance I had studied the ancient texts which talked of both merciful and vengeful gods and treated of the exorcising of demons. I had learned almost two thousand pages of these books by heart, and in this respect my good memory had been of great advantage to me. I had acquired a fairly wide knowledge of the teachings of Padmasambhava, that Indian scholar who had come into Tibet in the eighth century and founded Tibetan Buddhism. Under the name of Lopön Rimpoche he was as highly honoured as Buddha himself, particularly in the monastery of Samye, the oldest monastery in Tibet, which he himself had founded. Of course, this short summary of what I had done so far does not by any means exhaust the whole curriculum of a young novice.

My teachers persistently refused to say anything definite about the date on which I was to be examined to discover whether I was yet fit to be accepted by the general assembly of monks, though the reader can perhaps imagine how desperately I longed for that moment after my long years of study. So much so in fact that I could hardly control my excitement when one day from my study I overheard a conversation between Lhagsam and the Steward of Tagtser Labrang, from which I gathered that they were in agreement that the time had come to ask the Khenpo for my admission into the Tsogchen. So at last I was to become a fully fledged member of the great college of more than three thousand monks. So far I had only very occasionally been allowed to be present, and then only as a visitor in the gallery. On those occasions I had followed the proceedings with eager eyes and the one great longing in my heart soon to be able to sit down there with the others.

I was indeed impatient for the great event now, for it was to represent the crowning reward of years of hard study. Of course, at the same time I was just a little anxious at the thought of the coming examination, but noticing this my teachers assured me that I had every reason to feel confident. However, not all the preliminary conditions had as yet been fulfilled, and the moment had not yet come when I should be entitled to make my way with my older companions to the great assembly hall in which so many interesting discussions were held and so many invaluable friendships begun.

There were various faculties, or Tratsangs, in Kumbum for those monks who devoted themselves to the scholastic life. Gyüpa Tratsang was for those who proposed to devote themselves primarily to meditation. Dükhor Tratsang was for those who wished to study mysticism. Medicine was taught in the Menpa Tratsang. And finally there was the Shadupling Tratsang which taught logic and the art of debate. Once I had passed my Düra I was to be accepted into the faculty for logic, the Shadupling Tratsang. For this I still needed a number of preparatory lessons, because the final part of my examination concerned itself with the elements of logic and debate. My teachers thought it would be a good idea for me to take these introductory lessons from a very famous professor of logic who was the permanent teacher of Akya Rimpoche, a very rich and highly respected monk of about thirty, who also proved sufficiently amiable to

Thubten Jigme Norbu and his mother Dekyi Tsering

Holy relics are preserved in golden Chörtens such as this one, which is at the gates of the holy city of Lhasa

give his professor, a highly intelligent Mongol named Ohön, special leave of absence to allow him to teach me. This Ohön had the title of Yongdzin, which means professor or teacher; and because he was the teacher of Akya Rimpoche, his full name and title was Ohön Akya Yongdzin. This very capable teacher quickly provided me with the necessary knowledge to carry me successfully through the entrance examination for the Shaduping Tratsang, and it was then arranged that he should keep an eye on my subsequent studies too.

Feverish preparations now went forward in my labrang for the day of my examination and my expected acceptance into the Tsogchen. In view of the great importance of the day for me my Steward spared neither trouble nor expense. He secured the services of the best tailor available, and this man came to the labrang and measured me for the red-brown dagam, a wide garment which is worn like a toga, and in which, when you sit down, you can completely muffle yourself. After my acceptance I was to wear it every day. And from one of the neighbouring villages came a famous hat-maker to measure me for the traditional pointed hat of yellow wool which is so reminiscent of an enormous coxcomb. And finally a new pair of leather boots was made for me, this time without any form of ornamentation.

The great activity in my labrang pleased and excited me, for any general movement is always catching; and I looked forward with impatience to the day when I should be entitled to wear my new clothes for the first time. From the early morning on now the most wonderful smells arose from the kitchen, and my cook had engaged a whole army of helpers to assist him in preparing the rare dishes which were to do him the greatest possible credit at the great celebration banquet.

Then on the eve of the great day my parents appeared, for naturally they did not intend to miss the great event. And finally the day itself dawned, the day on which my most heartfelt wish was to be fulfilled. At the appointed hour, and with a heart beating harder than usual, I presented myself to the Khenpo. In accordance with custom I went quite alone, and unaccompanied by either teacher or servant. Rather hesitantly I entered his quarters. As a general rule the Abbot Superior is a very famous rimpoche, but in my time the office was held by a lama who was highly respected for his great knowledge. He was seated on a raised cushion, and I greeted him by prostrating myself three times before him, and then I presented him with the traditional kata, or good-luck scarf. When he had blessed me by the laying-on of hands I took my place on a rug at his feet.

He first asked me whether I was still firmly resolved to take the examination, and if, in fact, I had prepared myself for it with appropriate thoroughness. My mood was very different this time, and, unlike the time I was ordained a monk, I answered with a determined "La-les, la-les." Then he picked up at random one of the books beside him, opened it casually without looking for any particular page, and read part of a passage out loud, inviting me to conclude the passage for him by reciting it by heart. For half an hour he tested me in this way from various books, and not once did I even hesitate; in each case I fluently completed the passage for him. My years of hard study had clearly been to some purpose.

When I was finally graciously dismissed from his presence I left with a surge of pride and pleasure in my heart. I had passed the first part of the Düra; the first stage on the road to the general assembly was now behind me. I had to take the second part of the first great test before the Shengo, the superior magistrate of the monastery. This Shengo had not only all the powers of a justice of the peace, but as a sort of Proctor, and with the assistance of certain monks, "Bulldogs" appointed for the purpose, he maintains law and order throughout the monastery, and, in particular, in the general assembly. He is responsible for seeing that each monk has his own proper place and that they all behave themselves in accordance with the rules.

I also had to prostrate myself three times before the Shengo, but as he was not a lama he could not give me his blessing by the laying-on of hands. Compared with the first part of the examination the second part was quite easy. I was examined out of three books only and at no time was I at a loss for the correct answer. When the Shengo had closed the third book he had used in my examination he called in my good friend Püntso, who was waiting in the ante-room, and then both of them congratulated me on my success. Püntso afterwards accompanied me back to the labrang, where my parents were waiting in some anxiety to hear the result. You can imagine how proud and joyful they were when I reported my success to them. They hardly knew how to express their delight, and my mother kept surreptitiously wiping her eyes. That evening when I went to bed it was in full and proud consciousness that the next day I should have the right to take part in the full assembly of my fellow monks.

I was already awake when the great conch horn sounded its deep notes from the roof of the assembly hall calling on the monks to rise. Püntso was already on the spot to assist me into my new garb and to hand me the traditional hat of yellow wool, which the young monk carries in his hand for the first few years, and then over his left shoulder. For breakfast in hall he handed me a bowl in which there was a small bag of tsampa, and then we made our way together to the Tsogchen. It was a wonderful feeling for me to walk through the streets of the monastery with the knowledge that I was now a fully-fledged monk, enjoying equal rights with all the other monks around me. Like me, they were all making their way to the great assembly hall. On a large covered veranda at the entrance to the hall we removed our boots and put them with the mass of other boots already standing there. Only the Khenpo himself was entitled to keep his boots on until he reached his throne. Although these boots with their yak-leather soles, their sheepskin shafts and their woollen fastenings at the top to keep them in place, all looked the same, when the monks came out afterwards each man immediately found his own pair without the slightest difficulty, though it was something of an achievement.

Once inside the hall, Püntso led me straight to the Shengo, who then led me in his turn to my place amongst the other rim-poches. As he walked ahead of me he held his four-edged metal sceptre in his hand as the symbol of authority. Generally speaking the seating order amongst the incarnations was according to the number of years each had sat in the Tsogchen. I was therefore placed beside my friend Chone Rimpoche, who had passed the entrance examination just ahead of me, and who was a little older than I was. On the other hand, my friend Seto Rimpoche, who had been a member of the general assembly for a much longer period, had a seat which was much nearer the altar. The innumerable monks in their red habits, most of them with the yellow hat over their left shoulders, made an impressive picture. Before they took their seats each man solemnly prostrated himself on the ground in the direction of the altar, before which stood the throne of the Khenpo.

In the beginning I was a little anxious at sitting for the first time with all these monks murmuring their prayers around me. Everything seemed strange to me: the great hall with its many columns, the babble of noises, and the peculiar and soon to be familiar smell which resided in the timber and the cushions, and had done so from time immemorial. I was glad that my friend Chone Rimpoche was sitting next to me and was thus able to give me a hint as to how I should behave during the individual ceremonies. However, we could only whisper softly to each other without moving our heads, because the slightest violation of the very strict regulations was sternly rebuked by the Shengo. In serious offences the guilty party had to come forward before all his assembled brethren to receive his punishment, which was often quite severe.

The prayer-leader, or Umdze, would pronounce the first prayers, and they were then repeated in chorus by the whole community. I was happy to be able to join in because I already knew them all by heart. We prayed for the spread of Buddha's teachings; we prayed for good weather for the harvest; and we prayed for good health and long life for man and beast. And one of our prayers was on behalf of the Dalai Lama who was at that time in the world as a baby, living unrecognised in some family or other. Without knowing it we were all praying for my youngest brother who was not far away in my home in Tengtser.

After the prayers came the interval for breakfast. Through the open doors came young monks carrying large cans of steaming tea. We held out our wooden bowls and they poured the strong tea into them, at the same time offering us generous quantities of butter. We now mixed the tea and the butter with the tsampa flour we had brought with us. This proceeding had to be carried out as unobtrusively as possible under cover of the dagam, and you had to be very careful not to spill anything. We were not allowed to talk even during breakfast; and if we did dare to whisper to each other now and again we would first cast an anxious glance in the direction of the Shengo to make sure that neither he nor any of his subordinate Geyos happened to be looking in our direction. These Geyos were all powerful men of a daunting exterior, and they were armed with six-foot-long staves which they would shake threateningly when the rules were broken, and use vigorously when they thought it necessary.

Occasionally it happened that one of the tea-distributors busily going backwards and forwards between the hall and the great kitchen to provide us with our tea would slip in a spilt pool of tea and measure his length, dropping his tea-can with a clatter on the floor. When that happened we were expected to control the muscles of our faces and not laugh. If anyone were caught laughing, or perhaps surreptitiously enjoying the joke with his neighbour, then he might well receive a painful blow from the staff of one of the Geyos for his pains—or from one of the Chabris, who were the assistants of the Geyos. The younger monks, who were naturally far more lively than the older men, were the normal recipients of such hefty blows, and they would do their best to dodge them by ducking, or to reduce the force of the blow by pulling the dagam over their heads.

The tea was prepared in the ground-floor kitchen next to the assembly hall. Enormous copper kettles stood on even more enormous stoves, and each kettle held more than a thousand gallons. In addition there was a series of smaller kettles. The beautifully shaped brass tea-cans with their ornamental copper bands would all be standing ready in long shelves against the wall. The greatest cleanliness was the rule in the kitchen, and the tea-cans were always very carefully washed out when breakfast was over.

After breakfast there was usually a sermon or a lecture given by the Abbot himself, who was a very fluent speaker, and to whom I would listen with rapt attention. But very often he would give one of the lamas the floor, and I would listen equally devoutly to him. They would talk on a great variety of subjects, from articles of faith to proper behaviour, and I was already firmly resolved to base my conduct on their example. Very often the Umdze would read out long passages from our holy writings, the Kangyur; and when the booming voice fell silent we would repeat his words in chorus. Our sacred book, the Kangyur, consists of one hundred and eight volumes having a total of forty-five thousand pages. The figure one hundred and eight is a sacred one for us, and you come across it again and again in the life of any pious Tibetan. There are even Tibetan women who braid their hair into one hundred and eight small plaits.

One day in the Tsogchen I accidentally came across this sacred figure in an unexpected fashion. I was listening to a lecture which did not much appeal to me either in its content or its form, and I therefore withdrew my attention to say my rosary. As the one hundred and eight wooden beads passed steadily through my fingers I mechanically counted the columns in the great assembly hall, and to my astonishment the architects had kept to the sacred number even in that respect—there were one hundred and eight columns exactly.

The first morning spent in the great assembly hall impressed me deeply. Still deeply moved I hurried back afterwards with Püntso to my labrang where we had our midday meal with my parents who were still there. I was delighted that they had allowed themselves time enough to stay on after the examination for the celebrations, which lasted several days. We had not got that far

yet, but the great preparations made necessary by the many
invitations issued had now reached their peak. Everyone was
running around busily, and the kitchen staff had their hands full.
I enjoyed the last few peaceful moments in my rooms with my
parents.

That afternoon I presented myself in the magnificent building of the Shadupling Tratsang, or faculty, which had a large
gravel courtyard in which many trees with thick foliage were
growing. It was there I was to take the second part of my examination. I had to engage in a minor debate before an audience
of several hundred monks, and this went off to the satisfaction
of my teacher. After that I went straight back to my own labrang
where I prepared myself to receive the visit of the Abbot himself
who was coming with all due formality to congratulate me on
passing my examination. I awaited this great moment in some
excitement. Servants were posted in front of the house in order
to warn me in good time of the approach of the Abbot and his
retinue. When the announcement finally came I went forward
to greet him in the open air before the door of my labrang. He
handed me the traditional good-luck scarf with both hands, a
particularly choice gesture of politeness, at the same time con-
gratulating me on my acceptance into the general assembly. He
then took a light meal with me in my room, sitting on the highest
seat in the room, whilst I sat on the next highest. He did not
remain long, but his visit was followed by that of other dignitaries, led by the Shengo, in whose presence I did not have to
rise, as I was an incarnation. Amongst these other dignitaries
were representatives of the individual tratsangs and labrangs.
They were all invited to the subsequent meal, and formed an
illustrious company which my parents also joined.

When the official reception was over, and all the high dignitaries had left the labrang, my more intimate friends appeared
to congratulate me. They were welcomed only with tea, but
this did not dampen the cheerful spirit of the gathering;
and, in any case, they were all invited to the big celebration
banquets.

For several days in succession after that there were always at least a couple of dozen guests in my labrang. There was no necessity for anyone to bring along his own wooden bowl to these formal meals, because the tea was served in beautiful porcelain dishes with richly decorated covers. The Steward of the labrang used this special tea-service, for which there was also an appropriate number of magnificent silver stands, only on very special occasions. With the tea the series of preliminary dishes was opened, and this stressed the festive character of the meal. The cook then served a variety of pastries, of which the most popular were those fried in oil of mustard. With these pastries he also served dresi, a mixture of rice with melted butter, sugar and raisins. After these introductory dishes came the main courses which consisted of enormous quantities of mutton, rice and vegetables prepared in innumerable variations.

We usually ate in groups of six at a time: my parents, my friend Jangchub Nyendra, my brother and sister and myself sitting at the same table. After the meal we would go out into the courtyard and pass the time by playing dice games, and otherwise amusing ourselves. I was already so exhausted from everything that had gone before and the inevitable excitements, that these receptions were really something of a burden. Very often when the noise became too great I would have loved to withdraw into the peace and quiet of my own rooms, but politeness required that as host I should stay all the time with my guests until the evening meal was over, a meal at which enormous quantities of momos and shabagle were served. Momos are small pieces of meat rolled in dough and then either boiled or steamed. Shabagle is much the same thing, except that the form is flatter and the pieces are fried in oil. At the evening meals we also drank our tea out of the best tea-service.

When at last my acceptance into the general assembly and my entry into the Shadupling Tratsang had been adequately celebrated, my parents set off for home, and after the lively days of festivities and celebrations the everyday jogtrot started for me again. The mornings were spent in the Tsogchen, and the afternoons were devoted to a study of logic and the art of debate, and I was gradually to be introduced to every finesse of this form of dialectics. We constantly engaged in oratorical duels in which we had to confound our opponents with swift and carefully phrased questions, so driving them into a corner that they had no way out and were defeated. These debates were held not only between individual pupils, but between whole classes; and sometimes even between whole faculties. We usually assembled in the Chöra, the courtyard of the Shadupling Tratsang, for this intellectual jousting.

Each Tratsang had its own buildings and its own Dukhang, or great hall, in which all the members of the Tratsang could gather. However, only the Shadupling Tratsang had such a Chöra, where, in the warmer months of the year, open-air gatherings could be held and discussions conducted even in poor weather. All the professors and their pupils would assemble here, whilst the two superiors of the tratsang, who were also known as the Khenpo and the Shengo, would sit on a covered-in veranda.

I now visited the first classes of my faculty, the so-called Khadogkarma. In this basic course we did not work from books but from lectures, and we had to answer quite simple questions as quickly and as clearly as possible. The next stage of the proceedings was when the students were set to ask each other questions. Two adversaries would be chosen; the one would squat on the floor, now wearing the pointed yellow hat, and the other would plant himself before him and ask him a question, which the seated student had to answer as rapidly and as cogently as possible. One question would follow the other in this way until in the end the quicker and more intelligent of the two would reduce the other to silence. Then the roles would be changed, and he who had had to answer the questions would now rise to ask them of his rival. During this kind of exercise we would be working in pairs all over the Chöra, hurling question and answer at each other's heads, often to the accompaniment of a tremendous babble, because a raised voice was regarded as a perfectly legitimate means of plunging the enemy into confusion. The questioner was also entitled to use movements and gestures to press home his attack, though he was not allowed to touch his rival in any way.

In the beginning the questions would refer to the simplest things of everyday life and to the common vocabulary of everyday speech. Things and conceptions had to be defined and their application circumscribed. Very often in these duels one of the rivals had to get at the object or the idea by clever questioning, and this he would do by first seeking to discover its uses and qualities. Many of these exercises, both simple and complicated, are recorded in the textbooks and can be learnt by heart, but presence of mind and quick repartee can be perfected only in constant practice.

These subtly developed exercises aimed at sharpening our intellects were known as "Rigpa Chenpo Yongya" in Kumbum, or roughly "Intellect Sharpeners." They were certainly very helpful to us in our efforts to think rapidly and logically. Whilst these duels were going on we would be supervised by Gyurpön, who would go from one pair to the other, exhorting, correcting and encouraging. Very often such a class would have up to sixty members; and promotion into the next-succeeding class was according to scholastic progress and performance. Some pupils would be able to leave the Khadogkarma stage within three months; it would take others years.

Of course, these duels were practised only in a few courses because we needed a great deal of time to absorb other knowledge, and, for the most part, this had to be obtained from books, the study of which had to be carried on in the intervals between the individual lessons. But even during the vacations we still had to appear every morning in the Tsogchen.

My older friends were already in higher classes and I therefore did not see much of them, but in the first class I made the acquaintance of a lively and intelligent companion who was quickly to become my very close friend. This was Drotsang Khenpo, whom I had not met previously, as we lived at some distance from each other in the very extensive grounds of the monastery. We were soon fast friends, so much so that we were thick enough to allow us to practise a carefully planned deception which does not, I think, show us in our very best light.

From time to time the Shengo of the Tratsang would appear in the classes and call upon students to volunteer for debating duels before the assembled Tsogchen. When one day he called for volunteers from the first class for these so-called Tsolangs, Drotsang Khenpo and I and a number of others volunteered. But we were taken completely by surprise when the next day the Shengo arrived with a list of the competitors and informed us that we two should prepare ourselves to meet each other before the assembled Tsogchen in a few weeks' time.

At first we were at a loss: should we two close friends go for each other hammer and tongs before everyone else? But it did not take us long to make up our minds what to do, and so we spent the period of preparation carefully rehearsing what we were going to say and fitting question and answer together so that when the day came we should be word perfect. Our only fear was that someone would see through our little trick. We each remained as silent as the grave on the point, though neither of us found it easy to deceive our much respected teachers, or even our fellow-pupils, to whom we were greatly attached. And how embarrassing it was when Püntso would urge me again and again not to let my rival gather the slightest inkling of the questions I proposed to overwhelm him with when the time came! On the other hand, there was the great attraction which forbidden things always hold, and the pleasure of hugging a wicked secret to our breasts.

Perfectly confident we entered the Dukhang on the appointed day, dressed in new clothes from head to foot. There was solemn silence in the room, and every seat was occupied. The Khenpo sat on his throne, with the Shengo beside him on the one hand, and the Shungleba, or examining inspector, on the other. Then in a loud voice the Shungleba called out our names, and we walked together through our assembled fellow-students to take our places in the spot chosen so that everyone could see and hear us. On arriving there we divested ourselves of our dagams and prostrated ourselves three times in the direction of the Khenpo and the statues of the gods. Then we put on our dagams again and presented ourselves to the Khenpo to receive his blessing.

Afterwards each of us murmured a quiet prayer and then we once again removed our dagams. The Shungleba now called on me to begin the questioning. We had a strip of the floor about sixty feet long for our debate, and without hesitating I now advanced on my supposed opponent, driving him before me with vigorous gestures as I hurled my loudly shouted questions at him. After a little while the Shengo silenced me and called upon Drotsang Khenpo to take up the questioning in his turn. As we had prepared ourselves down to the slightest detail, question and answer followed each other like lunges and parries in a fencing match. We sprang forward and we leapt back, and we accompanied our carefully studied performance with dramatic gestures. Our debate was a so-called Gelmingel, that is to say it dealt with homonyms, words and ideas which sound similar but which in fact have different meanings.

Our duel was impressive—and small wonder!—and we earned a great deal of praise for our performance. At the end of it a general murmur of approval went up throughout the hall. If we had failed or done badly that would have been borne in on us by laughter and derision. But we were not feeling particularly proud of ourselves, or altogether comfortable, when we finally received the congratulations, because inwardly we knew only too well that we had done so impressively only because we had cheated.

The year was now rapidly approaching its close. Winter was at hand again and before long we found ourselves preparing for the New Year's celebrations once more. As they did every year, my parents let me know that they would visit me as usual for the festivities, and this time they told me that they were bringing my young brother the three-year-old Lobsang Samten with them, since he too was destined for the monasterial life. They proposed that he should stay on with me, and they thought that the sorrow of parting would be greatly diminished if he found himself at once in the care of an older brother; and that similarly on that account, he would settle down more quickly in his new surroundings.

My parents meant well, but in fact the first days and weeks without his mother and father were very difficult for Lobsang Samten, as I can very clearly remember. I had taken leave of my parents and my sister shortly before they left because I wished to accept an invitation from my friend Shelkar. When I returned towards evening to my own labrang I found a picture of misery awaiting me. On my couch sat little Lobsang Samten obviously feeling very sorry for himself. Big tears rolled down his chubby cheeks, and convulsed with sobs he was hardly able to utter a word. He just couldn't grasp the fact that his mother and father had left him behind alone in this strange place. I immediately did my best to comfort and console him, of course, but I was a little uncertain of the best way to go about it. I made little jokes with him and brought out toys for him. Yet how well I could understand what the little fellow was feeling! Suddenly all the misery I had suffered when I was in his situation revived in my memory again. And he was even considerably younger than I had been at the time. When all my well-meant efforts to comfort him were of no avail I lost my head too and there we sat locked in each other's arms and sobbing in concert until in the end we were both so exhausted that we fell asleep.

The next morning it was clear to me that something must be done. I could see no solution to the present, as it seemed to me, hopeless situation. Privately I even bitterly reproached my parents for having acted, or so it seemed to me, so cruelly. It so happened that I had an opportunity of sending a message to my grandmother at the time, and I begged her to use all her influence on my parents to persuade them to come and take little Lobsang Samten back home at once. However, they wisely ignored my arbitrary intervention, and my little brother came into the care of the Steward of Tagtser Labrang, who, after all, had had considerable experience in such matters. In fact, the little fellow settled down in his new surroundings more quickly than I should have expected. No doubt at first the many cases of toys helped him over his sorrow to some extent, and then came a most engaging four-legged playmate in whose company he would enjoy himself for hours on end.

Trari was a spotted dog, or rather a bitch, hence her name, and I had begged my teacher Minyag Rimpoche to give her to me, which he did when she was a month old. I brought her up with great care and lavished attentions on her, and before long she was the favourite of everyone in the labrang. Even Lhagsam would quite frequently find time to come and play with her, whilst Püntso and the Steward himself seemed to be rivalling each other in spoiling the dog. And, of course, Trari was an ideal playmate for my little brother. But the next time my father came on a visit he asked me to let him have Trari for the yard at home, and that placed me in a very awkward position. For one thing I was very fond of the dog myself, and for another I didn't want to deprive Lobsang Samten and the dog's other admirers in the labrang of their pleasure. In addition, I feared that I might offend Minyag Rimpoche if I were suddenly to give away the dog I had so urged him to give me in the first place.

On the other hand, the possibility of doing my father a favour was very attractive too, and so in the end I decided to let him have the dog; but at the same time, in order that the others should not notice anything too soon, we worked out a veritable abduction plan. When early one morning, after having said goodbye to everyone, my father set off for Tengtser I surreptitiously handed him the dog through a window. Of course, the disappearance of Trari was soon discovered, and after a while I confessed the story of the successful abduction. After the first shock everyone got used to the idea that Trari was gone. And I persuaded Lobsang Samten to console himself with the thought that by letting Trari go to Tengtser we were giving the family there a pleasure. Minyag Rimpoche praised me for not having refused my father's request. Trari probably enjoyed herself more

in Tengtser than she did with us. When later on the family moved
to Lhasa Trari came back to me and became henceforth my constant companion. In the end she too ended up in Lhasa, where
I finally took her, and she died there at a ripe old age for a
dog.

9. My Youngest Brother, the Dalai Lama

AT an unusual hour the mournful tone of the conch horn called the monks to the general assembly. The Panchen Lama was dead. The news spread like the wind from village to village and monastery to monastery. Only a little while before we had had the Panchen Lama in Kumbum as a guest for a few days when he broke his journey from Pekin to Lhasa. And now he had suddenly died in Kantse, once again on a journey to Lhasa.

Since the Fifth Dalai Lama had given his great teacher, or Panchen Lama, the monastery of Trashilhünpo as a living and declared him to be an incarnation of Ö-pa-me, every incarnation of Ö-pa-me was the master of this great monastery. However, in the course of time this gesture of gratitude on the part of the Dalai Lama was to prove rather embarrassing. Although right down to our own day, as far as Tibet was concerned, the Panchen Lama had control only over Trashilhünpo, as the incarnation of Ö-pa-me he was a living Buddha, and, in addition, a Buddha to whom even greater reverence was shown than to Chenresi, whose current incarnation is always the Dalai Lama. As there were constant struggles for power between Tibet and China the Chinese naturally exploited the rivalry between the Dalai Lama and the Panchen Lama, which was, at first, tacit rather than open; and for generations they have played the one off against the other. Despite this, in Tibet, and by all Tibetans on Chinese territory, the Dalai Lama was always recognised as the supreme spiritual and temporal head. For this reason, and for as long as it suited their book, the Chinese did their best to avoid any direct clash.

Thus the journey of the Panchen Lama which I am about to describe here had its political aspect. Kumbum lies in Chinese territory, but, apart from certain administrative technical anomalies such as the payment of taxes to the Chinese administrative centre in Siling, it has always regarded itself as belonging to Tibet. It was one of the last monasteries the Panchen Lama visited. It is worthy of note that on leaving Kumbum he did not travel by the direct route to Lhasa, but continued his journey as far as possible along the Tibetan frontier; and Kantse, where he finally died, is in Chinese territory. The Chinese authorities had provided him with an escort of no fewer than a thousand armed men who were to accompany him to Lhasa. In answer to this plan the Tibetan Government announced that although the Panchen Lama would always be very welcome in Lhasa in his capacity as incarnation of Ö-pa-me, the Government could not see its way clear to giving his large Chinese escort permission to enter the country.

In these circumstances it will be no surprise for the reader to hear that the mourning celebrations for the Panchen Lama were not immoderately heartfelt. The ceremonial adopted was that usual on the death of a highly respected lama of a monastery, and in fact it was hardly as impressive as that which had marked the death a few years previously of Cheshö Rimpoche, the man who had ordained me as a monk. Nevertheless, it was quite a big and solemn affair with many butter-lamps and candles and a procession to the Serdong Temple, which is the holiest place in Kumbum.

Serdong means "Golden Tree," and the four-storeyed temple, which narrows as it rises to its crowning golden roof, is built round the tree which grew on the spot where our great Reformer Tsong Khapa was born almost six hundred years ago and where he was ordained. According to legend the roots of this tree are the hair of the young novice himself. A silver Chörten was erected round the tree, to which there is no access, and this

Chörten reaches right up to the fourth storey of the temple, and is hung with ornaments and jewellery presented by pious pilgrims from all parts. This Chörten itself was in an enclosed place surrounded by six other golden Chörten about five feet high, and twelve gold butter-lamps and a great number of silver ones each about six feet high. These lamps are so large that two men with outstretched arms can just about span them. In each lamp there were no fewer than fifteen lighted wicks daily replenished with butter. Around the temple, whose three lower storeys are covered with glazed tiles, stand a number of very old trees whose foliage provides agreeable shade in summer. I loved this place and I passed it every day on my way to Tsogtchen; perhaps I loved it in particular because in the best months of the year I used to meet my friends there.

Incidentally, in Kantse the Panchen Lama had met a Government Delegation from Lhasa. This Delegation had been sent out to find the new incarnation, or the Fourteenth Dalai Lama, and was soon after to light on my young brother Lhamo Döndrub. On his death-bed the Panchen Lama had drawn the attention of the leader of this Delegation to a small boy from Lönpa whose mother had brought the lad to Kumbum only a little while previously in order that the Panchen Lama might bless him. The child had seized the tassel with which the Panchen Lama was accustomed to bless all the faithful who solemnly filed past him, and had refused to let it go; an incident which had seemed significant to the Panchen Lama.

We learned about these and other details when the members of this Delegation, who, as guests of high standing, were welcomed on the Trashithang meadow, took up their quarters in Kumbum with the intention of remaining there for an indefinite period. The Government Delegation consisted of about forty members, and according to Tibetan custom it was under the joint leadership of a high ecclesiastical and a high civilian dignitary, respectively Kyetsang Rimpoche and Künsangtse Dzasa. In all the Delegation operated from Kumbum for two years in its search for the new incarnation of the Dalai Lama. It carried on its work quietly and unobtrusively, of course, but the general opinion in the monastery at the time was that the small boy from Lönpa—whose mother brought him with astonishing frequency on pilgrimages to Kumbum—would be chosen as the Fourteenth Dalai Lama, the incarnation of Chenresi.

Later on it filtered through to us that on its search the Delegation had visited our farm in Tengtser, and I found myself being eagerly questioned from all sides. The members of the Delegation had naturally nothing to say on the point, and it would have been foolish to question them. However, the next time my father came to visit me I told him of the rumour we had heard in Kumbum, but he refused to believe it. My parents were much too simple and unsuspicious to suppose for one moment that any of the travellers who had knocked at their door asking for food and drink and a night's rest could have been disguised members of the Government Delegation seeking the incarnation of Chenresi. In fact, the search for the Fourteenth Dalai Lama was such a delicate matter requiring such a great degree of conscientiousness and discretion that the individual groups of the Delegation were compelled to carry out their investigations in the guise of simple travellers.

Naturally the fascinating question of who was to be the Fourteenth Dalai Lama occupied our monastic community more and more the longer the Delegation maintained its headquarters in Kumbum—and, as I have already said, they stayed there for no less than two years. It was only much later that I heard the details of the visits paid by the ambassadors of the Government to my old home, visits which finally led to the declaration of my younger brother Lhamo Döndrub as the incarnation of Chenresi; and then it was in Lhasa from a monk named Kesang of the Sera monastery who was a member of the Government Commission which carried out the search. Kesang was in the retinue of Kyetsang Rimpoche when the Rimpoche subjected my brother to a searching interrogation and examination in our family home.

Kyetsang Rimpoche had gone to Tengtser with Kesang and

one or two others. They were travelling as merchants on their way to Chakhyung, and they asked my mother for permission to make themselves tea in her kitchen. In order to obtain the best possible insight into any circumstances he met with Kyetsang Rimpoche had chosen the role of servant to the rest, who were outwardly Bönpos, and thus his masters and superiors. On going into our courtyard for the first time he had been struck by the bizarre shapes of our wooden gutter pipes; the same that had so often stimulated the imagination of my playmates and me years before. It appeared that the Regent in Lhasa had had a dream in which he had seen the as yet unknown Fourteenth Dalai Lama standing under just such extraordinary roof gutters. In consequence Kyetsang Rimpoche now decided to subject the background, and in particular the little Lhamo Döndrub, to a much closer investigation. He therefore told the others to ask for lodgings for the night, and this was willingly granted to them by my parents. That evening he and his companions played for a long time with Lhamo Döndrub and were greatly impressed by him.

Now Kyetsang Rimpoche had a number of things with him which had belonged to the Thirteenth Dalai Lama, and the normal procedure was to bring them quite casually to the notice of such children of whom it was thought that they might conceivably be the long-sought-for incarnation. Now no sooner did Lhamo Döndrub catch sight of the rosary of the dead Thirteenth Dalai Lama in the possession of Kyetsang Rimpoche than he addressed him indignantly, declaring that the rosary was his; and he refused to let himself be persuaded, and continued to insist that the rosary was, in fact, his. Lhamo Döndrub was an unusually lively and high-spirited child, and he insisted that Kyetsang Rimpoche should hand over "his" rosary. But not only that, the child told the disguised Kyetsang Rimpoche to his face that he was a lama from Lhasa. And the visitors could hardly believe their ears when the child addressed them in Lhasa dialect. Then the same thing happened with a walking-stick and a damaru, or small double drum, both of which had previously belonged to the Thirteenth Dalai Lama. Lhamo Döndrub seized them, declared them to be his own, and refused to be parted from them any more. In fact he was so excited about the whole affair, and so indignant at what he regarded as the attempt to deprive him of his possessions, that he was near to tears.

My mother found the whole scene, which she was quite unable to understand, very embarrassing, and she tried to soothe the boy with promises of a new and much bigger drum at first opportunity; but it was the smaller drum the child wanted, and he insisted on taking it to bed with him. Afterwards it was gently extricated from his firm fingers whilst he was asleep and returned to the one whom my mother regarded as its rightful owner. Much impressed though he was, Kyetsang Rimpoche did not reveal the secret of the supposed travellers that evening. Instead he left the house before dawn without even taking leave of my parents.

Soon after that he returned with his assistants to my old home, but this time no longer incognito. He handed my parents presents and told them that he was an ambassador from Lhasa. My brother Lhamo Döndrub was now subjected to a very thorough examination. In addition to the rosary, the walking-stick and the damaru which had belonged to the Thirteenth Dalai Lama, the delegation also had with them his silver pencil, his spectacles and his eating-bowl, together with very clever imitations of them. When Kyetsang Rimpoche now received little Lhamo Döndrub he wore the real rosary round his neck, and held the imitation in his hands in prayer. But the child did not hesitate. He ran to Kyetsang Rimpoche and tried to take the rosary from his neck by force, once again insisting that the rosary was his. This time he was allowed to have it. The oral examination of the child was also completely satisfactory. The delegation then went away firmly convinced that in my brother Lhamo Döndrub they had found the fourteenth incarnation of the Dalai Lama. Such was the story as told to me much later in Lhasa by the monk Kesang. However, at the time those responsible maintained complete silence, though by 1938 rumours were coming thick and fast. Finally they had spread so far that Chinese photographers arrived in Tengtser to take photographs of Lhamo Döndrub.

It was at about this time that my well-beloved Püntso died. It was autumn and the mists were rising in the valleys, and it was not until midday that the heat of the sun managed to disperse them and leave the shining blue sky free. The leaves of the trees were putting on their autumn colours, and the landscape was beginning to glow in reds, browns and yellows, and in the early morning hoar-frost glistened in the meadows. Nature was preparing for her winter sleep and the year was going to its end. But the life of my faithful guardian, whom for a long time now I had called Agu Nagpo, or "Dark Uncle," on account of his swarthy nomad face, was also going to its end. He was only fifty-six years old, but he had aged himself prematurely by prayer and fasting and a never-ending devotion to the interests of his neighbours. He was often in Shartsong Ritrö on supervising missions and on the last occasion he fell seriously ill, and had to be brought back to Kumbum on a stretcher. I can see him now as they brought him into my labrang. The signs of death were already on him, but I did not realise that at the time. He lived on for two months, lying in my room and unable to get up. He fell away more and more, and his bones showed up with increasing prominence under his brown nomad's flesh, which began to look greyer and greyer. Towards the end every word he spoke cost him a tremendous effort.

But young people are never willing to acknowledge the empire of death, and Püntso clung on to life so long that when the end came it took me by surprise, and I was deeply shocked when one morning I found him lying back in the pillows, dead. For some time I was unable to grasp the fact that the one man in the whole monastery who had stood so close to me was now no more, and I was overcome by sorrow and suffering. Never once since then has death come so near to me and caused me to sorrow so keenly as I did when I mourned the death of the man who in my early childhood had replaced both mother and father for me. Now in his passing he gave me a final lesson: that death is the all-powerful ruler of us all. It was only after his going that I realised fully what a tremendous role the splendid fellow had played in my life. And the older I become the more I recognise and appreciate his virtues. His purity of heart, his affection and his kindness will remain an example for me all my life. We took his body up into the mountains and cremated it, but his memory will always remain undimmed with me.

In the meantime rumours still continued to circulate in connection with my brother, young Lhamo Döndrub. The boy from Lönpa had long ceased to be on the short list of candidates, because on the arrival of the Delegation to examine him he had fled shrieking. But as by that time he had already entered a monastery, he remained there and later became a monk. A third candidate died unexpectedly. And those who remained shortlisted were not thought to have much chance by comparison with my brother. As Tengtser was on Chinese territory the Chinese now began to take a serious interest in their small citizen, and at the beginning of the 1938–39 winter the Governor Mapufang invited my parents to come to Siling and bring their son with them to visit him. In receiving them there he advised them to place the boy in the monastery of Kumbum, which was, as we have seen, formally on Chinese territory.

My parents regarded this advice as an order, and on their way back from Siling, which took them in any case past Kumbum, they arrived one bright and tingling winter morning at the monastery with Lhamo Döndrub. We spent a happy few days together in my labrang until it was time for my parents to go back to their farm. My mother went first, consoling Lhamo Döndrub by telling him that she was only going to visit her parents. But then early one morning my father went off too, and Lobsang Samten and I were left to look after our small brother, who was naturally very upset when he noticed that his parents were missing and that he was to stay on in the monastery without them. Dissolved in tears he begged us to take him home to his mother and father. I was almost seventeen years old now, but I was still helpless in the face of such misery. Lobsang Samten was the first to join little Lhamo Döndrub in his sobs, but it was not long before I too dissolved into tears. A last attempt to distract my small brother by getting him to look at the dancing snowflakes outside the window naturally failed, and then we were all three in tears.

But Lhamo Döndrub was young enough to get over the absence of his parents very quickly, and he soon settled down with us in Kumbum, where he remained for six months, enjoying no particular privileges, because the final decision from Lhasa was long in coming. But the interest of world public opinion had now been aroused, and inquisitive visitors were becoming more and more frequent at Kumbum, and they all wanted to see the famous child. Many Chinese and quite a number of European photographers took pictures of him, and in the meantime Kyetsang Rimpoche turned up frequently in our monastery in order to supplement his reports to Lhasa.

That winter I agreed with my Steward that for the Festival of Light, on the fifteenth day of the first month, Tagtser Labrang should contribute an enormous and artistically decorated butter tower. The making of this butter tower was quite a complicated and expensive business. The costs for the raw material, the butter, and for the long hours of labour, came to far more than a thousand Gormo, a coin which was worth about one and eightpence. I now devoted myself with great enthusiasm to the interesting task of surprising the monastic community with an outstandingly large and beautiful butter tower.

In the Gomang class, which is a sub-department of the Shadupling Tratsang, I found a particularly gifted butter modeller who already enjoyed a high reputation for his talent, and with him I discussed the decoration of the butter tower I proposed to contribute to the Festival of Light. After long discussion and some hesitation I decided that it should represent a model of the town of Lhasa showing its most prominent buildings. The artist was delighted at my decision as giving him full scope for his talents. The centre point of the whole model was, of course, the

Potala, with the biggest flag in the world hanging from its windows, as it does for several hours every year for the minor New Year's Festival. Our model was to show the Dalai Lama sitting in his palanquin and just entering the Potala Palace in solemn procession. As each such butter tower was always intended to be a surprise for the other monks, my artist worked behind closed doors in my labrang for weeks. Above all, the other monks in the Gomang and Gyetsünpa classes, who were always trying to out-do each other in artistic achievement, had to be given no inkling of our intentions.

All Tibetan monasteries celebrate the Festival of Light, but Kumbum in particular always regarded it as a very special occasion and made its preparations accordingly. Even Lhasa itself could not compete with Kumbum on that great day, because Kumbum had always paid particular attention to maintaining and developing the art of modelling. Every day I went to see the progress of the work on my butter tower, and every day I was delighted anew to see the wonderful detail in the artist's work. The basis of the tower was a series of wooden frames, which, when placed one over the other, provided the body of the tower, and each one had to be separately decorated. The artist began by imitating the surrounding landscape, whereby he made liberal use of rich colours. Then followed the individual buildings, after which he began to model the small figures in the procession. I was particularly impressed by his work on the equestrian groups, and the great flag with its glowing colours was a tribute to the pains the artist had expended.

On the evening of the Festival of Light, the two great squares of the monastic town were a strange sight. Under cover of darkness the model sculptors were busily erecting their butter towers with the help of their assistants. From all sides surreptitious groups would glide by carrying wooden frames, ladders and scaffolding, because without such aids it was impossible to get the upper stages of the butter towers into position.

The weather was kind to us. The moon rose silver in the sky and bathed everything in a mild and gentle light. And now it was time for the sightseers to stream up, and with the normal inhabitants were many pilgrims who had come from the neighbouring villages, and they all jostled each other good-naturedly in the narrow streets and alleyways of the monastery. Then suddenly, as though a magic word had been pronounced, innumerable lights came on everywhere and cast a golden refulgence onto the seething crowds. The habit of the monks was maroon of course, and the peasants were mostly in dark-coloured furs, but their womenfolk wore the gay and brilliant clothing of high days and holidays, and proudly showed off the involved artistry of their headdresses with their one hundred and eight carefully braided plaits, glistening with butter and held in place with green and red ribbons. Together with the Tibetans and the Mongolians there were also Mohammedan merchants who were only too glad to let their caravans rest in the neighbourhood for a while whilst they went into Kumbum to enjoy the famous Festival of Light.

The lights on the actual butter towers were now lit and visitors and monks crowded delightedly round first one and then the other, out to enjoy thoroughly everything that was offered them. Their unsophisticated admiration and appreciation were expressed in constant oh's and ah's, to the great gratification of the artists and their patrons. Not that the audience was unsophisticated in its judgment. On the contrary, the people studied the models with an expert eye, and eagerly pointed out this or that carefully executed detail to each other—the impressive sweep of the landscape, the architectural accuracy of the buildings, the artistically modelled representations of man and beast. There were models of high dignitaries in their costly robes; figures of women displaying their finery, with their headdresses carefully copied down to the smallest detail; mettlesome horses stamping their hooves and covered with magnificent carpets. The crowds swayed backwards and forwards from one square to the other to compare the butter towers displayed in each, and the general spirit was gay and lighthearted. I joined the crowds together with my parents and my brothers and sister, and in the glow of ten thousand butter lamps and amidst the fanfares of trumpets and the sound of oboes we too made our way admiringly from tower to tower.

The festivities lasted until dawn, and when the crowds had seen all they wanted to see of the butter towers and their intricacies they moved on to the nearby village of Lussar where there were food and drink to be had in liberal quantities, and dancing throughout the night. On the way from the monastery to Lussar lines of stalls had been set up as though at a fair, and the vendors shouted their wares cheerfully as the gay crowds strolled up. There were small prayer-tablets with the *om mani padme hum* for sale, cheap jewellery, confectionery, dried cheese, and a dozen and one things the simple heart of the Tibetan holds dear. And barkers with stentorian voices tirelessly drew the attention of the crowds to the performances of the acrobats and conjurers who were hard at work contributing to the general gaiety. And, of course, there were innumerable beggars with their squeaking prayer-wheels.

Kumbum never presented a more beautiful and dazzling picture than it did on the night of the Festival of Light, and never, it seemed to me, did it bear its name—"A Hundred Thousand Pictures"—more worthily. By four o'clock in the morning the crowds had all left the monastery precincts to continue the celebrations elsewhere; and then all the butter towers and all the decorations which had been set up were taken down and destroyed. Tradition insists that they shall never see the light of day. By the time everything had been cleared away and the monastery wore its usual appearance only a few pale stars would be left in the morning sky.

10. My Family Moves to Lhasa

ONE day the great moment arrived at last: the Delegation announced its intention of taking Lhamo Döndrub to Lhasa. But even now it was not possible to discover for certain whether the final decision had really been taken, and not even the day of the departure was definitely fixed. For one thing, the Chinese authorities were making difficulties, as had been generally expected for some time. The Chinese Governor Mapufang demanded a sort of ransom payment of thirty thousand dollars, but when the Delegation paid this it merely whetted his appetite and he immediately demanded a further hundred thousand. The Delegation had not so much money in hand, and in consequence the negotiations dragged on. In the end the necessary sum was borrowed from Mohammedan merchants, and handed over, and the rapacious Mapufang concluded that he had gone as far as he could. But, then Kumbum made certain wishes known The Council of Twelve, to which the four Khenpos of the individual tratsangs belonged, declared the official proclamation of my small brother as the Fourteenth Dalai Lama by Lhasa to be a matter of prestige for Kumbum. Finally this problem was settled with the payment of a large sum to Kumbum too, and with that there were no further obstacles to my small brother's translation to Lhasa.

The preparations for the journey, which would take several months, had already been going on for some weeks. My parents, my brothers Gyalo Döndrub and Lobsang Samten (who had already become a monk), were to accompany Lhamo Döndrub on his journey to Lhasa and stay there with him. My sister was already married by this time so she no longer belonged to the more intimate family circle, and she and I—I was already in the fourth class of the Shadupling Tratsang, and deeply immersed in my studies—were not included as members of the party.

The parting with my family, who were now moving so far away from me, was very difficult. In my heart of hearts I was resentful at the decision which threatened to separate us not merely for the time being, but perhaps for ever. Together with many other monks I accompanied the great caravan for the first two hours of its journey, and my heart was heavy within me. Lhamo Döndrub sat with Lobsang Samten in a specially made palanquin carried by mules. My mother was also making the journey in such a conveyance. On a little hill we all embraced each other for the last time. Secretly I still harboured the hope that at the last moment I should be asked to go with them, but nothing came of that, though my father did seem to guess my feelings and promised that he would do his best to see to it that later on I too should be called to Lhasa. Then the caravan moved off leaving me behind sadly staring after it. For a long time I stood there and watched it as it moved on towards the blue-shimmering mountains in the far distance. Somewhere in that direction, far, far away in the West, must lie Lhasa. When the caravan finally disappeared from view I turned my horse about and made my way back to the monastery. It was only now that the tears came.

When I got back my labrang seemed empty and deserted. Only a little while before my brothers had played around joyfully within these walls, and there had been a constant coming and going. All that remained to remind me of them now were the toys lying mutely around. In the next few nights I often woke up suddenly with the feeling that Lobsang Samten had called out for me, or that Lhamo Döndrub had cried out in his sleep. But each time it was imagination, of course, and I had to do my best to get to sleep again.

The first news of the caravan was brought to me by a traveller who had met it crossing the high Tibetan plateaux, and he now brought me greetings from my family, together with an envelope

containing ten gormo, and a beautiful cream-coloured pony as a
riding horse. That horse was to render me faithful service for
many years. But we did not hear of the safe arrival of the caravan
in Lhasa until visitors who had read about it in the Chinese newspapers told us. A Cabinet Minister accompanied by a large
retinue had ridden far out to meet the caravan and to present my
small brother Lhamo Döndrub with a letter from the Regent
formally declaring him as the incarnation of Chenresi and thus
as the Fourteenth Dalai Lama. For the first time he was formally
honoured in that dignity, and on 7 October 1939 he made his
solemn entry into Lhasa in a golden palanquin which had been
sent out to meet him, amidst the cheers and prayers of the whole
population of Lhasa and the surrounding countryside. During
the great New Year's celebrations in the following February he
was formally enthroned and his new names announced: Ngawang, the Eloquent; Lobsang, the Wise; Tentsing, Defender of
the Faith; and Gyamtso, the Ocean.

The winter of 1939–40 was very severe in Kumbum and there
were unusually heavy snowfalls. Sometimes we had to climb onto
the roofs several times a day to clear away the great weight of
snow which might otherwise have caused the houses to collapse.
The streets were now only narrow passages for pedestrians, and
they ran along by the walls of the houses, whilst the middle of
the roads were so piled up with snow that the mounds were soon
taller than any man. The monastery looked wonderfully beautiful in its white mantle of snow, but it made things very difficult
for the servants. For one thing they had to go down to the water
sources below the monastery and break the ice cover, which was
so thick that it meant very hard work, after which they had to
toil up again carrying the water.

We suffered a good deal from the cold too, because we were
not prepared for such long or such severe winters. The temples,
the great meeting-halls and the cells were not heated; and only
very few rooms had properly installed firebrick stoves with
permanent chimneys of sheet iron to carry the smoke away. To
install more of these stoves would have taken time and been

expensive, so we had to get on as well as we could with large copper fire-pans which were taken to the kitchens to be filled with glowing embers and hot cinders. At least they had the advantage that you could carry them around and put them down wherever you needed them most. When the cold showed no signs of abating we bought more of these fire-pans in the market of Lussar, which was quite close to us.

The visit to the market was always a pleasure in itself, and we would take our time choosing just what we wanted amongst the many fine fire-pans exposed for sale there. Spare parts for the firebrick stoves were also to be had there. But despite all our efforts we could not master the cold, and when the icy wind howled round the monastery buildings we huddled up inside shivering miserably. Even in the small classrooms it was not possible to stand it for long, and to put out your hand merely to turn over the pages of a book made your fingers freeze. I would sit in the lotus position on my mattress, my cold toes curled up against my thighs, and the good Tsöndrü Gyamtso would look after me to the best of his ability, bringing in hot tea and frequently replenishing the glowing coals in the fire-pan.

On such occasions my friend Döndrub Gyantsen, a monk of my own age, would often keep me company; and he soon became my loyal servant and devoted friend. He was to prove himself a a reliable helper in both the easy and the difficult hours of my life. At that time I was secretly occupied in making plans for getting to Lhasa, and as I knew that he was seldom at a loss for good advice it was then that I took him into my confidence for the first time.

A few weeks before the enthronement of the Dalai Lama I received the first direct news of my family. Tsering Döndrub, one of my father's cousins, had taken over the farm at Tengtser, leaving his wife and children there whilst he went off with the others to Lhasa. He now arrived in Kumbum with many servants and in the company of Chandzö Jampa, a monk from the monastery of Sera, who occupied the position of Steward there, and who had, it appeared, been of assistance to my parents on their arrival in Lhasa. My father's cousin and this monk had used camels on the return journey, and thanks to the endurance and speed of these animals they had very quickly crossed the snow-covered plateaux. My father had given them four gyamars for me, and they were particularly fine examples of the Tibetan hound, much sought after because of its size and temperament, though its long, shaggy hair, and a reddish ringe at muzzle and eyebrows, give it a rather alarming appearance.

My father's cousin had been instructed to bring my sister Tsering Dröma and her husband from Chungtsi to Lhasa, and also to buy a large number of horses at the Siling horse-fair, as they were both better and cheaper in this part of the world than in Lhasa. When he had visited Tengtser to see that everything was in order there, fetched my sister and her husband from Chungtsi, and bought the horses he wanted in Siling, he came to see me again in Kumbum. I begged him urgently to do his best when he got back to Lhasa to see that before long I was called there too. In the early summer of 1940 his caravan set off with thirty horses, and over a hundred mules and draught, leaving me looking sadly after him. Apart from myself the whole family would soon be assembled in Lhasa. How long should I still have to wait before my turn came?

The understandable wish to start off on the long journey to rejoin my family as soon as possible, and the previous excitements in connection with the successful search for the Dalai Lama, had not exactly been conducive to study, and it was with mixed feelings that I now looked forward to the examination which followed the completion of the first five classes of the Shadupling Tratsang. A few weeks after the departure of the caravan for Lhasa the Shengo appeared in my labrang and informed me officially of the date of my examination. On five afternoons in succession I should have to submit myself to questioning before the assembled Tratsang on all the subjects I had studied during the past few years; and any member of the five lower classes would be entitled to ask me questions. Once again I plunged with determination into my studies, but the few weeks which

From Lhasa, which is already lying in the shade here, the eye sweeps over the Turquoise Bridge away to Mindrutsari, almost twenty thousand feet high. The ropes serve to fix the marquees which protect the houses from the heat of the sun

Every day Tibetans pay honour to their gods with incense and prayer flags, as they are doing here on a ridge of Chagpori, or the Iron Mountain. In the background is the Potala, the Winter Palace of the Dalai Lama, with its golden roofs.

Entrance to the Norbu Lingka, the Summer Palace of the Dalai Lama in Lhasa. In 1959 many thousands of people gathered on the great square in order to prevent the Chinese from entering into the residence, thus giving their ruler the opportunity to flee to India

were left were hardly enough to allow me to catch up entirely, because of late my work had been rather neglected.

Ohön Yongdzin, who had supervised my studies, recapitulated zealously with me and did his best to fill in the gaps in my knowledge; and not without a certain degree of success, because I actually passed my examination, though not with any particular distinction. In fact I felt a little embarrassed on this account when, in accordance with tradition, I had to accept the congratulations which the Khenpo and the Shengo conveyed to me in person in my labrang. But by the time the subsequent celebration banquet was held I was again in the best of spirits. After all, I now had the first half of my education behind me.

But my desire to rejoin my family intensified almost to the point of obsession. I couldn't see why I shouldn't be allowed to go to Lhasa and complete my studies there, and when my Steward pointed out very reasonably that I must not neglect the Tagtser Labrang in Kumbum I was unwilling to concede his point. They could not accept my point of view, and I could not accept theirs, so I began to work out a way to circumvent the impasse. It was really a plan of escape. If the journey along the caravan route over the Tibetan high plateaux was to remain closed to me then I should have to try another route, that was all. For example, via Siling to the coast, and from there by ship to India, and then over the Himalayan passes to Lhasa. The fact that this circuitous route would take three times as long as the direct way along the caravan route did not worry me in the least, and I started to make my practical preparations; through a Mohammedan friend who was employed by the Siling administration I actually obtained a passport and other necessary documents. It was impossible for me to conceal my preparations for long, but at least their discovery had the advantage of persuading my superiors that as I was so determined to have my own way in the matter the best thing to do would be to give me official permission to go to Lhasa, and this they now did.

I was overjoyed, and assisted by Döndrub Gyantsen, who proved himself a tireless and ingenious helper, I plunged with enthusiasm into my preparations for the four-month journey, and, needless to say, my studies were once again badly neglected. We had already made the first of the necessary purchases and given the craftsmen their instructions when one day Chandzö Jampa again appeared in Kumbum. He had already twice made the long journey to and fro with my uncle, and now he brought me a letter from my father in Lhasa. I crowed with delight when I read what he had to say. He told me that he was now able to keep the promise he had made me, and proposed to do so. He would leave the final decision to me, but frankly he would prefer me to stay where I was for the time being. However, if I decided otherwise Chandzö Jampa had instructions to accompany me to Lhasa. I found little to give me pause in that. My father had now, if reluctantly, given me permission to come to Lhasa, so what was there to keep me in Kumbum? I could hardly summon up enough patience to wait until I was once again reunited with my family, whose members I had seen so frequently previously and who were now so far away. My family was the most valuable thing on earth to me, and I loved my parents and my brothers and sister more than anything else in the world. The thought that I might never see them again had filled me with gloom. It was my mother whom I missed above all. No one else could ever replace her deep love for me, her great goodness of heart, and her instinctive understanding of everything that ailed me. How long would it be before I could again hug her in my arms?

11. Caravan Journey from Kumbum to Lhasa

THE preparations for my departure now went forward very thoroughly and in great detail. As much of the route passed through terrain which was practically uninhabited, a very large part of the provisions we needed for the journey had to be taken along with us. In addition, it was always very advisable to get into touch with other travellers in order to make the journey together, as the possibility of attacks by bandits had to be taken into consideration. I had to make arrangements for twenty-two people with the necessary riding animals, pack animals, tents, equipment and provisions. Once on the way, you were at the mercy of the weather and all its vagaries, and there were wide rivers to be crossed, which meant that the provisions we took with us had to be so packed that water did not get into them and spoil them.

I had strong leather sacks made and rendered waterproof by being rubbed with oil and fat. Such a leather hold-all will take about seventy pounds, which means the amount of tsampa necessary for one person, sufficient wheaten flour for four persons, or stone-hard rolls for two persons. My cook was occupied for many days baking enormous quantities of these rolls which were made from a particularly nourishing dough and then fried in deep fat. They were made quite small in size, not much larger than cherries, in order that they could be conveniently dropped into tea to soften before being eaten. The rest of our provisions consisted of butter, dried vegetables, turnips cut up small, dried onions, and beetroots, pickled radishes in wooden tubs, herbs and tea. Most of the caravans also took at least some meat along too, but generally speaking it was possible to obtain meat on the way either by hunting or by buying it from nomads. As there was not always enough grazing to be found on the way a sack of dried peas was allowed each animal as supplementary fodder.

In view of such loads the reader will hardly be surprised to learn that for my party of twenty-two men I needed a hundred and twenty animals, including about forty horses, because on such a journey one must always reckon with losses; and even apart from this, sometimes an animal will fall lame or go saddle-sore and have to be rested. In addition to my own group, which included Döndrub Gyantsen and an uncle of mine from Balangtsa, named Sönam Norbu, with whom I had always been on very friendly terms and who had immediately accepted my invitation to come with me to Lhasa, there was Chandzö Jampa's party. He had not failed to take advantage of the opportunity to buy horses and mules in the neighbourhood of Siling, for they could be sold at a good profit to the nobles and officials of Lhasa where horses and mules fetched much higher prices. In addition, my father, who had always been an amateur of good horseflesh, had given him instructions to buy one or two particularly fine horses, so that all in all Chandzö Jamapa's caravan included about one hundred and fifty horses alone.

All journeys along this caravan route—unless undertaken under the pressure of great urgency—were always begun at one or other of the two main seasons of the year, summer or winter; and this had been the case for centuries. The individual groups of travellers would assemble separately and then join each other on the way. My party and that of Chandzö Jampa left Kumbum together with the caravan of Matsenshi, the Mohammedan official in Siling who had been so obliging in the matter of my passport and other documents. In addition there were smaller groups of monks and families of nomads who wished to make a pilgrimage to Lhasa. By the time we reached the last caravan assembly point, which was in Tsaidam, our caravan consisted of about twenty thousand animals.

Naturally, such large caravans do not make very rapid progress, but at least they offer the traveller the greatest possible degree of safety and the advantage of immediate assistance in case of need. However, even caravans of that size are sometimes attacked by bandits, who have often learnt a good deal from civil-war tactics; and sometimes the caravans suffer bloody losses before getting through.

The astrologers had decided that the nineteenth day of the fifth month was the best time for my departure. And we were certainly fortunate with the weather. A fourteen-day period of rain had just stopped and so we had every reason to look forward to a period of better weather. In the fifth month the rainfall in that neighbourhood is very violent. When the sun has parched the earth for weeks, causing deep cracks to open in the ground, huge dark clouds suddenly begin to gather in the previously blue sky. At the sight of them man and beast hurry for shelter before the heavens open their floodgates. The rain then pours down in torrents, and the cracked earth eagerly sucks up the longed-for water. In a matter of moments the whole area is turned into an enormous Turkish bath. The cool rain falling on the hot ground sends clouds of steam up into the air blotting out valleys and hills, and it does not dissipate until the rain has ceased to fall. Then it rises into the sky to form new clouds which bring further rain. This impressive spectacle is repeated several times in succession until finally the sun comes out again, lighting up the green layer of vegetation which has sprung up in the meantime under the encouraging effect of heavy watering. The young green which grows out of the previously parched earth is of an unbelievable brilliance, and at such times one can almost literally "watch the grass grow." In an incredibly short period the tan-coloured earth is covered with a bright green carpet in which innumerable flowers blossom gaily.

It was on such a day that we left Kumbum. The pack animals had gone on ahead very early, and the mounted party followed them later in the morning. From my window I thoughtfully watched the final preparations for departure. At last I was going to attain my objective, but on the other hand I was leaving good friends behind. The years I had spent in Kumbum represented a decisive period in my life, and I had more to thank the place for than I as yet altogether realised. Even so, I was certainly grateful both to Kumbum and to those in it, and I was keenly aware that I should never be able to repay the debt I owed. The previous evening I had given a farewell party at which I had said good-bye to the Abbot, to my teachers and to all my friends. I had been deeply moved by the tangible evidence of their regard for me. The Abbot had given me a warm fur coat for the journey; my friend Seto Rimpoche made me a present of butter, tea and meat to take with me; and my old teacher Minyag Rimpoche, who was now white-haired, and whose once stern features were mild and serene, made me a present of a magnificent lambskin coat to protect me from the icy winds we should meet with on the high plateaux. With profound emotion I accepted their presents and their good wishes, and thanked them from the bottom of my heart.

Otherwise departure from Kumbum was very similar to my arrival ten years previously. I rode slowly forward followed by a monk carrying a large yellow umbrella behind me as the symbol of my rank, passing through long lines of monks silent or praying. The lugubrious sound of the oboes and of those four-sleeved trumpets, which can be fitted into each other, got on my nerves now, and I breathed with relief when we finally reached the tent where I was solemnly offered the last bowl of tea. When I had emptied it they filled it again and let it stand there, a custom which expresses the hope that he who is departing will soon return to drink the second cup. And now the tears did rise to my eyes and my feelings threatened to overcome me. Was it happiness, pain or gratitude? I thrust my hand into the broad pocket of my coat and grasped the small yellow case in which I carried the effigy of my protective spirit around with me, and silently I begged for help and support. After a last farewell to those who had assembled there to see me off, we went on.

Lhagsam had begged permission to accompany me to the first caravan assembly point, and we reached it that same evening after a long upward haul. The Trekhog plain is surrounded by wild and deeply fissured mountains and watered by one single river. Far and wide there was no sign of human habitation apart from one or two nomad tents, though we knew that human beings lived in the fastnesses of those mountains. In order not to break into our supplies unnecessarily we bought milk and meat from the nomads. Trekhog lies over twelve thousand feet up and when we lit fires we had to use our bellows in order to keep the fires alight.

We remained three days there waiting for other groups to join us, and by the evening of the third day there were no fewer than forty tents set up in the plain. Lhagsam now said good bye to me. It was a bitter moment for both of us, and we stood there and hugged each other, tears in our eyes. I found it terribly difficult to part from this old guardian and friend who had stood by my side for so many years and to whom I had become very deeply attached. After the death of Püntso, Lhagsam had taken over his responsibilities too, waking me up in the morning, inquiring amiably as to my well-being, and massaging my head. He had been my teacher and guardian—but even more than that he had been my confidant and friend. When we finally released each other he gave me a towel as a parting present together with fifty gormos, at the same time solemnly urging me always to remain pious and honourable. The following morning he embraced me quickly for the last time, mounted his horse and rode off at once without even looking back. Whilst my people were making preparations to get under way I stared after him until he was only a tiny point in the distance, a point which finally disappeared altogether from view.

After going forward for several hours we came to Tongkhor where there is a small monastery built on the mountainside. We pitched our tents below it and spent the night there. Three days later we reached the Ko-Ko-Nor, or Blue Lake. Its deep brilliant blue has made it justly famous, and it is surrounded on all sides by snow-capped peaks which are reflected in its salty waters. Its surface is gently ruffled by constant breezes in the warmer months of the year, and sometimes whipped up into real waves in stormy weather. When I stood for the first time on the shores of this enormous lake, about whose beauty and immensity I had heard so much, it no longer seemed incredible that the way round it would take three weeks. Monks had built a monastery on a rocky island in the centre of the lake, and they lived there so completely cut off that they did not even possess a boat with which they could have established contact with the outside world. But in winter, when the lake, which was approximately ten thousand feet above sea-level, was frozen over they would tramp over the ice to the shore and beg for alms. The riparian inhabitants fished only in the cooler months, and avoided the eating of fish in the warm weather.

We remained for a few days on the shores of Ko-Ko-Nor, where we were joined by a number of other caravans, and then we pushed on to Tsaidam, which we reached a week later. Our way lay through uninhabited steppes with yellow, brown, red and violet vegetation on to the high mountains which separated us from the marshy plains of Tsaidam on the other side. Our progress was now hampered by broken terrain and the presence of many watercourses, and all our attention had to be concentrated on crossing them safely. But the flat steppe terrain had its difficulties too; almost everywhere it was undermined by the burrowings of the rat-hare, and we constantly found ourselves breaking through into its burrows. These animals, sometimes called piping hares, are quite tame, and they sat at the entrances to their burrows and watched us, indulging in a whistling concert all the time, a concert in which from time to time the carolling larks joined in.

Before we made our way through to the marshy plains of Tsaidam we first had to go over some very mountainous terrain, but at least we had solid ground under our feet and we made better progress. We went through a number of passes until finally we saw the enormous marshlands of Tsaidam spread out below us. Its dull and gloomy coloration made a striking and disagreeable contrast to the bright and amiable steppe landscape through which we had just passed. Going forward along the eastern edge of the marsh area we approached the great nomad camp of Tsaidam, the last caravan assembly point on our route.

A veritable tent town had been erected at the foot of barren, weather-beaten rocky salients in which eagles and vultures had their eyries. During the next few days further caravans and troops of horses were to arrive to join us, and they too would need ground for their tents and for grazing. Before long the noise and confusion were enormous, and in the general hubbub it was often not easy to hear yourself speak. Men and animals crowded together haphazardly whilst with the help of his servants each Bönpo desperately tried to keep his own party together. However, the chaos was all very good-tempered, and there was a great deal of joking. The final preparations had to be made for the journey through the barren high plateaux; necessary repairs had to be carried out now; and each party helped the other. In- numerable fires were burning, and the cooks were busy preparing solid meals for their parties, something which was made easier because the nomads willingly sold us butter, meat and milk. Along the shores of the nearby salt lake some of the men were breaking up the thick salt crust and putting the pieces into sacks for the long journey. I bought a dozen sheep from the nomads for my group; they were to trot along with the yak caravan and be slaughtered for food at need.

It was long after dark before the camp was quiet. Once the sun had gone down behind the snow-capped mountains a cold breeze sprang up and encouraged the stragglers to seek out their sleeping-places and muffle themselves up warmly. I put on my lambskin coat and retired to my tent. Only the Bönpos, or the quality, slept in tents; the others spent their nights in the open warmly wrapped up in coats and blankets. Tents had to be pitched with some care, as otherwise some sudden cloud-burst might sweep them away, or high winds cause them to collapse. But even those who slept under the stars were careful about choosing their sleeping-places, and every small depression in the ground was taken advantage of. For the most part the servants and the herdsmen would camp round a large fire in the centre of a square formed by the loaded bags; and when the night was particularly cold relays of hot tea would help to keep everyone from freezing.

The yak caravan went on ahead at midnight. The yaks grazed on the way and managed to find some sustenance even in very barren areas, but because of this grazing time they made much slower progress than the horses and the mules, and we usually caught up with them before the whole caravan arrived at the next camping site. We left the nomad camp at Tsaidam and started on the first really dangerous stretch of the way which went through totally uninhabited areas in which for weeks on end we should not see even a nomad tent, much less a house. In addition to being dangerous it was also difficult. Although caravans had passed this way from time immemorial and the route was clearly visible, it nevertheless happened quite frequently that a yak or one of the other pack animals would get bogged down in a swamp; and because there were so many animals it was not always noticed immediately. When the herdsmen did spot the unfortunate beast it could usually be extricated by head or rump, but sometimes it was too late. In this way the swampland claimed its steady quota of victims.

So far we had been able to arrange our times and our camping places very much to suit ourselves, but now we had to take the movements of the other caravans into consideration, and to make our arrangements to fit into theirs. In other words, the normal safety routine of the caravan route had begun. We had already been on the way long enough for me to have had ample opportunity to confirm that the preparations for our journey had been very thorough and painstaking: nothing had been forgotten; we had adequate supplies; and our equipment was excellent. Apart from very unforeseen circumstances we could look to the future with confidence. In a few days now we should have left the marshlands behind us, though they still stretched away to the west for hundreds of miles. All this was very satisfactory, and I turned in early, because I knew that in the next few weeks the nights would be short and there would be less time for sleep.

Preparations to move off usually began about two o'clock in the morning, but I would lie on for a while wrapped in my saddle-cloths listening to the voices of the busy servants and herdsmen before I finally forced myself to get up. It was very cold outside the tent, the ground was frozen hard, and an icy wind dissipated the last remnant of tiredness. Our animals were saddled, and the pack animals fitted with their loads. Döndrub Gyantsen, who was always cheerful even so early in the morning, struck my tent, packed it up expertly and fastened it to the back of a mule, whilst I saddled my own horse. All this had, of course, to take place in the dark, or at least by the light of the stars, and, occasionally, the moon. We did not even stop to have tea. Each herdsman had to attend to twelve mules apart from his own animal, but his task was made easier by the fact that the animals were docile and only too anxious to be on their way. There was no trouble, and all you could hear was the occasional chink of harness buckles and the dull thud of hooves on the ground. In fact we would break camp and move off with what seemed to me astonishing rapidity. Each pack animal carried two equally heavy saddle-bags which were so expertly fastened together that two herdsmen could easily lift them over the back of the animal and secure them readily by a strap under the animal's belly. The rope with which the beast had been hobbled in the night was quickly released, a smart slap on the haunches and the animal would rise at once and move off after the others. In the meantime the leading animals would have had their special collars fixed, and as they moved you would hear the cheerful jingling of the bells attached to them. The horsemen were always the last to move off, each man leading two spare horses.

From the first awakening up to the time of moving off hardly more than half an hour would pass.

By the time the main caravan had moved off only the cooks and the Dangkyabkhens, or scouts, were left. It was the task of these Dangkyabkhens to collect the pegs and ropes to which the animals had been attached during the night and to load them on particularly powerful mules; those which wore the biggest collars with the loudest bells, and were decorated with a scarlet bobble of yak hair. We set off without breakfast as the cooks had packed their utensils the evening before. It was the business of the Dangkyabkhens to decide on the next camping place, and the business of the cooks to have hot tea and food ready by the time the caravan arrived. A large caravan would often have up to forty or more such scouts and cooks who had to be mounted on very good horses as they were last away from one camping site and first at the next.

Unless particular circumstances were involved, a day's march meant between five and six hours in the saddle, and the first preparations for the reception of the caravan had been made before it arrived. The tether rope was stretched in a large rectangle on four strong pegs whose upper part was protected against fraying by thick pelt. It was a particularly powerful rope made up of many individual strands of yak's-tail hair. At appropriate intervals shorter lengths of rope with wooden pegs were spliced into it for fastening the individual animals. I had caused all this equipment to be specially made by handicraftsmen in Kumbum before we left, and it was all new—and I had not economised in the making. We also had reserve pegs made of the toughest thorn and rosewood hardened with oil and dried out in the sun.

We usually camped on ancient sites where innumerable caravans had preceded us down the years. They were camping places which had been tried out and found suitable. The animals of previous caravans had richly manured the grazing places, and there was still enough dung around to provide our cooks with fuel. For this reason and because they hadn't to bother collecting the stones they needed to build their fires, they too preferred the old camping sites; everything they needed was already there. Sometimes such an ancient caravan site even had a stone wall which offered protection against the wind. It was therefore not surprising that sometimes the Dangkyabkhens would squabble over the best spots, since each man was anxious to secure the best site for his particular group. But such squabbles usually took place only early on, because before long the more experienced, quick and competent Dangkyabkhens gained the upper hand, and invariably secured the best places, the richest grazing spots and the shortest way to water.

The cook of each individual group would be ready with steaming hot tea for his people when they arrived, and that would be all the more welcome because it was the first hot drink we had had since the evening of the previous day. Only after we had drunk this long-desired and refreshing stimulant would we set to and release the animals from their pack saddles and let them loose to graze. After that fuel had to be collected for the fires. You took a sack and grabbed whatever came to hand as long as it promised to burn: roots, tamarisk branches, thorn thickets, and any dung left over by the beasts of previous caravans. Sometimes too there was dung dropped by the drongs, the wild yaks, or by the kyangs, the wild asses. After that there was usually only a short pause for food, and we would eat just enough to take the edge off our appetites; some tsampa, dried cheese and perhaps a piece of meat—washed down, of course, with tea. After that we would set to work to examine every piece of equipment, and if anything was found damaged—sack, harness, rope—it had to be repaired at once. When it grew dark the animals would often return from the grazing grounds on their own and loudly demand their ration of dried peas, which was then given to them in nosebags.

Once they were all attended to and safely tethered to the common rope, the men could at last begin to think of their own solid evening meal, which usually consisted of meat, tsampa, rolls and tea. As soon as darkness had fallen everyone prepared to sleep. The great dogs, without which no caravan would dream of setting out, were then attached to the corners of the baggage, which had in the meantime been piled up into a sort of protective wall. The horses were covered up with their saddlecloths, and the mules would be content with the protection of the loosely strapped saddle against the cold of the night. Before long there would be complete silence as the caravan slept, broken only occasionally as some animal stirred in its sleep.

I began to enjoy the journey more and more as we went along; for one thing I was to get to know quite a considerable part of my own country I had not known before. For years I had never gone beyond the general neighbourhood of Kumbum, and now in the first few days of our journey to Lhasa I had already seen a good many new things. And even that was nothing compared with what lay ahead: the great richness and variety of the land-scape, the different plants and animals, the constantly varying coloration, and the many tones and half-tones. In fact it was on this journey to Lhasa that I first obtained some idea of the fascination of my own country, and it heightened my feeling of intense communion with the soil. Of course, all this was not immediately clear to me then, but I sensed the depth and per-manence of the impressions which were crowding in on me, and I eagerly bombarded those who had already made the journey with questions concerning every detail that occurred to me.

Before long I was to see the vast herds of drongs with my own eyes. The sight of those beautiful and powerful beasts who from time immemorial have made their home on Tibet's high and barren plateaux never ceased to fascinate me. Somehow these shy creatures manage to sustain themselves on the stunted grass roots which is all that nature provides in those parts. And what a wonderful sight it is to see a great herd of them plunging head down in a wild gallop across the steppes. The earth shakes under their heels and a vast cloud of dust marks their passage. At nights they protect themselves from the cold by huddling up together, with the calves in the centre. They will stand like this in a snow-storm, pressed so close together that the condensation from their breath rises into the air like a column of steam. The nomads have occasionally tried to bring up young drongs as domestic animals, but they have never entirely succeeded. Somehow once they live together with human beings they seem to lose their astonishing strength and powers of endurance; and they are no use at all as pack animals, because their backs immediately get sore. Their immemorial relationship with man has therefore remained that of game and hunter, for their flesh is very tasty.

The kyangs, or wild asses, live together in smaller groups each headed by a stallion, lording it over anything from ten to fifty mares. I was struck by the noble appearance of these beasts; and, in particular, by the beautiful line of head and neck. Their coat is light brown on the back and whitish below the belly, and their long thin tails are almost black; the whole representing excellent camouflage against their natural background. They look wonderfully elegant and graceful when you see them darting across the steppes like arrows, heads stretched out and tails streaming away behind them in the wind. Their rutting season is in the autumn, and then the stallions are at their most aggressive as they jealously guard their harems. The fiercest and most merciless battles take place at this time of the year between the stallion installed and interlopers from other herds. When the battle is over the victor, himself bloody and bruised from savage bites and kicks, leads off the mares in a wild gallop over the steppe.

We would often see kyangs by the thousand spread over the hillsides and looking inquisitively at our caravan; sometimes they would even surround us, though keeping at some distance. And it happened again and again that our own animals, attracted by the cavorting kyangs and their strange neighings, would gallop off to join them. Now and again chaos would result, and we would have a tremendous amount of trouble to separate our own animals from their wild friends and bring them back again. At such times the steppe would be almost hidden by clouds of dust. Despite their loads our animals would try to compete with the kyangs in speed, and in their efforts they would often scatter sacks and cases on the ground. It even happened occasionally that some of our animals would stay with the kyangs, loads and all, and we would never set eyes on them again.

The worst enemy of both the drongs and the kyangs is the wolf of the steppes, the most feared predator of the Tibetan high plateaux. The kyangs defend themselves by forming a protective circle as soon as they spot a wolf. Heads down in the middle they lash out wildly with their hooves, and woe betide any inexperienced wolf who comes too close. But generally speaking a wolf knows better than to try conclusions with such a group; he much prefers to pull down a single kyang who has been foolish enough to wander too far away from the main body whilst grazing. But the undisputed king of the Tibetan fauna is the rat-hare bear, so-called because these delightful little beasts are his main source of sustenance. On many occasions on our journey we would see these bears working away furiously, digging up the ground with their forepaws and throwing up the earth behind them into clouds in their efforts to get at the rat-hares in their burrows, whilst steppe foxes would prowl around at a respectful distance from the bear, knowing from long experience that some of the dug-out rat-hares would escape the bear and flee blindly in all directions—often to fall an easy prey to their own snapping jaws.

A Tibetan would never dream of hunting a bear. In Tibetan tradition the bear holds a high place in the animal kingdom; and his strength, his wisdom and his powers of endurance are admired and praised in many folk-tales. I was to learn later that the bear is just as much feared and respected amongst other peoples too. The very appearance of a bear, its astonishing ability to stand and walk on its hind legs like a clumsy giant, its voracity, and its fearlessness towards man all combine to make it awe-inspiring. Whoever comes across the marks of its hind paws in the snow, looking like the footmarks of some giant, as indeed they are, knows the eerie shudder which goes through everyone who knows the beast and the stories current about it.

Amongst the most difficult phases of our long journey were the crossings of big rivers and the climbs through high passes.

The highest pass we had to negotiate was across the Burhan-Buddha Mountains. As at that height there is neither vegetation nor water for the animals a caravan has to do the climb and the journey down the other side in a day. We rested at the foot of the mountain for a whole day before attempting the climb in order that the animals could graze peacefully and be fresh for the effort, and we started only when the sun had disappeared behind the snow-capped peaks in the evening. At first the long and arduous haul up through the rocky pass helped us to ignore the increasing cold, but by midnight, at which time we reached the highest point of the pass, it was so intensely cold that it almost took our breath away, and everyone complained of shortness of breath and giddiness. A traditional specific against this sort of trouble is to chew a clove of garlic, and many did so; others sat the wrong way round on their horses in order that the icy wind sweeping through the narrow pass should not interfere with their breathing. We used to believe that the mountains emitted poisonous emanations to rob us of our senses, but since then, of course, I have learnt that what we were really suffering from at such heights was a shortage of oxygen. Early the next morning we reached the first water-hole and good grazing grounds on the other side. By this time both man and beast were so exhausted by the sustained effort of getting over the pass that we now took another rest day in order to recover.

A week later we reached the banks of the River Togtog. It was beautiful weather and it did not take us very long to get across. The clear water and the rather low surface level helped us considerably, and our animals, which had to swim part of the way, carried us and our baggage across calmly and without difficulty. I must say I was thrilled at the magnificent sight of hundreds of animals crossing the river, which was not far short of five hundred feet across at this spot. Horses, yaks and mules stretched their heads as far as possible out of the water which gurgled and frothed around them. In a moment or two their hooves had stirred up the mud at the bottom of the river, and from the point of our crossing the water was suddenly transformed into brown and yellow mud as it coursed on downstream, and it was some time after the last animal had scrambled up the bank on the other side before the water settled down and became clear again.

Once over we stopped to examine our baggage to find out whether any water had got into our stores. Cases, sacks and bags were all carefully checked, and if anything was found to be damp it had to be unpacked and spread out in the sun to dry; after which it had to be repacked. In fact as far as our baggage was concerned, Döndrub Gyantsen and the craftsmen he had instructed and supervised had done a good job, and our careful examination showed that everything had come across the river safely. Other groups were not so lucky with their equipment, and found they had to spend the greater part of the day in unpacking, drying, and repacking.

It was when there were rivers to cross that the experience and knowledge of our Dangkyabkhens came in most useful, for it was they who chose the places at which to ford the rivers, and they who guided over the individual groups. For all those who were inexperienced it was a good thing that the first big river to be crossed was the comparatively undangerous Togtog, and that the great River Chumar, which flows into the Drichu, the upper course of the Yangtse-kiang, came only later when they had already had a little experience of fording rivers. Even so, the sight of the great Chumar, or Red River, when we saw it a couple of days later was intimidating enough, for heavy rainfall had caused it to overflow its banks in places, and its reddish-brown masses of water carried river rubble and mud along with it and rolled over the dangerous rapids with a tremendous rushing noise. The sight of exposed sandbanks here and there in the wide river raised our hopes, because they seemed to offer some hope of doing the crossing by easy stages, but our hopes were immediately dashed by our more experienced scouts who informed us that those sandbanks had to be avoided at all costs because our animals would just sink into them and disappear.

This time we were unable to cross the river on horseback, and we had to go naked into the water, our clothes tied in bundles on our backs, and cling to the manes of our animals. It was anything but a pleasure to wade up to our necks in that ice-cold water from the mountains, but once you had gone thoroughly under the worst was over. Under the experienced guidance of our Dangkyabkhens we crossed safely to the far side and scrambled up the bank shivering with the cold. This time too the baggage of my group was carried across almost without trouble, and the routine examination showed that there was very little to unpack and dry.

Our way now lay through a green and pleasant landscape with gently sloping hills and many sparkling streams, until two weeks later we came to the River Drichu, the upper course of the Yangtse-kiang. "Drichu" means "River of the Yak Cows," and you could easily understand why, because as far as the eye could see there were vast herds of drongs grazing along its banks. The sight of the swollen Chumar had frightened me, but it was just nothing by comparison with the vast masses of water being carried downstream by the Drichu. It looked absolutely impossible to me that we could ever hope to cross that enormously broad stream with its four great arms each over four hundred yards wide. A glistening expanse of water that looked endless stretched away ahead, and I was almost in despair, because I suddenly had the feeling that I would never get to Lhasa at all, that some grim guardian of the door was barring my way.

When our group reached the bank early in the morning it was as though we were standing on the shores of the sea. Ahead of us innumerable heads of men and beasts were bobbing up and down in the water without making any apparent progress. I had to force myself to unstrap my saddle, which was what our Dangkyabkhen advised in order to give my horse greater freedom of movement on the long stretch ahead. Ragpa, the beautiful creamcoloured pony which my father had given me, was to carry me across, whilst my spare horse, the black Nagpo, was to make the crossing together with the other reserve horses. I knew that I could rely completely on Ragpa, and, of course, from early youth I had been used to horses; but when Ragpa now carried me into the water I was seized with a terrible and unexplainable fear. I don't know whether it was fear of the depths ahead, or merely of the water itself, that strange element to which I now had to trust myself over a very long distance.

My uncle, who had already done this journey several times before, and Döndrub Gyantsen, who had not lost his cheerful confidence even in these conditions, both spoke encouragingly to me, and I really think that if they had not been there to keep me in countenance I should have panicked. Desperately I clung on to Ragpa's mane, and everything around me seemed to be spinning. I had the feeling that the broad stream which was slowly and powerfully moving away to the east would drown me and everything around me. I closed my eyes, and trembling with fright I listened to the splash and gurgle of the water, the snorting of the animals, and the calm, encouraging shouts of the drivers as they guided the beasts across. I seemed to be the only one of our party who was not soothed and reassured by the matter-of-fact behaviour and obvious competence of these long-experienced men. My thighs gripped so desperately and tightly to Ragpa's flanks that I began to feel my muscles getting painful cramp in the ice-cold water. The cheerful shouts of the others and the crack of the whips as they lashed through the air sounded like mockery to me. Of course, the aim of all those shouts and words of encouragement was to prevent a panic from breaking out amongst the animals in this enormous waste of water, because at such a moment panic would have led to a terrible catastrophe.

In actual fact, the crossing of the Drichu, as wide as it was, was not so dangerous as the crossing of the Chumar which had been in spate. But when after an hour we finally reached the other side safely I had to be lifted from my horse. I was completely exhausted and incapable of uttering even a single word. But my gallant horse was also trembling in every limb. The intense cold and the great effort required to carry across a panic-stricken rider clinging on like a limpet had exhausted him. I let myself sink to the ground with a deep sigh of relief; secure in the knowledge that we had now crossed the last great river which barred our way to Lhasa.

But my relief at being able to rest and recuperate at last was ill-founded. Although there was good grazing land for many miles around our Dangkyabkhens considered it highly inadvisable for us to stay where we were and enjoy a well-earned rest because the notorious Gologs, a particularly savage tribe of robber nomads, had pitched their tents a little way off and it was their herds we could see grazing everywhere. They had come this far in their flight from the troops of our Governor Mapufang, with whom they had but recently engaged in a bloody skirmish. Although we greatly outnumbered them and were altogether better armed and equipped, it really did not seem advisable for us to pitch camp in their neighbourhood, so we pushed on grimly until we had put a respectable distance between us and them and found suitable grazing ground for our animals. Even then we did not altogether trust them, and so we pitched our tents close together and kept sentries on the lookout all the time. We rested from our excessive exertions for a couple of days, and when we finally moved on both men and animals were completely recovered—and the dreaded Gologs had made no attempt to interfere with us.

Gradually we made our way forward through barren, gently rising terrain towards the Tibetan frontier, which runs between the Drichu and the Dang Pass. It was becoming noticeably colder now, and summer was giving way to autumn. At nights we huddled up even closer into our fur coats and pulled our fur hats closer down over our ears. Then, on a clear day glistening with frost, we reached the first Tibetan frontier post, and thus the realm of the Dalai Lama. The frontier guards, or Apohors, belong to the Tibetan nomad tribe of Horpas, and they are regular soldiers under the orders of the Tibetan Government in Lhasa. The thirty members of this frontier guard live in baghurs, dark tents made of coarse yak-hair weave. They were armed with modern rifles and mounted on excellent horses.

From these wild and tough fellows I learned that my father had sent a man named Trangsi to meet me with presents, and that he had gone as far as the banks of the Drichu, where he had waited for me for a month and then given up and returned, leaving most of the food which had been intended for me to the frontier men—including no doubt some of the wonderful pastry my mother made. Incidentally, these frontier guards might well be wild and tough, but they were disciplined, and they took their duties seriously: they examined all baggage, checked the number of travellers and the number of animals, and questioned everyone concerning his objective and the purpose of his journey. There was nothing astonishing about the fact that our caravan with its thousand human beings and its twenty thousand animals was one of the biggest which had crossed the frontier for a long time—after all, Tibet had a new Dalai Lama, and pilgrims were streaming into Lhasa from all parts to celebrate that event.

Right here on the frontier I was made aware at once of the privileges which were due to me as brother of the Dalai Lama. The officer in charge of the frontier post had received instructions from Lhasa to provide soldiers for a personal escort to accompany me over the Dang Pass. We started the ascent that afternoon amidst a light fall of snow, and accompanied by my military escort. An icy wind swept down on us from the snow and ice-covered mountain peaks ahead, but we rode on and up without pausing until by midnight we had reached the highest point of the pass, a stony desert under a glacier over which a veritable storm howled. We were shivering with cold now, and already very tired, but there was no question of resting, so we started the descent on the other side at once. By the time we had reached the bottom of the valley the next morning the weather had cleared. Brilliant sunshine now lay on the mountainside over which we had passed, and in the clear frosty air we could see white clouds of steam rising from the hot springs of Dangla-Chutsen.

Very tired indeed from our night march we now rested. Just as I was about to go into my tent a man arrived saying that he wished to speak to me. He turned out to be the Trangsi who had already ridden once as far as the Drichu to meet me, and he had waited for me here in this beautiful spot. He conveyed the affectionate greetings of my parents and welcomed me warmly to Tibet. I immediately invited him to join our caravan, and the next morning we took leave of the soldiers and went on under his guidance.

Four days later we reached the nomad settlement of Shag-chukha, where we saw the first permanent human dwellings we had seen in a march lasting two months. We now felt that we were on safe ground again at last, and we gave thanks to the gods for having spared us from thirst, bandits, wild animals and sickness on our long journey. Now that there was no longer any danger to be feared there was no reason for the individual caravans to stay together, and each caravan leader did whatever he pleased. For example, some continued their way at once. However, we preferred to stay for a few days in Shagchukha and enjoy a modest share of that simple domesticity we had so long been compelled to do without. The settlement had big, strong tents in which the drivers and the servants could be accommodated, the cooks had proper fireplaces to cook at, and the nomads willingly sold us the curdled milk and fresh meat we had gone without so long.

Then we started off on the two-day journey to Nagchukha. We had not yet come in sight of the town when ahead of us we saw a very smart cavalcade approaching. Even at a distance you could see the broad-brimmed red hats of gentlemen's servants. I rode forward to meet this cavalcade and to my delighted surprise I recognised the man who was riding ahead of the others as my father. He had obviously spotted me too for he now urged on his horse to greater speed. What a great change had come over the simple peasant Chökyang Tsewang since I had last seen him! His upright bearing and his natural air of authority had always impressed me even from early childhood. But now, seated on a fine horse and clothed in splendid silk garments, he bore himself with the dignity of a king or a duke. In fact in the magnificence of his appearance he quite outdid the Legate of the Dalai Lama who was his companion. Deeply moved we now fell into each other's arms and I was so stirred that I could not find words to express my feelings. It was altogether a great moment for me, for I had now obtained my heart's desire; that my father should bring me back into the bosom of our family! And as we rode into Nagchukha together I could hardly take my eyes off the splendid figure beside me.

Nagchukha was only a small town with a few clay huts but it was the headquarters of the District Officer, the Dzongpön, in whose official residence, the Dzong, my father and I were given rooms. The whole population of the town was assembled to witness the formal reception which had been arranged for me by the Legate of the Dalai Lama, himself a high prelate. Solemnly he handed over a letter and a gift from the Dalai Lama and formally welcomed me into Tibetan territory. The monks of a small monastery not far away from the town had also hurried in to take part in the reception, and when the Legate of the Dalai Lama had welcomed me, they handed me curdled milk and tsampa flour, and greeted me with the sound of trumpets and oboes as due to me as an incarnation, whilst the assembled populace avidly murmured prayers.

When my father and I had refreshed ourselves a little in the Dzong, we both paid a visit to the nearby monastery where I gave thanks to the gods from the depths of my grateful heart for their goodness to me. I burnt incense and lit a butter-lamp before the statue of each god, and I gave each monk a present of money with the request that they too should thank the gods for my safe arrival. After that I remained there for some time immersed in prayer.

When we returned to the Dzong I settled down comfortably. For the first time since my departure from Kumbum a hundred and twelve days previously I now had a proper roof over my head, and my sufferings from the cold and the damp were over. We proposed to stay here and rest for ten days, and to my great delight I discovered my old friend Tentsing amongst the servants. Tentsing was the youth who had fled from Kumbum some years before. I was lost in admiration as I looked at all the presents I had received—my mother, for example, had sent me a costly silk coat to wear on my entry into Lhasa—and I left it completely to Döndrub Gyantsen to look after our caravan.

After our long rest in Nagchukha we set out happily on the rest of our journey and before long we came to the monastery of Reting. Whilst our animals were grazing in the meadow below the monastery, my father and I paid a visit of respect to the former Regent of Tibet, Reting Rimpoche, who was now in residence there, and I was enormously surprised when in the middle of a barren and broken landscape we suddenly came into a garden which was more beautiful and more neatly kept than any I had so far seen, though indeed the whole layout of the monastery reminded me strongly of Shartsong Ritrö. Juniper bushes and Himalaya cedars grew around the residence of the former Regent, and I had plenty of time to look round the wonderful garden on my own because my father and Reting Rimpoche plunged at once into an interested discussion about their joint hobby, horseflesh, and I might as well not have been there. After a very good meal my father and I undertook the customary tour through the monastery, making our offerings in each of the temples. Then, followed by the blessings of the former Regent, we returned to our caravan, part of which had already moved on, and continued our way.

In Penpo Dzong a deputation from the famous monastery of Ganden was awaiting me to pay me all the honours due to me as the incarnation of Tagtser. The grave of our great reformer Tsongkhapa is situated in this monastery. That same evening we reached Phödo, our last stop before we arrived in Lhasa. My mother had sent my brother Gyalo Döndrub and my brother-in-law Püntso Trashi out to meet me here. I hardly recognised either of them at first because they were so splendidly clothed. With cries of joy we fell into each other's arms, and then they led me into the bedroom which had been set aside for my use and showed me the magnificent garments my mother had sent with them for me. I stood before them almost at a loss for words. What riches and what plenty now surrounded me after the hardships of the long journey! And then Gyalo Döndrub produced a basket of freshly baked pastries which my mother had sent with them, and smilingly he handed them to me. My mother had not forgotten to provide her eldest son at first opportunity with those delicacies he was so fond of. It was late that night—the last before arriving in Lhasa—before we all got to bed.

12. Arrival in Lhasa

THE astrologers had chosen what they regarded as a promising day for my arrival in Lhasa, and as far at least as the weather was concerned they seemed to have chosen well. Preparations for our formal reception had been made in Rigya, about an hour's journey from the capital. I was assisted from my horse and led into a tent where another high prelate welcomed me on behalf of the Dalai Lama, and handed me a white good-luck scarf and a sungdü, a short red ribbon which is worn round the neck. Its knots had been tied by the Dalai Lama himself. Instead of the milk and flour which had previously been given to me as gifts of welcome I was now presented with lengths of magnificent wool and silk, since such things were more appropriate than food.

After the representative of the Dalai Lama had concluded his greetings, I was welcomed by deputations from the nearby monasteries of Drepung and Sera. In accordance with boundaries drawn up as early as the days of the Fifth Dalai Lama, Tengtser, my home village, belonged to Drepung, the superior monastery of Kumbum. The Shengo of Drepung now handed me a large good-luck scarf. I felt a trifle constrained in my new clothes, and I was also mildly confused by the solemn formality of my reception.

The many dignitaries who were assembled there together with their servants now accompanied our caravan into Lhasa where the Dalai Lama awaited us in his summer residence of Norbu Lingka, a name which means more or less "Garden of Jewels." But when the Potala, the Winter Palace of the Dalai Lama, whose golden roofs dominate all the other buildings in Lhasa, loomed

up in the distance my heart was full of joy. At last I was about
to set foot in the town I had longed for so eagerly! Before long
the whole of Lhasa with its many splendid houses and beautiful gardens was spread out before us. We approached from
the north, so we crossed the Lingkhor, the exterior pilgrim's
ring round the town. Great crowds of people had assembled
and from everywhere still more sightseers ran up. My impressions
were so overwhelming that I hardly knew where to look first. My
father pointed out a great park and informed me that a large
house was about to be built there for our family. Passing along
the south front of the Potala and going through a Chörten gate
we came to the Norbu Lingka, which is in the west part of the
town. In the warm bright rays of the afternoon sun the golden
roofs of the Potala glowed as though they were on fire.

Stone lions stood at the gates of the summer residence of the
Dalai Lama, and on duty were sentries in European uniform
armed with modern rifles. At the orders of my father we now
dismounted, and the guard presented arms. My father then led
me to the small house which had been placed at the disposal of
our family. We were met on the threshold by my mother, and
once again I was struck by the great outward change in my
parents. My mother had always been the dominant personality
in our family, though without ever questioning the authority of
my father as head of the family, and now, apart from her splendid
clothes, she looked just the same to me. Even as Gyayum Chemo,
or Great Mother of the King, Dekyi Tsering behaved in a
simple and modest fashion, but at the same time she radiated a
quite impressive grandeur. I now flung myself into her arms.

After the months of uncertainty in Kumbum, the hardships
and privations of the long journey, and the excitements of the
past few days, I was once more back in the safe and protective
bosom of my family. Wordlessly my mother handed me a bowl
of curdled milk and soothingly she stroked my hair. It was like
old times, when, overheated from wild play, I would run to her
in the kitchen. I hadn't yet finished greeting my mother when
my younger brother Lobsang Samten rushed into the room

followed by my sister Tsering Dröma. To my surprise my
sister held two children in swaddling-clothes in her arms; they
were her own child, Tentsing Ngawang, and my younger sister
Jetsün Pema, who had been born to my mother in Lhasa.

In the afternoon I was allowed into the Norbu Lingka to see
the Dalai Lama. My father took me through a door in the Yellow
Wall which surrounds the inner precincts and the buildings of
the Dalai Lama, and into the Kesang Potrang, and led me to a
small room in which my brother was doing his lessons. The
three abbots who were entrusted with supervising his studies
were all present: Simpön Khenpo, the Master of Robes; Söpön
Khenpo, the Master of Religious Ceremony; and Chöpön Khenpo,
the Master of Tea. I prostrated myself three times on the ground
before the Dalai Lama as tradition requires, and then I handed
him a white good-luck scarf. My brother, who was now a lad
of six and a half, wore a simple red garment like any other monk.
In the presence of the three abbots he remained formal and
inquired politely about my journey, but then he took me by the
hand and led me out into the garden, where wonderful flowers
were blossoming in the shade of magnificent trees. Radiantly
he introduced me to all the wonders of this small paradise: the
flowers, the pond, the tame animals, and the nuts, which were
just ripe. Gleefully he showed me the best way to crack them.
He also told me about his teachers Yongdzin Rimpoche and
Tagdra Rimpoche. The latter was also serving as Regent until
my brother reached his majority. My brother also told me that
he could read and write already. After an agreeable hour we had
to part because he was then taken off for religious instruction.

When evening came the whole family was assembled for the
final meal of the day. How long was it since I had last sat down
like this with them all. Father and I as the eldest male members
of the family sat in the places of honour, then came my mother
with Gyalo Döndrub and Lobsang Samten, who were already
quite big boys, and then my sister Tsering Dröma with her
husband. Only one was still missing, the one to whom we owed
it that we were all sitting here in this beautiful house before this

richly decked table. It was already dark when the door opened
and the Dalai Lama came in and greeted us all cheerfully. We all
asked him to take the seat at the head of the table, but this he
refused to do, saying that it was due to his father or to me as the
eldest. Finally he sat down on a costly silk cushion and we all
squatted on woollen cushions. After our meal the time went very
rapidly with happy family chatter, and all too soon our young
brother was taken away from us again.

That night it was a long time before I could get to sleep. I had
thanked the gods in deep gratitude for the rich harvest they had
poured out for us all. By their inscrutable wisdom we had all been
transferred from a modest peasant homestead in the province
of Amdo to Lhasa the capital of Tibet, where we had achieved
riches and high honour beyond our dreams. No greater good
fortune could have come upon us. Deeply moved I now prayed
for health and a long life in peace and harmony for me and mine.

Quite early the following morning a party of monks put in an
appearance and brought an invitation to an official audience with
the Dalai Lama for both my father and me, for he had been
absent from the capital for some time. Such solemn receptions
for highly placed visitors to Lhasa always took place during the
daily Drungja, a ceremony for which all the monk-officials
gather in the great hall of the Dalai Lama. A special Letsenpa,
or guide, had been sent to me and he explained the details of the
strict ceremonies at the court of the Dalai Lama. He helped me
to put on the court clothing, a brown silken coat and a short
yellow jacket, and he then accompanied me to the plinth of the
temple before the Kesang Potrang, where about six hundred
pilgrims were already waiting to be let in to the audience room
to receive the blessing of the Dalai Lama. A little later the
Drönyer Chemo, the High Chamberlain and Master of Ceremonies of the assembled pilgrims, invited me as the highest in
rank to accompany him into the Small Palace. At the head of the
troop of pilgrims I now followed him into a larger room, where
the monk-officials had already taken their places on their rugs.
At first I had felt a little uncomfortable, but now I was more at

my ease because so much reminded me of what I was used to in Kumbum.

Hardly had the last pilgrim entered the hall when the Dalai Lama himself appeared. Looking ahead thoughtfully he went up the steps of the throne with confident, deliberate strides. Everyone present had risen and was bowing low. When the Dalai Lama had taken his seat on the throne all the others also seated themselves. My father and I now slowly approached the throne and prostrated ourselves three times before the Dalai Lama. The ceremony of Mendel Tensum then followed. A statuette of the God of Long Life, a small religious book and a Chörten symbolising the body, word and spirit of Buddha were pressed against our foreheads and then blessed by the Dalai Lama. The room was sparsely lit from above, and in the flicker of the butter-lamps the faces of all those around me seemed to fade away and I saw only the face of the Dalai Lama shining in the golden light before me. Respectfully I handed a costly scarf to the High Chamberlain whose duty it was to accept all gifts for the Dalai Lama. Then I went up close to the throne to receive my brother's blessing. As he blessed me with quiet dignity by laying his hands on me I noticed for the first time how really beautiful they were.

Then I followed my father to the seat of the Regent, where the ceremony of Mendel Tensum was repeated, another kata handed over, and a sungdü received in exchange; a brilliant red ribbon which could be worn round the neck, carried as an amulet, or laid on the altar of the house chapel. Afterwards we moved to one side and waited until the long file of pilgrims had passed by the Dalai Lama and the Regent. Only highly placed personages, high officials and monks were honoured by being blessed with the laying-on of hands; the other faithful were blessed by being touched with a tassel by the Dalai Lama.

I was completely absorbed by the solemn ceremony when the High Chamberlain and a monk carrying a large silver tea-can approached me. As soon as the last pilgrim had received his blessing I went forward to the throne again as I had been told to do by my Letsenpa, prostrated myself three times in the regulation fashion before him, and then stood there in a bowed position holding my wooden tea bowl in my hand. Even here I carried it in my habit above my belt. Strong butter-tea was now poured out for me and I drank it all, wiped the bowl with a piece of white cotton, wrapped the bowl up again in its yellow silk covering and put it away in my habit. When I had again prostrated myself three times before the Dalai Lama I was allowed to return to my place and sit down on my cushion.

In the meantime the Dalai Lama had also drunk his tea, and now the monk with the tea-can poured out tea for the other monks present. I was also given another bowlful. A distribution of rice followed the tea. The Dalai Lama was served first, then the Regent, and then me, as highest-ranking amongst the guests. Custom demands that one should take a few grains of rice from the bowl and offer them to the gods. During the ceremony of tea-drinking and rice-eating, the servants of the Dalai Lama kept bringing in presents from him to me: sacks full of rice, butter, tsampa flour; thick bales of sheep's wool and silk. Steadily they piled up in front of me. I gave thanks for them by prostrating myself before the Dalai Lama once more. It was only now that the High Chamberlain put the white good-luck scarf round my neck. Then the Dalai Lama immediately arose and left the room with the Regent and the other dignitaries of his court whilst everyone else present bowed low reverentially.

Deeply impressed I returned from this audience to my parents' house in the company of my father, and I had hardly arrived there when the first visitors began to put in an appearance to pay their court to me as the eldest brother of the Dalai Lama. Each visitor brought me a kata, and I blessed each one by the laying on of hands. These visits went on steadily for several days, and amongst the visitors were a number of Cabinet Ministers. I had to give an account of my journey again and again, and to tell them about Kumbum and Siling, whilst I returned the compliment by asking them questions about Lhasa. The Dalai Lama was in the house every day, but only for a short

His Holiness the Fourteenth Dalai Lama with his mother

Kündeling nestles in the mountains. It is one of the many monasteries in the neighbourhood of Lhasa

In the centre Norbu's mother; on the left his older sister Tsering Dröma

time, because his many duties and his lessons completely occupied the rest of his time.

When the stream of visitors to see me was finally over I went out into the town for the first time, accompanied by my parents and my brothers and sister, making a great Chömche, or sacrificial tour, of all the city's temples, leaving my offerings in each. In the largest and most famous of Lhasa's temples, the Tsuglagkhang or Jokhang, and the Ramoche, we burnt incense and lit butter-lamps. The sensible layout of the town and the riches of its buildings and gardens made me suppose it must be the most beautiful town in the world. Three sacred circular streets divide it. The first surrounds the sanctuary itself, an area in which the whirring and squeaking of prayer-wheels turned by many hundreds of pilgrims and visitors from all parts never cease. A second ring, the so-called Barkor, runs round the Tsuglagkhang and several blocks of houses and many shops. The outer ring, the Lingkhor, is, as the name indicates, a park ring, and it runs for about five miles right round the city, which is dominated by the vast Potala Palace with its golden roofs.

Most of the houses are two-storeyed structures, and they do not differ a great deal from each other in colour and form. Now and again you come across a splendid small temple with precious decorations. I was particularly struck by the beautiful gardens around the Potala Palace, and I was delighted at each new rain-water gulley ending in the form of a golden dragon's head jutting out from the eaves, and at every prayer-flag on the many roofs all around. This rich and beautiful city struck me as the most wonderful culmination of many thousand years of development on the part of a peaceful people fundamentally opposed to war. Finally my parents took me back for a snack and a short rest to the house which had been temporarily placed at their disposal until our own town house was ready, a building which was subsequently taken over by the Chinese Legation.

A visit to the Potala had been arranged for one of the next few days, and again my parents and my brothers and sister accompanied me on the great sacrificial tour, during which I made the

acquaintance of the whole enormous complex, in which there
are many residences and also a large school. The western wing
includes the Namgye Tratsang Monastery with its two hundred
and fifty monks. We had to pass through many corridors, and
climb up seemingly endless stone steps until finally we clambered
up a rather steep flight of wooden steps up to the highest observa-
tion point of the palace. The view from the parapet there took my
breath away. The magnificent panorama was beyond even my
expectations. The great city of Lhasa lay whole and entire at our
feet like a vast toy town. The caravans passing into the city
through its gates, the crowds of people in front of the temples,
and the stalls of the vendors on the streets, all looked tiny, and
reminded me of the butter-tower I had had made in Kumbum
for the Festival of Light. Wisps of smoke rose into the clear air
from innumerable fire-centres and sacrificial altars and moved
slowly across the town in transparent swathes.

In particular I could follow the course of the silver-glinting
River Kyichu, which touched the southern part of the city, for
a very great distance. Conical Chagpori, or the Iron Mountain,
with the Government Medical School on its peak, dominated the
mountain line which bordered the broad plains with an autumnal
brown; and in the distance you could see the Sera and Drepung
monasteries. Quite carried away by the beauty of the panorama
I took my mother's hand and listened to her as she explained
the details to me.

So long as it had not been decided where and how I was to
continue my studies I had plenty of time in which to look around
in the city. I strolled through the streets and the alleyways, and
I discovered new wonders almost at every step. Everything in
Lhasa was so different, and so much more rich and exciting than
in Kumbum, and when before the beginning of winter the Dalai
Lama was carried in solemn procession to take up his residence
in the Potala Palace I was given some idea of the tremendous
pomp which accompanies the celebration of feast days in the
capital. Everyone taking part in the procession was dressed in
brilliantly coloured and costly clothing. My father rode a splendid

horse, and the Dalai Lama was carried in a palanquin covered with yellow silk and borne by thirty-six uniformed attendants. Following the palanquin was a monk carrying a precious umbrella of peacock's feathers, which were ruffled gently by the breeze.

My mother decided to stay for the time being in the small house in the Norbu Lingka, and to move into the house in Lhasa only when the cold weather began. Of the family, only my brother Lobsang Samten accompanied the Dalai Lama into the apartments of the Winter Palace. The rooms in which they lived there were quite modest. Apart from the living-room, from which there was a fine view out over the city, there were only a small bedroom, a study and a house chapel. During my visits I usually saw the Dalai Lama only for a short time, but I spent hours with Lobsang Samten on the great terrace, a point of vantage from which we could study the life of the city below us through field-glasses and point out to each other every coloured paper dragon that people sent up from their flat roofs.

Lobsang Samten was only two years older than the Dalai Lama, and their interests were therefore quite similar. They already talked to each other exclusively in Lhasa dialect, whereas all the other members of the family spoke to each other in the Amdo dialect, and were only gradually accustoming themselves to High Tibetan. However, in the presence of the Dalai Lama we all did our best to speak it in the polite Lhasa fashion, making as few mistakes as possible.

13. Studies in Drepung Monastery

TOWARDS the end of the year a family council under the chairmanship of my father decided that I should continue my studies in the monastery of Drepung, the superior monastery of Kumbum, which was about five miles away from Lhasa. Once the decision was taken the preparations for my instalment there were started at once. My uncle, the one who had made the long journey to Lhasa with me, now left for Drepung, and returned after a while with the information that I could study in the Gomang Tratsang and find quarters in the Chupa Og House in the Samlo Khangtsen wing. However, first of all the house would need a thorough overhaul before it would be ready for me. Whilst the workmen were busy carrying out this job my father negotiated with the representatives of the Samlo Khangtsen concerning the size of the kugye I should have to raise.

This kugye is the name for the round of visits a newcomer has to pay, taking in each monk in the monastery in turn to ask for his prayers. And "pay" is the right word, because each monk has to receive a present of money. Now Drepung is the biggest monastery in Tibet, sheltering something like ten thousand monks within its walls. About eight thousand of these would be entitled to a present from me on my kugye. Thus, in addition to everything else, the undertaking was no mean financial problem. Finally it was agreed that each monk should receive a present of one gormo. In addition to the total sum involved for these presents there would be the cost of the katas, the butter-lamps, and the receptions I should have to give after my instalment in Drepung.

On a day worked out by the court astrologers as auspicious I set off for Drepung accompanied by my parents, Tsering Dröma, Gyalo Döndrub and a large number of friends and servants. In a magnificent tent not far from the monastery we were received by the Drepung Lachi, the Chief Abbots of the monastery, and the representatives of the Gomang Tratsang and the Samlo Khangtsen. After we had solemnly exchanged katas we all went together into the vast cloister city which clustered in a half-circle round the foot of the mountain. The golden temple roofs glistened in the winter sun, and a large number of monks were assembled to welcome us, but they remained silent. The monastery of Drepung was famed for the strictness of its rules, and, amongst other things, it renounced the music of trumpets and oboes.

I was taken to a five-storeyed house, where, on the top floor, an apartment of three rooms with a kitchen had been prepared for me. There was also a broad veranda from which I could look out over the greater part of the monastery. I had brought Döndrub Gyantsen, my cook and another servant with me. My party was now enlarged by the addition of a monk named Tseten, who was appointed by the monastery to be my mentor during the first period of my stay within its walls, and also by a Mongolian scholar named Ngawang Nyimala, who was to be my teacher in Drepung.

I found that everything was bigger than in Kumbum, and in some matters the monastic authorities were stricter here than in Kumbum, but on the whole the differences were not very great. Full of pride, Tseten explained to me that Drepung, which, together with Sera and Ganden, was one of the "Three Pillars of the Land," had six abbots and four tratsangs, whereas the Sera monastery, which was almost as big, had only four abbots and three tratsangs, and Ganden even only two abbots and two tratsangs. The names of the Drepung tratsangs were Loseling, Deyang, Ngagpa and Gomang, and each was divided into about twenty khangtsens, to which the monks were alloted according to what part of the country they came from.

The next morning, instead of the conch horn which was used in Kumbum, a clear penetrating boyish voice sounded from the roof of the great assembly hall to call the monks to prayer. In the enormous hall the Shengo immediately led me to my place amongst the incarnations. From the gallery, my father and Gyalo Döndrub watched my first appearance in the Tsogchen at Drepung. This gallery went round the whole of the first floor and it was provided with hassocks to sit on and small tables at which tea was served to visitors. Afterwards they accompanied me on my kugye and went with me into the many temples I visited to make my offerings, and in the afternoon when I entered the hall of the Gomang Tratsang for the first time they were once again in the gallery to witness my reception. As an incarnation and a brother of the Dalai Lama one of the front seats was made available for me. When they left the monastery that evening the parting was not sad this time because I was now living only an hour away from them.

Before long I had to take the entrance examination to the sixth class of the Gomang Tratsang, and it was held in the Chöra. On the morning of that important day a messenger arrived from the Dalai Lama bearing presents for me consisting of new top boots with sheepskin shafts and leather soles, a wine-red dagam and a yellow hat. I set off to take my examination dressed in these new things, but I must confess that after such a long pause the thought of an examination worried me a little. My mood was not improved when I learned that a monk with far more years of study behind him than I had was to be my rival in the decisive dispute. As it turned out, my fears were unfounded. On the whole the authorities seemed to regard the matter as more or less a formality, and the questions I was called upon to answer were not particularly difficult. However, from the answers given by my partner I realised that I had to do with one of the keenest minds in the tratsang. The examination did not take long and then I received the congratulations of my superiors on my success. I had already asked that the usual reception given in a newly furnished house should be allowed to coincide with the celebration of my successful entrance examination. A great number of officials, nobles and friends of the family now came to Drepung from Lhasa to congratulate me, and it was not long before I began to make new friends in the monastery itself.

I now plunged once again into my studies with zeal and enthusiasm, because they had been neglected for so long, and only on special occasions did I take part in the general assembly of the Drepung monks. The Chuke, or call to prayer, sounded at four o'clock every morning. I certainly never missed a single lesson or discussion in the two Chöras of my Tratsang; and we were called to our joint studies by a kind of gong or cymbals made of two big keys. The lessons lasted until late in the evening. We assembled in the morning for joint study and for joint exercises, and this was followed by a short break for tea, which in good weather was served in the Chöras, and in inclement weather in the Dukhang. At four o'clock in the afternoon I had two private lessons with Ngawang Nyimala, who would go through religious texts with me, though at this stage I no longer had to learn them by heart. After that I would take my main meal, and then before long the improvised gong would sound to call us together again for debate and discussion in the Chöra. When this was over we would say prayers together, and then the various classes would assemble separately for the evening lessons. There were about a hundred pupils in the sixth class, and we were taught by two monks from a much higher class. It wasn't often that I got back to my quarters before nine o'clock at night, and even then I would almost immediately get down to my books again by the light of the mustard-oil lamp.

However, before long this period of intensive and onerous study was to be pleasantly interrupted: our great New Year's Festival was approaching, the so-called Mönlam Chenmo, a feast which was celebrated with great pomp in Lhasa and extended over many weeks. My request that I should be allowed to watch the far-famed celebrations on the spot was immediately granted. It was in any case a holiday period in the Tratsang so I went off to Lhasa with my servants. As the house of my parents was not large enough for me to stay there as well I rented a small place of my own in the capital.

When the three of us left Drepung the normally so quiet and peaceful monastery was hardly recognizable. After the strict discipline of the school year the students were now allowed to give free rein to their long-suppressed desire to be noisy and joyful. Shouting and cheering, and singing high-spirited songs they marched through the streets of the monastery, letting off fireworks and getting up to all sorts of harmless mischief.

14. New Year's Festival in Lhasa

ALTHOUGH Lhasa lies about twelve thousand feet above sea-level its winters are very mild and snow hardly ever falls. For example, when the city was preparing to celebrate the Great New Year's Festival the usual sandstorms were already announcing the approach of spring.

The New Year's festivities begin on the twenty-ninth day of the last month of the old year with the Torgya celebration in the Potala. Greatly excited I accompanied my parents and my brothers and sister to the Dalai Lama, who welcomed us in his apartments and then had us led to the balcony which had been prepared for us. He himself was also present at the celebrations, which were held in one of the vast palace yards, the Deyangshar. And together with his teachers and guardians, he occupied a place prepared for him behind a curtain of yellow silk on the highest of the balconies. The members of his family and his officials had seats in the lower rows, for no one might occupy a place higher than that of the Dalai Lama.

On the flat roofs of the neighbouring buildings were jostling throngs of gaily dressed and excited spectators. Everyone was waiting with impatience for the beginning of the very diversified spectacle, which was arranged exclusively by the monks of the monastery in the west wing of the Potala. Jokes were cracked gaily, people talked about the possibilities for the coming year, and expressed delight at the boisterousness of the wind, which was flapping the silken curtains of the Dalai Lama's balcony—since this was taken as a good omen for the New Year.

Then suddenly a murmurous hubbub arose from the crowds,

followed by complete silence as everyone stared with con-
centration at the steep wooden steps on which the first group
of actors was now visible. Escorted by seven masked monks
came Hashang, a Mongolian of enormous stature, but as
good-natured as he was powerful. He was now wearing such
a huge mask that it was difficult for him to see, and his
escort had to lead him slowly down the steps. When the actors
reached the centre of the courtyard they all prostrated themselves
solemnly in the direction of the Dalai Lama. Then they began
their dances, which mimed various legendary events in the
country's history. When the traditional and unchanging part of
their performance was at an end they began to gag and improvise
amusingly, urged on by loud shouts of encouragement from the
audience. Soldiers dressed in the chain-mail which their pre-
decessors had worn hundreds of years previously now fired off
ancient muzzle-loaders until there was so much smoke in the air
that now and again you could hardly see.

The next group of performers consisted of a number of monks
wearing animal masks. Their ludicrous cavortings were welcomed by a delighted audience with loud laughter and much
applause. Most of the spectators were not aware of the deeper
meaning of the many masks and figures, and they just enjoyed
the colourful and amusing spectacle and left it at that. However,
each individual figure had a symbolic significance and a long
history, though in the course of time it had fallen largely into
forgetfulness except for a small circle of cognoscenti. During
the long series of these Cham, or dances, which lasted for
several hours, there were many masks whose meaning was lost
on the great majority of the spectators but which represented a
fantastic delight to the eye and were therefore welcomed with
delighted laughter and frantic applause. But when the black-hat
dancers appeared it was different. A visible throb of emotion
went through the whole audience, because it was still generally
known that this group of dancers represented demons, and their
costly and ancient costumes were amongst the unforgettable
impressions of the whole spectacle. The leading dancer of this

group, who was taller than any of the others, played the role of
the demon king. Over their dark-coloured costumes the individual dancers wore artistically worked chains made of human
bones reaching almost to the ground. During the dancing these
grisly chains, which are called Rügyen, make a strange and
eerie noise, and at the sound the audience fell completely
silent.

One dance group followed on the heels of the other; and good
and evil, beautiful and ugly masks gave way to each other in a
long succession. Behind a handsome person moving gracefully
across the courtyard would come a gruesome, revolting skeleton.
The best dancer of all was wearing the mask of a deer, and he
performed such wild leaps and twirls that the audience grew
giddy watching him.

A symbolic pantomime concluded the spectacle. A very large
sheet of rice paper with a male figure painted on it was laid out
in the courtyard; and, led by the Chief Magi, all those who had
taken part in the previous performance now danced around it to
the sound of trumpets, drums, oboes and cymbals, making it
very clear in dumb show that everything evil in the Old Year
now coming to an end was being loaded onto the figure represented on the rice paper.

Gradually the dance became more and more wild, and the
dancers leapt higher and higher into the air. In the background
in one corner of the courtyard a bright fire was burning under a
cauldron of oil. The music now rose to a crescendo, the dancers
leapt and gyrated furiously, and then amidst great applause
from the audience, the Chief Magi seized the rice-paper image,
screwed it up and threw it into the boiling oil, then took a scoop
of raw spirit in a bowl, which was a human skull, and threw it
onto the fire so that the flames leapt up even higher than the
dancers; and with this all the evil of the Old Year was symboli-
cally dissolved into nothing.

This spectacle was the peak and at the same time the end of the
festivities. We thanked the Dalai Lama for his invitation and
then went back to my parents' house. On this evening every

Tibetan family has Gutug for supper, a thick soup with dumplings floating in it, and kneaded into the dumplings are small stones, pieces of wood, wool, dice and coins, or perhaps only a little salt or paprika. All these concealed things are regarded as more or less favourable omens. The soup and the dumplings are ladled out amongst those present, and then the various finds in the dumplings are interpreted amidst much laughter and joking.

The first two days of the New Year in Lhasa were celebrated only by the Government and the ordinary civilian population, but on the third day the Mönlam Chenmo, or Great Prayer, begins. This is a three weeks' succession of large and small prayer meetings, and the monks of the immediate neighbourhood all take part in them. Quite early in the morning thousands of monks begin pouring into the town from all points of the compass until with the twenty-five thousand ordinary inhabitants, and the many pilgrims who come into Lhasa on high days and holidays, there would be perhaps a hundred thousand people in the capital all joining in the Great Prayer for man and beast, and asking the gods to grant happiness and prosperity to their country.

The small house I had rented lay in the centre of the town only a stone's throw from the Temple of Tsuglagkhang, and every morning I would take part in the great meeting there, together with about twenty thousand other monks. Whoever was unable to find any more room inside the temple itself would climb onto the neighbouring roofs, or stand in the surrounding streets and courtyards saying his prayers. A great number of servants were always at hand busily keeping the assembled monks provided with tea and soup. This soup, which was made with rice, meat, butter, dried fruit and cheese, always tasted a little burnt, but no one seemed to mind; in fact that particular taste almost seemed to belong to the celebration. Tea was consumed in vast quantities and there were also large amounts of butter, some of it not very fresh. Each of those present would produce tsampa flour from a little sack he had brought with him, and mix it with the tea in his wooden bowl.

Following on the great meeting came the Sungchöra, to

which monks who had completed their studies came from far and wide to win themselves the title of Lharimpa. The theological disputations of these experienced and learned men always attracted large audiences. The wordy duels were fought out in the presence of the abbots, and a jury decided on the rank due to each participant according to his performances. There were twenty-two degrees of Lharimpa; the first five invested the holders with the dignity of a Khenpo at one of the big monasteries, and even opened up the possibility of the regentship. The general public in the body of the hall and the gallery would follow the proceedings with passionate interest, particularly as the honour of the various monasteries from which the monks came was also involved. Outstandingly brilliant performances were rewarded with great applause, whilst the man who finally had to acknowledge himself defeated was jeered at good-humouredly.

On some days the Dalai Lama himself would leave the Potala and visit the Tsuglagkhang. Ceremoniously escorted by abbots he would be carried in solemn procession through the crowded streets followed by his teachers, the Chief Abbots of the monasteries, the members of his Cabinet, and various Rimpoches, of whom I was entitled to be one. A throne was made ready for him in the temple, and as soon as he was seated a vast concourse of people would stream past him in order to receive his blessing. These ceremonies, during which each of the faithful who had been blessed received a red ribbon, would last practically the whole day.

So long as the Dalai Lama, the Regent, or other high dignitaries were in the town there was always the utmost discipline and order, and during the procession of the Dalai Lama soldiers would line the Barkor. But once the various dignitaries had gone back into the Potala and the soldiers had been withdrawn, then the Dopdops, the police monks with the blackened faces, the broad shoulders and the thick staves, would have their hands full controlling the crowds. For the New Year holidays the ordinary secular administration did not operate in the city, and the maintenance of law and order was left in the hands of this police force of monks made up of contingents from each individual tratsang.

The soldiers in their ancient uniforms made a special splash of colour in the already colourful crowds, and whenever they appeared so attired the people would stream together to marvel at them. Their generals, or Yasos, wearing splendid brocade cloaks and costly black fox fur hats would ride with them to the banks of the river where ancient mortars would be discharged, and enormous clouds of smoke produced in order to drive the evil spirits away from the city. The butter ornaments which had been used during the holidays were now solemnly burnt on the riverbanks in the same way as after the Torgya ceremony in the Potala.

On the fifteenth day of the first month of the New Year the individual households and tratsangs would seek to outdo each other with their high butter towers, and the Government gave a special prize for the one adjudged the best. Many of these butter towers were much larger than those we had been been used to in Kumbum, but they certainly could not rival ours in the skill and ingenuity lavished on them.

As the incarnation of Tagtser I had a place of honour everywhere, and I was also in the habit of attending the sports meetings which used to take place in Lhasa and were very popular. There were competitions in running, wrestling and weight-lifting, and, as the culmination, there was horse-racing. Although the prizes to be won were only katas, all these competitions were very popular, and people would flock to watch them being fought out, so that often there were as many as fifty thousand spectators present.

Once the three weeks' New Year's holidays were over, the town would empty very quickly. The visiting monks would leave in large groups, making their way in all directions to their own monasteries. The noise and hubbub would subside, and the street traders would put up their stalls again. Once more peace brooded over the city, and it seemed almost as though after the exertions of the festivities it was anxious to rest and recover its strength for the Tsogchö Mönlam, the Small New Year's celebration, which started twelve days later.

When that came round the streets were once again filled with a tremendous mass of people for another twelve days on end. The most interesting tradition of this second celebration of the beginning of the New Year was the holding of theological disputations between the monks anxious to attain the highest possible degree of the title of Tsokrampa. This was not so high a title as that of Lharimpa, but it also invested its holder with the dignity of a Geshe, or an acknowledged adept in the religious sciences. The culmination of the whole New Year's festivities was the great procession ending with the display of the enormous flag, or banner, known as the Ghöku. An endless procession of gaily dressed people would pass over the turquoise bridge towards the Potala; many of them carrying huge papier-mâché figures representing fantastic demons and animals, whilst here and there powerful monks would carry temple and monastery flags and banners, umbrellas of silk and brocade, and other good-luck symbols.

The vast crowds would then gather before the Potala and dance happily to the sound of drums. And finally, as the highlight and conclusion of the whole festivities, the two-hundred-foot-wide banner, which had in the meantime been taken for this one morning out of the special house in which it was kept, would be lowered from the windows of the Potala in full view of the masses, and attendants would carefully draw the protective covering away from its costly embroideries and its gold brocade ornaments. When the Ghöku with its wonderful colours was fully visible a great cry of admiration would go up from the assembled people, only to die away in a sigh of regret that the happy festivities for the New Year were at last over. After hanging exposed to the view of the people for a few hours, the Ghöku would then be hauled in and carefully rolled up in its protective covering once again.

15. The Death of My Father

MY duties as a monk recalled me to Drepung, where long years of study still lay ahead of me. The monotony of my life was interrupted from time to time by the arrival of relatives on a visit, or by my own departure from the monastery to be present at family celebrations. I also went regularly into Lhasa on high days and holidays, when we were always the guests of the Dalai Lama. I took an active interest in the well-being of my various relatives and I kept myself closely informed on all matters of interest to my family.

The building of the house into which my parents were ultimately to move dragged on for longer than expected. There seemed no sense of urgency, and the authorities invariably moved only slowly. However, in the end, when I had already been in Drepung for three years, it was ready at last. There it stood in a large garden amidst fine old poplars and willow trees, a big two-storeyed house surrounded by a high brick wall. The first time I entered it I could not help thinking of our modest old farmstead in Tengtser. What a difference there was! A few weeks later I was present at the solemn ceremony in which the house was formally handed over to my father. The house, which was built at the orders of the Government, was called Changsaipshar, but before long ordinary people never called it anything but Yabshi Sarpa, or New Father's House. All the workmen who had taken part in the building and decoration of the house were present at the house-warming; and in addition to a splendid meal my father handed a good-luck scarf and a sum of money to each man.

My parents and my brothers and sister soon settled down in their new house. Gyalo Döndrub proved himself to be an excellent nurseryman, and in the favourable climate and on the fruitful soil he produced turnips eighteen inches long, large tomatoes and fine cabbages. But he was happiest of all at his gardening, and he obtained his seeds specially from the gardens of the Norbu Lingka. The representative of the British Government in Lhasa, Mr Sheriff, and his wife, grew very interested in Gyalo Döndrub's garden, and gave him every assistance in his hobby. They themselves had a lovely flower garden and a quite magnificent lawn, which was kept regularly cut with a mower, a completely outlandish machine for us. Incidentally, it was in the house of the Sheriffs that we first made the acquaintance of Western culture and civilisation; learning, for example, to use a knife and fork, and to sit upright in a chair. We also first made the acquaintance of sugared tea in their house and we liked it so much that afterwards we often made it that way at home.

Early one morning when I was in my third year at Drepung, Gyalo Döndrub, who was now sixteen years old, and my brother-in-law Püntso Trashi, arrived on a visit, and they informed me with great delight that they had been given permission to make a pilgrimage to India and China. In fact, the object of their visit was to say goodbye to me. I was proud and moved that two relatives of mine were to make a pilgrimage to the holy places abroad, and I blessed them and wished them luck. Secretly I longed to go with them and visit the sacred Buddhist centres in those two great countries, but for the time being my duties did not allow me to be away so long. I buried myself more and more in my studies, for I was preparing to take the second of the five great examinations of the Tibetan monk, the Parchin; and during this period I rarely left the monastery, and then only on very special occasions. When my brother Lobsang Samten was twelve years old he too entered Drepung, and after his arrival the visits of relatives became more and more frequent. In the first month of the Fire-Dog year my mother gave birth to another boy, who received the name of Tentsing

Chögye, and was later recognised as the incarnation of Ngari
Rimpoche.

A few months after that—I was already almost twenty-four
years old—I went with the Parchin class into the Parchinlingka,
the beautiful little wood below the monastery, in order to perform the traditional prayer exercises before the examination.
For many days we went out in this way into the peace and
quiet of the countryside, saying our prayers as we walked over
the greensward and under leafy trees. When this period of
interior recollection was at an end I once again invited my parents
and a number of my friends from Lhasa to come to visit me in
Drepung. When their visit was over I withdrew into the strictest
isolation for two months and went conscientiously through the
whole curriculum of the forthcoming examination.

The Parchin took place in the Loseling Tratsang, that is to
say in surroundings which were strange and unfamiliar to me.
As examinees from all the tratsangs were present to take part in
the disputations and test their controversial prowess, candidates
were fighting not only for their own hands but also for the honour
of their particular tratsang. Although I really had prepared myself very thoroughly for the examination this did not prevent my
suffering from examination nerves when I found myself face to
face before the assembled Parchin class with the opponent
whom the jury had chosen to dispute with me. We were given
the theme "Kabshipa" for our dispute, and when I heard this
all my nervous excitement was allayed, because I had conscientiously mastered this particular discipline and I knew that
no one was likely to be too dangerous for me in it. And, in fact,
I was never at a loss for an answer to my opponent's questions,
whereas I was able with my questions to plunge him into ever
greater confusion; with the result that I sailed through the first
part of the examination amidst general applause.

The next day there was a kind of team dispute in the great
general assembly. Each examinee chose one of the most formidable Geshis from his own tratsang whose task it was to drive the
rival from the other tratsang into a corner by propounding knotty

questions. Enormous audiences would listen to the individual verbal duels with fascinated interest. Once again I did very well, and the second and concluding section of the Parchin now concluded with joint prayer exercises. In the following days came the big parties and receptions traditionally given by the successful candidates to congratulate each other on their passing.

During the holidays I then revealed to my parents and to the Dalai Lama my long-cherished ambition to undertake a pilgrimage to the holy places in China and India. My wish was granted and I then began preparations for the long journey, which was to start after the New Year's festivities. In the meantime I wound up my small household in Drepung and moved into my parents' new house. I should have been completely happy about my approaching pilgrimage but for one thing: for some time my father had not been very well. He complained of severe pains in the stomach, and generally he was beginning to look ill. Shortly before the New Year's festivities the pains became worse, and we relieved each other in day and night vigils at his bedside, much exercised because we had to stand there helplessly and watch him as he writhed in pain on his bed. Doctors were called in, of course, and they prescribed medicines, but none of them did him any good, or even greatly alleviated the pain; and on the last day of the Old Year his condition worsened to such an extent that we sent a messenger to the Dalai Lama asking to be excused from participation in the New Year's celebrations.

After a terrible night in which we hourly feared the worst, my father suddenly felt so very much better that he insisted on making the traditional New Year's offering on the house altar himself. This naturally gave us renewed hope, particularly when he subsequently drank tea with us, and seemed well on the way to recovery. In these more heartening circumstances I actually dared to make the traditional New Year's visits to a number of my friends. But I had hardly sat down in the house of my friend Shabdrung, a Mongolian monk from the Sera Monastery, when a messenger arrived with the news that my father had suffered a serious relapse, and would I return at once. Of course I hurried back to the house immediately, but my father was dead when I arrived. My mother, her face a mask of sorrow, sat beside his death-bed with my youngest brother in her lap. Crouched by her side were Lobsang Samten and Jetsün Pema. It appeared that in the end my father had died a quick and painless death.

A lama, Gönsar Rimpoche, who was a friend of ours, said the prescribed prayers for the dead, and many monks came to the death-bed to pray for my father, whose body was now dressed in new clothes and lifted into a sitting position. Before sunrise on the third day his mortal remains were carried up into the mountains and solemnly cremated. We spent the prescribed mourning period of forty-nine days praying and fasting. Then my mother, who was sorely in need of a change and a rest, went off to one of our properties near Gyantse, a place on the caravan route to India, and I moved into the small house in Lhasa which I had already occupied from time to time and where I now proposed to devote myself once again to the necessary preparations for my pilgrimage. However, man proposes . . .

An insurrection now took place and resulted in a minor civil war. The centre of the insurrection was the monastery at Sera, and its instigators were the supporters of the former Regent Reting Rimpoche, whom we had visited during my father's life-time. He had, it was true, voluntarily abdicated, but he had many friends, and in secret he was determined to overthrow his successor, the Regent Tagdra Rimpoche. The bomb explosion which was to have been the signal for the revolt was a failure, and the conspiracy was revealed. A small army under the command of a Cabinet Minister marched to Reting Ritrö, and arrested the former Regent. When the news of the arrest reached Sera Monastery the monks there rose in revolt and martial law was proclaimed in Lhasa; shopkeepers put up their shutters and there was hardly anyone to be seen on the streets. Only when artillery was brought into position to threaten Sera Monastery did the monks there surrender. Many of them fled to China, and in the resulting confusion the former Regent lost his life in circumstances which were never entirely cleared up. His great wealth was sequestered, and his splendid house in Reting Ritrö was razed to the ground. The beautiful trees which I had so much admired on my visit there were uprooted and planted in other gardens.

Owing to these happenings my departure on my pilgrimage was postponed indefinitely. I took up residence in Drepung once again and waited for the next opportunity to ask the Dalai Lama for leave. It arose in connection with the Chöshu Tshibgyor, the pilgrimage of the Dalai Lama to the big monasteries in the neighbourhood of Lhasa. The sky was deep blue and cloudless when the procession of the Dalai Lama made its way across the plains to Drepung where he was to take up his residence for a month in a palace specially built for the occasion. Once again Lobsang Samten and I had ample opportunity of being together with our brother. We took part in all the ceremonies, and we also accompanied the Dalai Lama on his visit to the nearby monastery of Nechung, where the State oracle lived. This oracle was a monk who would fall into a state of catalepsy and then give inspired answers to important questions concerning matters of State.

Once the Dalai Lama had left Drepung for Sera I went back to Lhasa where I made the final preparations for my departure on my own pilgrimage. This included a farewell visit to Mr Richardson, who had in the meantime taken the place of Mr Sheriff as representative of the British Government in Lhasa. On my visit to him I obtained permission to put up in the British Government bungalows along the caravan route from Gyantse to the Indian border. Mr Richardson was thoughtful enough to present me with a pair of sunglasses for use on the long journey. They were the first I ever possessed.

16. My Journey to India and China

THE astrologers had once again worked out the most favourable day for my departure, and so I took leave of the Dalai Lama, who gave me his blessing for the journey. On the appointed day I said farewell very early in the morning to my mother and to my brothers and sisters, except Gyalo Döndrub, who was still away on his pilgrimage and was expecting me to meet him in China. My brother-in-law Püntso Trashi had hurried home as quickly as possible on the news of the death of my father, and he was now to accompany me on my journey and give me the assistance and support of an experienced pilgrim. My mother solemnly handed me a little bag in which my father's ashes were preserved. Carefully I took charge of the precious remains and stowed them away safely in my amba, the fold in my garment above the belt. On my return from China I was to remain for some time in my own labrang in Kumbum, and from there I was to go to our family burial place in the neighbouring mountains and deposit my father's ashes there side by side with the ashes of my younger brother who had died as an infant.

One last farewell and I swung myself into the saddle and set off in the direction of Drepung followed by Püntso Trashi and my servant and friend Döndrub Gyantsen. At the foot of the mountain a tent had been erected, and there the Drebung Lachi, the abbots of the monastery, gave me a farewell banquet. After that we made our way along the caravan route to the south, passing through territory which up to then had been unfamiliar to me. When we had passed over the mountain chain we were ferried across the Brahmaputra in a large boat; after which we skirted the Yamdrok Lake, went through the Karo Pass and arrived at my family estate outside Gyantse, where we rested for two days. It was in Gyantse that I saw my first European soldier. Although the garrison which the treaty of 1904 entitled the British to maintain there, in order to protect their trade, was only small, there was a military band, and its playing made a deep impression on us.

Beyond Gyantse the bungalows maintained by the British Government were at our disposal, and from our point of view at least they were very comfortably furnished. These bungalows are situated at a day's ride from each other all along the excellent caravan route. What a contrast there was between this comfortable ride and my journey by caravan from Kumbum to Lhasa: That had involved so many hardships and privations, but now, even when we were overtaken by a sandstorm, at least we knew that we should have a comfortable roof over our heads by nightfall and be able to sit in front of a cheerful fire and relax from the exertions of the day's ride. Püntso Trashi's experience proved of great value to us. He knew many people who could be of assistance to us, and his shrewdness and his talent for getting on with people made him an excellent guide and manager on our journey.

In Sikkim I made the acquaintance of jungle terrain for the first time. The oranges were just ripe and we greatly enjoyed their delicious flesh. In the capital Gangtok I paid a courtesy visit to the representative of the British Government there, a certain Mr Hopkinson, whose acquaintance I had already made during his visit to Lhasa. I handed him a white good-luck scarf and thanked him for the hospitality his government had placed at our disposal in the chain of government bungalows. During my visit he showed me photographs he had taken whilst he was in Lhasa, and I was greatly touched to see my father in them, still hale and hearty. In Gangtok I also met my friend Telopa Rimpoche, who had gone on pilgrimage before me and was, for the time being, travelling separately.

We travelled from Gangtok to Kalimpong, the first large

Indian town, by motor-car. Shortly before entering Kalimpong we fell in with a party of officials from Lhasa who were just starting out on a world tour. There was a friendly meeting by the wayside and then our car carried us off to the magnificent house which had been placed at our disposal in Kalimpong by one of the richest men in Tibet, the noble and merchant Pomdatsang. It was also his car that brought us the following day to the Mount Everest Hotel in Darjeeling where for the first time I made the acquaintance of Western hotel comfort. But I was also to notice that such comfort can be deceptive; despite the electric fire which was put in my room I shivered miserably that night.

Once again we got into a car, which took us from the mountains down into the warm and fruitful plains to Siliguri. A silvery cloak of mist lay over the whole vast expanse of this country, which is very low-lying to our ideas and has a very humid climate. How different the skies were here compared with our skies at home. And how heavy and relaxing the air was. The transition from a barren, little-populated countryside into the overflowing riches of this unfamiliar land was an experience in itself, and new impressions crowded in on me. Wherever I looked there were things I had never seen in my life before—things I should not have believed possible. My brother-in-law answered my astounded questions as well as he was able, but again and again we both had to turn to our chauffeur for information, and he did his best to satisfy our insatiable curiosity.

From Siliguri we travelled to Calcutta by train, and the Government had provided us with a special coach. I almost jumped out of my skin when, before leaving the station, the locomotive suddenly let off steam with a tremendous hissing, stamping sound. My eyes and my ears were unused to all these new impressions and experiences and they pursued me even into my dreams, and it was a good thing that we were left to ourselves on the long railway journey to Calcutta, since it gave us a little time to sort things out. In Calcutta we were met by a representative of the Governor of Western Bengal. Shekapa, the leader of the Tibetan party we had met outside Kalimpong, was also on the platform to welcome us. My brother-in-law and I accepted the invitation of the Governor, Rajagopalachari, to take tea with him. We stayed in the town for a week, visiting the big temples and seeing the sights, and whilst we were there the representative of Chiang Kai-shek's government conveyed us an invitation from the Chinese Department for Tibetan and Mongolian affairs to make a tour of China.

We were to fly from Calcutta, but at the last moment bad weather delayed the take-off. I was secretly thankful for the post-ponement and I returned almost out of breath to the Grand Hotel where we had been staying, still overwhelmed by my first glimpse of the monstrous silver birds of the international air lines on the airfield. To my great delight I found my friend Telopa Rimpoche at the hotel with his servant, and they now joined our party.

When the weather improved sufficiently we flew to Hongkong. At first I did not feel too comfortable in the air, but after a while I began to enjoy the experience. Two days later we flew from Hongkong to Shanghai, where I was met by my brother Gyalo Döndrub, and a relative named Lhamo Tsering, During the five days we spent in China's great port my brother proved an excellent guide, and thanks to his linguistic ability he was also a very useful interpreter during the many visits we had to make to Chinese official institutions.

From Shanghai we went on to Nanking, the seat of the Kuo-mintang Government, and I stayed there for almost six months. As the Chinese authorities placed a car at our disposal I had ample opportunity to visit the surrounding countryside and to get to know the land and its people. One of my first visits was to the head of the department for Tibetan and Mongolian affairs, a certain Mr Shu, who proved extremely obliging, and also arranged a long audience for me with General Chiang Kai-shek. The General, whose forces had taken the capital of his communist opponents in March 1947, seemed very optimistic, though since that victory his forces had suffered a number of heavy defeats. However, at that time his position still looked unassailable. The following year the Chinese National Assembly elected him the first constitutional President of China and gave him exceptional powers for a period of two years. But in 1949 he was compelled to flee, together with his nationalist government, to Formosa; and Mao Tse-tung, as the head of the new Chinese People's Republic, became the undisputed master of the whole Chinese mainland.

When I flew alone to Pekin in 1948 I had obtained a modest knowledge of the Chinese language, and I had familiarised myself to some extent with the country and its people. Telopa Rimpoche had gone on ahead and I met him again in the Tibetan monastery of Yinhakön, which was run by Mongolian Buddhist monks. I put up at the Pekin Hotel, but although the town with its splendid architecture and its great Temple of Heaven, made a deep impression on me I did not stay there for long, because the rapidly changing situation made it seem advisable to break off my stay in China. The artillery of the advancing communist armies could already be heard in the town, and the railway line was cut. I therefore flew via Shanghai to Nanking, the Kuomintang capital, where I joined the other members of my party. The journey back to Kumbum by road was out of the question now, and we were therefore given permission to fly by military plane to Lanchow, which lies several hours by car to the east of Siling. Unfortunately military flights were very irregular and we often had to wait for days, and sometimes weeks, before we could continue our journey; and even then a plane would perhaps have room for only one person in addition to the war material and other goods being flown out. However, in the end we all arrived safely in Lanchow.

Mapufang, who was still Governor, had us transported in an army car from Lanchow to Siling, and from there we went on to Kumbum in a jeep. It was a warm summer's day in the Earth-Mouse year when I once again entered Kumbum, seven years after I had left it to go to Lhasa. I was wearing ordinary civilian clothing, and my monastic habit was still packed up with my things, but although my arrival lacked all formality I was soon recognised, and there was a warm welcome from all my old friends. The worthy Lhagsam and my old teachers Minyag Rimpoche and Ohön Yongdzin greeted me with radiant faces. When I was once again installed in the Tagtser Labrang I made the traditional sacrificial tour of the temples, and then formally handed over a present from the Tibetan Government to the monastery, a sum of money amounting to 30,000 gormos. There were not many of my generation left in Kumbum now. Most of them had left the monastery, some of them were away on pilgrimage, and a number had died.

I quickly got used to the old familiar surroundings, and the next few months were spent chiefly in journeys into the immediate neighbourhood. My first longer trip was to our family burial place in the mountains above Tengtser. The moment when I buried the little bag containing my father's ashes, consigning his mortal remains back to the earth from which in long years of toil he had earned the daily bread of all of us, was a very moving one for me. I knew that despite the privileged position he had latterly occupied in Lhasa he had always felt himself primarily as a son of the remote mountain village of Tengtser, which he loved above every other place. The wheel had now turned full circle and the dead son of Tengtser had come back to his native soil. My eyes were glistening when I straightened myself and looked down at my native village lying there far below. That small village with its neat and spotless houses perched on its gentle hill looked more beautiful to me than anything I had seen on my long journey abroad; and with gratitude in my heart I turned towards Kyeri, whose snow-clad peak shone above me in the sun.

Once again I received an enthusiastic welcome in Tengtser; and it was with deep emotion that I met my one-time playmates and was received by old Pasang, the former village headman, who once more spoke for the whole village. His hair was now white and his cheerful face was full of many wrinkles. He bombarded me with questions, asked about the well-being of the Dalai Lama, about Lhasa, about the Potala, about the details of the famous festivities in the far-off capital, and about all the details of the new life of my family in Lhasa. In succession I was the guest of every family in the village, and I had to spend at least one night under each roof; and everywhere I went I had to give a detailed report of my experiences and answer innumerable questions, most of which referred to the Dalai Lama and the conditions under which he lived, for everyone was tremendously proud that the Dalai Lama was a son of their own village.

I also made a trip to Shartsong Ritrö where I had once been prepared for the monastic life. As the master of Tagtser Labrang I once again inspected the hermitage which belonged to my ecclesiastical benefices; and now that I was older and more mature I appreciated its romantic seclusion more than I ever had done at first. For a long time I stood on the terrace in the evening and looked out over the magnificent landscape all around, sunk deep in thoughts of my childhood days.

17. Abbot of Kumbum

TOWARDS the end of the year the Abbot of Kumbum, Choni Rimpoche, announced in the general assembly of monks that it was his intention to resign his abbotship.

In accordance with the traditional procedure he then formally begged the monks to spare him from carrying the heavy burden any longer, and left the hall. The monasterial council immediately came together and short-listed the names of twenty candidates who were regarded as having the qualifications necessary as the successor of the retiring abbot, who would then choose his successor from amongst them. One of the factors which had to be taken into consideration was that the successful candidate must have sufficient wealth to uphold his position with dignity, and, in particular, to meet the heavy expenses in connection with the Tongo ceremonies. A newly installed abbot has to lay good-luck scarves on all the altars of the monastery, burn incense, set up butter-lamps, and present each monk in the monastery with a certain sum of money. Choni Rimpoche, whom I had formerly known quite well, had carried out the duties of his office for three years with skill and sagacity, and there was nothing extraordinary about the fact that he now wished to resign from his office, perhaps to go on a pilgrimage or to withdraw into his own labrang, although he was still young; not very much my own senior in fact.

The Abbot of Kumbum was the highest authority in the monastery both in ecclesiastical affairs and in all questions of administration. He took the chair at all meetings, supervised all examinations, represented the monastery to the outside world, and had the last word in everything that was ultimately decided upon in the affairs of the monastery. His position was certainly no sinecure though it was entirely honorific, bringing him in no emoluments whilst at the same time involving him in heavy expenditure. In addition, a Khenpo had little or no free time, because even during the normal school holidays he had to make a tour of inspection of the thousand or so houses and the thirty temples which made up the monastery, and to attend to all the administrative business which had accumulated in the meantime.

It came as a complete surprise to me when after the New Year's festivities my old teacher Minyag Rimpoche approached me and formally offered me the post of Abbot of Kumbum in the name of the Tsongdü, or monasterial council. The suggestion caused me a great deal of perplexity, and at first I declared that I felt myself too young to accept such a great responsibility, and doubted whether I should be able to fulfil all the demands which such a post would place on its occupant, particularly in such troublous times as those in which we lived today. But, ably supported by my good friend Lhagsam, Minyag Rimpoche refused to accept my denial, and in a solemn speech he sought to convince me that all my fears as to my own abilities were baseless. In particular, he pointed out, it would be of inestimable advantage to the monastery if, above all in such troublous times, its abbot were the eldest brother of the Dalai Lama. In the end I allowed myself to be persuaded and I formally declared myself ready to accept the high and responsible office which was being offered me.

I was now given two months in which to prepare myself to take over, and there was a great deal to do. For one thing, although Tagtser Labrang was very rich, I was not in a position at such short notice to raise all the cash necessary to pay for the many ceremonies involved, and the supplementary amount I needed had to be borrowed through the good offices of a friend, who had once administered the property and benefices of the highly respected Amdo Künkhyen Rimpoche in Labrang

Trashi Khyi, the second-largest monastery in the province of Amdo.

I was formally inducted into my high office on the ninth day of the third month of the Earth-Bull year. Wearing the yellow Khenpo dagam, and followed by the members of the monasterial council and my personal friends, I walked into the general assembly of monks under the silk umbrella of my new dignity and accompanied by the strains of musical instruments. Almost four thousand monks were assembled there to meet their new abbot. Apart from the monks of Kumbum itself, many other monks had come in from the approximately seventy hermitages which belonged to Kumbum in order to be present at the cere-mony. In my speech I promised to do everything possible to the best of my ability to serve the interests of the monastery, and after this came my formal induction. Choni Rimpoche took his place beside me. His ministrants held the carved and well-worn wooden cases which had already held the insignia of the Abbots of Kumbum for hundreds of years. First of all they handed over to my ministrants the long shallow cases, which they had already opened to reveal the brittle and crumbling dark yellow silk scrolls which proclaimed their possessor for the time being the highest authority in the monastery of Kumbum. Then they transferred the smaller case containing the four-inch-long, finger-thick monasterial seal wrapped in an ancient kata. In another piece of ancient cloth was a piece of sealing-wax. And finally, the keys of the cases, wrapped in almost crumbling pieces of red silk, changed hands too.

I then mounted the throne of the Khenpo, and all those present filed past me and handed over their katas. Great piles of good-luck scarves rose by the side of my raised throne until before long I sat in the middle of clouds of white tulle and silk. When I had received the last congratulations I was escorted in solemn pro-cession to the bright-red painted house of the Khenpo in which I was henceforth to reside. There I immediately carried out my first official action: the installation of my closest collaborators. It was customary for the new Khenpo to appoint men of his own choice for all the important and responsible positions in the monastery, including a new Chandzö, or treasurer, a new Nyerpa, or steward, and, in addition, two new secretaries and six new members of the council. Lhagsam, my old friend and teacher, had promised me to accept one of the vacant seats on the council. My loyal servant Döndrub Gyantsen I appointed my Simpön, a sort of chamberlain responsible for my official wardrobe. With this the most important formalities were complied with.

My daily programme now left me very little free time. In the morning I took the chair at the general assembly of monks, at which I also had to deliver the sermon. The afternoon was spent in administrative work and in preparing the sermon for the next day. But it was not long before further and unusual burdens imposed themselves. At about the middle of the fourth month the political situation grew more and more tense. The so-called Chinese People's Army had forced Chiang Kai-shek's troops out of North China, and in the following spring the communists crossed the Yangtse-kiang on a broad front a million strong. It was inevitable that our neighbourhood should be affected by the revolutionary events in the East. For example, the Governor, Mapufang, was demanding more horses, more foodstuffs and more money at ever-shortening intervals in order to resist the advance of the communist forces; and the more critical the situation became the more he asked for. But to ask was one thing, and to obtain quite another, because by this time our resources were almost exhausted. A request for the supply of five hundred horses soon became a mere nothing in the endless series of demands imposed on us, but before long we were unable to provide him with any horses at all because we had none ourselves, and no more money to buy them with even if they had been obtainable. In the meantime the communist troops relentlessly continued their advance.

In the seventh month, which was always reserved for the strictest prayer exercises, the Chinese People's Army occupied Lanchow. Despite the many disturbing rumours, life in the

The Potala, the Winter Palace of the Dalai Lama, rises steeply like a fortress above the city of Lhasa. Its full golden beauty is to be seen in the autumn

Many thousands of effigies of Buddha are carved in the rock face along the
great caravan routes and decorated with prayer flags

Thubten Jigme Norbu in everyday Tibetan clothing. His homeland lies beyond the snow-capped Himalayas in the distance

monastery went on for the time being very much as usual. The monks continued to assemble silently both morning and evening in the Tsogchen, and their voices were raised only during the period of common prayer. Apart from this no word was spoken during the day and no visits were paid; each monk kept himself apart from his fellows. During the whole month not a soul left the monastery except the water-carriers, and even the cattle were not driven out to the pastures. Then on the last day of the month all the monks left the monastery and went up into the mountains to give thanks and make sacrifices to the gods. That was the last organised exodus into the countryside that the monastic community of Kumbum ever carried out. For several days the smoke of sacrificial fires rose into the sky from the hills around Kumbum and new prayer-flags fluttered in the breeze. The members of the Menpa or Medical Tratsang clambered high up into the mountains with their tents, and stayed there for a while collecting herbs, roots, flowers and seeds with which to make their medicines. In a splendid procession I went with the Shengo, the steward and all the members of the Council to the Heart Mountain, so-called because of its strangely evocative shape. As soon as the sacrificial fires had burnt out we pitched our tents and sat down to a formal banquet. Afterwards the monks sang, played and wrestled with each other, and were happy and carefree once again. This trip into the countryside was the annual farewell to the warm season of the year. This time it was also to be the farewell to a long period of peaceful contented years.

In the subsequent weeks there was an endless amount of work for me to do: one examination followed the other, and I had to be present at each. I must confess that I found it very difficult to concentrate properly on each individual examinee in those times when almost every hour brought its new and disturbing news. I felt deep sympathy with them as they stood before me striving desperately to find the right answers, and I made things as easy for them as I could. I passed all the monks of the lower classes, because a word of rebuke from me would have meant severe punishments for them from their teachers. Sometimes in memory of my own examinations, I pretended to be absent-minded, which gave me an excuse for overlooking their wrong answers. It was very much more difficult when monks from classes which I had not yet myself attended appeared before me for their examinations. I would then often have difficulty in following the examination at all.

In addition to my proper burdens I was now forced more and more to occupy myself with the news from the outer world. After his final defeat in the battle of Lanchow, Mapufang had fled. It was reported that he had made his escape in an aeroplane, taking with him all the portable treasures he could lay his hands on. His leaderless units now disintegrated and dispersed in all directions. As stragglers and in small groups the disbanded soldiery flooded back from the western districts to their own homes, carrying their booty or dragging it along behind them on the backs of mules. What Mapufang had been compelled to leave behind was now sacked and pillaged, and robbers and bandits made the neighbourhood unsafe.

More and more fugitives sought asylum in the monastery. They were mostly Buddhists from Mongolia or Lhasa who had been taken by surprise by the rapid advance of the communists. So far the Red Chinese had not shown themselves in Kumbum, but we had to reckon with their imminent appearance any day now. The strangers who sought asylum with us told alarming stories of communist outrages, of their contempt for existing institutions, and their ill-treatment of the civilian population. We already knew how badly they had behaved towards our co-religionists in Mongolia and China proper, and we were well aware that our high dignitaries and wealthy monks in particular had every cause to fear them. Many Tibetan Buddhists in Mongolia and China had even lost their lives on account of their religion, and we were sorely afraid that the communists would persecute us and forbid us to continue to practise our religion. Under these circumstances it was not surprising that numerous monks left the monastery and sought to go underground in the nearby villages. In fact some monks even joined the nomads in the hope that the Communists would not suspect them of having fled to the wide open spaces, and would not be able to find them there even if they did. In consequence, the number of those who had decided to stay in the monastery and await whatever was coming grew smaller and smaller.

When Red Chinese troops finally entered Siling we decided that I, together with the monasterial council and one or two high rimpoches, should pay the new masters of the country a preliminary courtesy visit. It seemed to us to be wise to avoid anything which might exacerbate the situation, and we decided that as far as possible we would attempt to meet our enemies halfway and give them no excuse for proceeding against us—because the Chinese were our traditional enemies, whilst all communists were, of course, our ideological enemies.

We arrived in Siling late in the afternoon, and we noticed at once that the blood-red flag of the new rulers was already waving from the roofs of many houses. Hanging around aimlessly in the streets were poorly clothed and obviously ill-fed soldiers, who very often even had no boots. Altogether they looked bored and disinterested. But the headquarters of the Red Chinese commander, General Ye-chuntang, made a very much fiercer impression, and grim-looking sentries led us into an untidy room in which the General himself received us. One or two orderlies handed us dirty china tea dishes, which were then filled with hot water. With due formality we handed the General a good-luck scarf, whereupon he stuck out his chest and treated us to a bombastic speech which he obviously had off by heart. Vulgar abuse of Chiang Kai-shek and his supporters, who were described as chagpa, or criminals, alternated with exaggerated promises. The Chinese People's Army had come to us as liberators, he declared, and the age-old persecutors of our people had now been driven off for good and all. At last we were free and in a position to do what we wished; for example, practise our religion in peace and without interference. In fact, it appeared, our every wish was to be fulfilled under the new dispensation, and the General concluded his tirade with the assurance that our country was now on the threshold of vastly better times.

As a matter of fact, we were all rather dismayed by this bombastic speech, which, despite its promises, we felt boded us no good. However, I thanked the General politely and invited him to pay the monastery a visit; an invitation which he accepted with another flow of turgid oratory. Actually we were never to see him in Kumbum. The moon was already rising in the darkening sky as we rode through the streets to the house which belonged to the monastery. A strong wind arose and caused the many red flags on the roofs to snap and crack like whiplashes, and the eerie sound struck us as a foreboding of evil. Mapufang's last-minute flight had saved the town from destruction, but nevertheless it made a very disheartening impression on us. We sat together discussing the situation before we retired for the night, and we were unable to conceal our anxieties from each other. It was a long time before I could get to sleep that night; I was too worried about the future of Kumbum, and about the fate of our religion at the hands of our new rulers.

We had been back in Kumbum for several days when a detachment of about five hundred Red soldiers arrived there. They halted before the big labrang of Minyag Rimpoche and demanded accommodation, but fortunately the wily steward of the labrang was clever enough to persuade their officers that they would find more suitable quarters in Lussar, the nearby village in which pilgrims coming to visit Kumbum always found shelter; and so they went off. The first attempt of the "liberators" to settle themselves in Kumbum had been warded off. A little later an order was issued calling on everyone, including the inhabitants of the monasteries, to surrender all firearms. The occupation authorities even offered to pay between ten and fifteen gormos for a rifle. Many people did hand in their weapons, but others hid them carefully instead, feeling that they might need them again. One decree followed quickly on the heels of the other now, and events hurried forward. In the circumstances it was difficult for us to carry on as usual in the monastery and to persuade those monks who were still with us to adhere to the normal daily programme.

Alarming reports were coming in all the time, and one of them in particular greatly depressed me; it was that a communist-led mob had attacked the monastery of Shartsong Ritrö and razed it to the ground. The bridge which for so many years had kept unwanted guests from the hermitage and turned it into a safe haven for its inmates, and, at need, for the local inhabitants, had not been sufficient to keep off hordes with modern weapons and modern equipment. The monks of Shartsong Ritrö had fled into the mountains whilst the mob roamed through the monastery desecrating its sacred treasures, plundering and destroying. What they could not carry away with them they threw over the rocky precipices into the gorge beneath, and finally the monastery buildings themselves were burnt to the ground. Similar mobs were known to be ravaging and plundering elsewhere, and before long we learned that the monasteries of Serto Ritrö and Tongkhor had suffered the same fate.

I had just received these alarming and depressing reports when I was honoured by the visit of a young man named Shu, who was, it appeared, the chairman of the new Red Chinese Tibet Commission. He arrived in Kumbum with his collaborators in three army jeeps. It was the first time that I had met a civilian communist official. His invitation to go back with him to Siling for a discussion just suited me and I agreed at once because I wished to see General Ye-chuntang again and remind him of his assurances in the matter of the freedom of religious observances and to protest vigorously at the destruction of Shartsong Ritrö and the two other monasteries. I was also anxious to get to the bottom of rumours to the effect that Kumbum itself was to be the next monastery to be handed over to the fury of the mob. I was determined to do all I could to save Kumbum from suffering once again the fate which had overtaken it during the great Hu-hu insurrection in the nineteenth century.

The new Governor listened to what I had to say without moving a muscle of his face, and then assured me that Kumbum was under the protection of the garrison which had been quartered in Lussar. At the same time he also promised to investigate my complaints with regard to the three other monasteries and to punish those who were guilty. Is it necessary to say that he did not keep his word?

The chairman of the Tibet Commission now asked me to take up my residence in the house of the monastery in Siling until further notice in order that I should be available whenever he needed me. For four days after that I was subjected to the closest questioning. A Tibetan from the province of Kham named Trashi served as interpreter. This man had been with the communists since the legendary "Long March," thirty years before. He had since lived in Manchuria, where he had been trained, and he was now acting as a Party secretary. The interrogation, for that is what it really amounted to, took place in the offices of the Tibet Commission. Everything had to be written down word for word, and things were made rather difficult by the fact that Trashi spoke only Khampa dialect, which differed in certain respects quite considerably from the Amdo dialect, whilst my Chinese was not sufficient to answer all the many and detailed questions which were put to me.

For one thing, I had to provide them with a meticulous account of my life and my career, and submit a detailed list of all the properties of the monastery and of the nobles. I was also asked searching questions about the rank, property and activities of everyone I knew. As I often understood the questions before the interpreter had translated them for my benefit this gave me time to think over my answers and formulate them in such a way that the wretched Trashi had the greatest difficulty in translating them clearly for the benefit of my questioners. Of course, my long years of dialectical training in the monastery stood me in good stead in this respect. On the other hand, I could not, of course, plead ignorance to any great extent, because it was a matter of course that as Abbot of Kumbum I must have a wide knowledge both of persons and things connected with my office.

Incidentally, the interrogations were carried out with formal politeness, and when they were at last over I was driven back to Kumbum in a car—to find on my arrival that everyone there was greatly worried at my unexpectedly long absence. I immediately called my closest friends and confidants together and reported in detail on my experience in Siling at the hands of our new rulers. They heard what I had to say with mounting dismay. There was no room for illusions, and we were all well aware that we should now have to deal with people whose regime would make Mapufang's look like child's play. It was quite clear that communism represented a deadly threat to our religion, our land and even our very lives. And now for the first time we had received a foretaste of its methods. They were still treating us with reasonable civility, but the news from Mongolia and China left us in no doubt as to what we had to expect, and we knew that our enemies would stop at nothing to gain their ends. For example, during my stay in Siling I had observed that the "re-education" of the population was already in full swing. The people were brought together at meetings, games and dances, and indoctrinated with communist propaganda texts, and I even heard young girls singing political songs in Tibetan.

The meeting in which I reported on my experiences in Siling was held behind closed doors, because even in the monastery itself we were no longer safe from prying eyes and eavesdroppers. There were a good many people now inside the monastery walls who had sought and been granted asylum, and it was to be feared that amongst them there were communist agents. In addition, during my short absence, quite a number of doubtful characters had wheedled their way into the monastery and settled down under all sorts of pretexts in the quarters vacated by those monks who had fled. These characters were constantly trying to draw the remaining monks into political discussions, and before long they appeared in my official Khenpo residence. There was no way of ridding ourselves of these burdensome interlopers for they were all provided with Red Chinese documents and they insisted that they were acting under orders. I raised the matter when I was once again called before the Tibet Commission in

Siling, but I obtained no satisfaction. With extreme politeness I was assured that all the measures taken by the Red Chinese authorities were intended in our own best interests.

However, it was on this occasion that for the first time frank words were exchanged. I had a long interview with the newly appointed Governor, a certain Tang Tushi, who first of all repeated the assurance of General Ye-chuntang that the Red Chinese Army had come to Amdo as liberators. But then he let the cat out of the bag by declaring incautiously that not only the province of Amdo but the whole of Tibet was to be freed from the yoke of the oppressor. He also pretended to be astonished that the Tibetan Government in Lhasa had not yet officially recognised and welcomed the communist liberators. When he talked like this it was quite clear to me that he was addressing not the Abbot of Kumbum but the brother of the Dalai Lama, and it was not long before that impression was amply confirmed.

Circumspectly I pointed out to him that the journey from Lhasa to Siling never took less than three months, and that there was no other and more direct means of communication with the administrative centre. Further, I ventured to suggest, the appearance of Red Chinese communist troops in the province of Amdo must naturally cause great concern in Lhasa. He should not forget that the regrettable treatment accorded to Tibetan Buddhists in Mongolia and in China itself by the Chinese communists was still fresh in everyone's memory. Age-old experience had taught the Tibetans to regard every Chinese penetration into Tibetan territory with the greatest possible misgiving. The former Governor Mapufang had not behaved altogether in accordance with the wishes of Tibetans either, but at least he had not interfered with the religious practices of the inhabitants, and on the whole his régime had been a mild one. Outrages such as had happened quite recently in the province had never occurred under his rule.

Such talk clearly upset the Governor who insisted irritably that the Chingtrö, or great liberation action, of the communists would be continued, come what may. I pointed out that it was not quite clear from whom Tibet was to be liberated. There were no foreign enemies installed in Lhasa; the Dalai Lama, who was greatly loved by the people, was the legitimate ruler of the country and recognised as such by the whole Tibetan people. To this the Governor replied that the influence of the chagpa, the criminals—which was the way that he too invariably referred to Chiang Kai-shek and his followers—and also of the Americans and the British in Lhasa, must be broken. When I pointed out that Chiang Kai-shek's representative had left Lhasa two years ago, he had nothing to say. At the end of our discussion, which confirmed what I already knew, namely that we were separated by a great and impassable abyss, the Governor completely changed his tone and politely invited me to a celebration banquet together with many other guests. As a matter of discretion I accepted the invitation, and we were entertained with dance and song, and the beer flowed in streams.

Soon after this the Governor appeared in Kumbum with a retinue of a score or so. I made use of the occasion to protest against the intolerable conditions which had arisen under the new régime. Not only was our freedom of movement, even within the monastery, being intolerably hampered by the innumerable agents of the Communist Party, who dogged our every step, but the old lines of communication had been cut. Never had I known so many doubtful characters making the neighbourhood unsafe as at present. It was impossible to get labourers, the fields could not be properly tilled, and what meagre harvest there was had to be sent into Siling. The many beggars who had formerly managed to get their food in the monasteries or from the peasants were now quite destitute and become a public plague. And in conclusion I told the Governor very firmly that something should be done at once to remedy a situation which made a mockery of his claim that he and his friends had come to liberate the country.

But the Governor had his answer ready: the difficulties could be solved in the twinkling of an eye; all that was necessary was that the land should be distributed amongst the people, and then no one would go hungry. The responsibility for the present situation rested on the monks and the out-dated economic structure of the country. The monasteries must now distribute their lands amongst the people and the monks must be integrated into the labour process. It could no longer be tolerated that many thousands of valuable labour units were kicking their heels uselessly in the monasteries.

I uncompromisingly rejected his picture of the situation, and I pointed out that there had been no shortage of food and supplies until the communists had arrived. The country had lived in peace and prosperity for hundreds of years with its many monasteries. I also pointed out that many monks were first-class artisans and that they had learnt their trades in the monasteries, but when I said this his face went blank and it was as though I were talking to a brick wall.

Then he repeated all his old reproaches: we should have put the beggars to work; we wasted large quantities of butter by burning it after our religious ceremonies; we frittered away our money on incense and good-luck scarves. My answers were like water on a duck's back. He could not or would not understand that almsgiving was one of the fundamental obligations of our religion, and that the beggar was therefore fulfilling a useful function in society. He could not understand that the sacrifice of butter and incense satisfied a deeply rooted need of the Tibetan Buddhist and gave him happiness. The Governor knew and understood only that form of happiness and satisfaction which his own doctrine preached.

We were therefore talking at cross-purposes, and I suffered that feeling of depression that invades you when you find yourself appealing in vain to the understanding and goodwill of an opponent. The Governor wanted me to issue an order at once forbidding the burning of butter for religious purposes; and to listen to him you would have thought that this measure represented the solution of all problems, or at least the problem of the alarming shortage of food. I resolutely refused to do as he said, and I pointed out that such an action would be regarded as an unforgivable sacrilege; that if I issued any such prohibition the monks would look upon me as the destroyer of their religion instead of its protector; and that they would undoubtedly fall upon me and kill me. In fact, I declared, I was committing an offence by even consenting to discuss such a matter with him. However, if, despite what I said, he still wished such a prohibition to be issued then he should summon the monks and issue the order to them himself. This clinched the matter for the time being. The Governor shook his head and declared that he had no such intention. If the situation were as I described it then other measures would have to be adopted. The authorities would just have to go forward step by step.

Before taking his leave he told me bluntly that he was leaving two of his men with me, and that he thought it best in the interests of the community, and particularly in the interests of my own security, that they should henceforth never leave my side. I protested, of course, but it was no use. I was now a guarded prisoner within my own monastery walls. My two warders never let me out of their sight, and as they gave no indication of whether they could understand Tibetan or not I was hardly able to exchange a frank word even with my closest friends. In addition, the two were always trying to involve me in political discussions; if not the one, then the other, and sometimes both together. Before long it became clear to me that they were following a previously arranged plan; and today I realise that they had been given the job of re-educating me, using particularly subtle means; that, in fact, they were subjecting me to that devilish procedure which has since become known as brain-washing.

We talked to each other in Chinese, and at least that had the advantage that it helped to improve my knowledge of the language. Again and again my two tormentors returned to the attack, condemning my views as false and obsolete, and saying that as monks we were wasting our lives. With fear and anxiety my friends observed the systematic siege to which the two were subjecting me. If my friends could often not understand the words, they could certainly hear from the tone of voice and see from their expressions that the two were deliberately and persistently keeping me under sustained pressure.

If they came upon me in prayer they would ask sarcastically whether prayer had ever filled anyone's belly. At first I tried to make them understand that prayer gave me serenity and confidence, and that a life without it was just unthinkable for me. But they mocked at our beliefs and at our gods, and they insisted that it was men like Stalin and Mao Tse-tung who had put food into the bellies of the starving millions, not our gods. I quickly realised that it was pointless to try and make them understand what life meant to us, and what Tibet had owed to its monasteries and its monks for many hundreds of years. Again and again they reproached me with standing in the light of progress, and declared that the monks exploited the people and wasted the national patrimony.

In particular, they were always trying to involve me in contradictions, and they never tired of setting traps for me. Looking back on it all today I think that they must have had a copy of the protocol of my interrogation in Siling; and that their questions were based on that document and formulated with the intention of proving that I had not told the truth or, at least, that I had been inaccurate. But for the fact that I had studied dialectics for many years and was therefore well able to look after myself in discussion I would undoubtedly have found myself in serious difficulty.

The merciless and exhausting pressure to which I was constantly subjected by my two shadows sometimes brought me to the verge of despair and desperation. I now hardly had time to carry out my most elementary duties because the two, who took it in turns to attack me, hardly gave me a moment's respite. The burdens of my high office weighed more and more heavily on me, and often in the night when I was unable to sleep I would ask myself how much longer I would be able to carry the responsibility for the community on my shoulders, and be worthy of the trust of those who anxiously looked to me for guidance.

Towards the end of the year there was bloodshed. One night

I was woken up by the sound of rifle-fire. It was obvious that there was trouble in Lussar. The shooting went on sporadically for the rest of the night, and continued during the day. The villagers who flocked into the monastery for safety reported that the Hu-hus had revolted against the communists and taken up their positions on the hills around Lussar from where they were firing on the communist troops in the village. The Chinese Red forces brought up artillery, but after four days' bitter fighting the Hu-hus took the village by storm and killed all the Red soldiers who fell into their hands. But they did not enjoy their victory for long. Powerful communist reinforcements arrived from Siling and there was more fierce fighting. From the roofs of the monastery buildings we could see the explosion of shells in the night and hear the sound of firing. In the end the Hu-hus were defeated and the village of Lussar was destroyed. Some of the Hu-hus succeeded in escaping to the hills, and the others were taken into Siling as prisoners.

Once again the time for the New Year's festivities was approaching. I discussed the matter with my advisers and we decided to refrain from any general celebrations this year in order to avoid all possibility of clashes. Each person would make his own sacrifice on his own house altar, and say the traditional prayers for himself. This difficult decision was made easier for us by the fact that in any case we no longer had sufficient resources to celebrate on the usual scale. In fact we found it difficult enough to obtain sufficient food to feed everyone. And for the same reasons our most beautiful celebration, that of the butter-lamps, held on the fifteenth day of the first month, could not be held either. Our life had become grey and barren, and we lived on as though under a leaden weight, hardly daring to talk to each other for fear of the communist spies, who would turn up suddenly in the most unexpected places.

In long and sleepless nights I came to the conclusion that the additional burden placed on my shoulders by the constant presence and persecution of my two warders rendered the situation intolerable, and that I was therefore no longer in a position to carry out my duties properly. A year ago it had seemed to be an advantage for Kumbum that its abbot should be a brother of the Dalai Lama, but now it was quite clear that this very circumstance made it impossible for me to carry on any fruitful labours on behalf of the monastery. In one of those few unwatched moments which arose from time to time and permitted a friendly chat or a serious talk, I confided my thoughts and feelings to my old friend Lhagsam. At first he sought to encourage me to carry on, but before long he was unable to withstand the force of my arguments, and in the end he agreed that I was right. I then sent for my steward and informed him that I had decided to relinquish the abbotship on the first anniversary of my induction, and I instructed him to make the necessary arrangements for the appointment of a successor.

On the ninth day of the third month of the Iron-Tiger year there was beautiful spring weather. At the usual time I informed the Shengo that I would appear in the general assembly; and then, with my yellow dagam thrown around my shoulders and the pointed yellow woollen cap on my head, I walked in solemn procession to the Tsogchen. There was complete silence, for I had ordered that the anniversary of my induction as Abbot of Kumbum should not be celebrated in any way, and so the musician monks had not brought their instruments. I ascended my throne and there I said the usual prayers for the favour of the gods on behalf of the monastery and its monks. The congregation, which by this time had greatly shrunk, answered in unison. The soft murmuring, which became louder from time to time, suddenly reminded me of the rushing noise of the great sandstorms which announced the approach of spring and were supposed to be of good omen. Might it please the gods that better times were in store for Kumbum!

The prayers ceased and the moment came for me to inform the general assembly of my decision. For a moment or two my voice threatened to desert me, but I quickly had myself under control again. I told them that I had carried out the duties of my high office to the best of my ability, but that my intentions had been constantly frustrated during the past few months and I had therefore been unable to place my poor powers completely in the service of our religion and of our monastery. An endless series of outside encroachments had progressively limited my freedom of movement. Further, my persistent efforts to defend Kumbum and its monks against everything which was not in accordance with our beliefs had made me the target for attacks which almost completely prevented any fruitful activity on my part on behalf of the community. Because of all these circumstances I had been forced to the conclusion that the best thing in the interests of the monastery would be for me to resign my high office. In conclusion I begged them to accept my resignation and release me from my duties.

The assembly heard what I had to say in dismayed silence. Everyone knew that my two guardians were treating me as though I were a prisoner, which, indeed, I was; and that they searched through my possessions, censored my correspondence, and kept on my heels persistently so that I was hardly ever out of their sight. My successor could scarcely be more hampered in the carrying out of his tasks; and it was, in fact, a reasonable assumption that a new Khenpo who was not a brother of the Dalai Lama, and whose activities were therefore not of such direct interest to the new rulers of the country, would enjoy greater latitude.

I descended from my throne and with trembling hands I laid a white good-luck scarf on its cushion. It was the most painful moment of my life, and everything went misty before my eyes. I felt like a traitor betraying the trust that had been reposed in him, and abandoning those who had been entrusted to his care. Perhaps after all I should have held on and used all the influence I could muster in Lhasa to support my efforts? But then these sudden doubts were dissipated. No, I was quite sure that I had done the right thing, and the council of the monastery had endorsed my decision only after careful consideration. The procession of dignitaries now formed and I placed myself at its head and was the first to leave the hall.

It was now my task to appoint a successor from amongst the candidates whose names were on the list before me. My choice fell on Shabdrung Karpo, a young lama—he was only twenty-five years old—from the monastery of Lhamo Dechen, a few days' journey away from Kumbum. Despite his youth he was already greatly respected. I now sent him a letter through my steward requesting him to accept the abbotship of Kumbum. To my great pleasure and relief he declared himself willing to do so, and it was not long before he arrived in Kumbum where he took up his quarters in one of the houses which were used as residences by the monks. In the meantime I continued to attend to the affairs of the monastery as well as I was able. Shabdrung Karpo and I met daily and I familiarised him with his new duties, and, as far as that was possible in the presence of my two shadows who very rarely left us alone, I gave him some idea of the difficulties he would be called upon to face when he took office.

A few weeks later his formal induction as Abbot of Kumbum in my stead took place. The ceremony was in every way the same as usual. He delivered his inaugural speech to the general assembly, the insignia of Khenpo power changed hands, and I congratulated him on his appointment and wished him good fortune and the help of the gods in the conduct of his difficult and responsible office. Everything took place in exactly the same way as it had done the previous year when I had succeeded Choni Rimpoche—except that the line of those who filed past to congratulate the new Abbot of Kumbum was by no means so long as it had been then. Not one of those monks who had fled, fearing that the horrors of the Hu-hu rising of the previous century were about to be repeated in this, had returned for the ceremony. I left the hall behind Shabdrung Karpo, followed by the council and dignitaries of the monastery. In the residence of the Khenpo the Steward handed over the formal inventory to the new Abbot. With this my task was over. Once again I wished my successor well in his new office and then in the company of Lhagsam, Döndrub Gyantsen and a few other friends, I left the Khenpo residence to go to my own labrang.

Wherever the Dalai Lama appeared with his retinue on his flight in the winter of 1950 – 51 he was honoured by monks (wearing the typical yellow woollen hats) with prayer flags and good-luck symbols

The monastery of Dungkhar lies in the Chumbi Valley near the border of India. In 1951 it served the Dalai Lama as a provisional residence during his flight. It was from here that he negotiated his return to Lhasa with the Chinese

It was a sad homecoming to my old house. My friends sought to cheer me up and console me, but I hardly heard their well-meant words, and I soon withdrew to my room and abandoned myself to my distress. I said my prayers almost mechanically that night and then, completely exhausted, I sank into deep slumber.

18. Alternate Threats and Promises

MY fears that my tormentors would soon follow me into my own labrang were realised the very next day. It was quite clear now that I owed their special attention to the fact that I was the brother of the Dalai Lama. Their object was to win me over to their side, or, failing that, then to make me subject to them and useful to their plans. Shabdrung Karpo, the new Abbot of Kumbum, was naturally not left altogether in peace either, and he too suffered from the attentions of those who had already made our lives a misery in the monastery for months, but, as I anticipated, they did not persecute him quite so intensely as they did me. He, too, was supervised of course, but he was able to move about more freely than I had been, and, above all, he was able to attend to his religious and administrative duties as I had latterly not been permitted to. He was visited only from time to time, and the control exercised over his doings was not systematic and permanent as it had been with me; they just checked up from time to time. But as for me, now that I no longer had any official duties I found it more difficult to shake off my persistent shadows than ever before.

At first they adopted a conciliatory tone towards me and contented themselves with describing the great progress allegedly being made in communist China. They bombarded me with statistics, particularly with regard to the increase of industrial production; and they informed me in great detail of the wonderful plans of the Chinese People's Republic for the future.

Altogether it was a picture painted in very rosy colours. The next stage was more critical: it consisted of an attack on our institutions and on our way of life. As far as possible I avoided any open disagreement with them, and I usually just listened wordlessly to what they had to say; which was by this time not in any way new to me. They praised the totalitarian State, which, so they declared, was realising the ideal of human equality; and in which, so they assured me, private property for the few was giving way to the joy of the many in the common ownership of the good things of life. In the future the State would take care of everything and everybody, and an egalitarian system of distribution would make the use of money unnecessary. Everyone would be drawn into the process of production, and women too would work with the rest, because henceforth they would have no housework to do and their children would be put into children's homes from the time of their birth, and there they would be much better looked after than they could be in individual homes.

Although by this time I had already heard this sort of thing often enough before, the thought of such a State never ceased to horrify me anew. It was a conception in crass opposition to everything we held dear; and as they described their paradise it sounded like hell on earth to me: a life of grey, uniform dullness, without warmth, without individual human love and affection, a life not worth living, and a world not worth living in.

Finally, the pair of them suggested that I should set my countrymen a good example by handing over the Tagtser Labrang and all its benefices to the State for the good of the people. I firmly rejected this monstrous proposition, and I pointed out that I was not the owner of that property, but only its temporary beneficiary, and that it was my duty to hand it on to my successor unimpaired. Obviously, my attempts to defend a system of society which had answered so well in our country from time immemorial were not received with any favour, and everything I put forward was just dismissed with a wave of the hand.

Greatly distressed I had to admit to myself that I was defending

things which were disintegrating more and more rapidly with
the triumph of our new masters. The decrees of the new Red
Chinese authorities had already brought about new conditions,
and what had only shortly been the existing order was now slid-
ing rapidly into dissolution and chaos. In the village cunning
and experienced propagandists were confusing the minds of the
peasants, and only the nomads were being left in peace for the
time being. A new system of taxation had already been introduced, and it was quite clearly intended to drive the peasants
to the verge of ruin and prepare the way for a communist land
reform. For example, each peasant now had to deliver his taxes
in kind direct to the authorities in Siling. Formerly he had
delivered a fixed amount to the local monastery, and if the authorities had subsequently made increased demands—which they
often did—the monastery had usually met them from its own
resources without having recourse to the peasants. But now
nothing stood between the peasant and the arbitrary demands
of the authorities, whose rapacity steadily increased. In despair
the peasants resisted, and the authorities replied with threats,
increased demands and punishments—and in the background
there was always the Red Army to enforce their will. Robbery
and murder had become common in a once peaceable countryside. Dissatisfied elements banded together, and the once much-
feared robber bands became a reality again. Hordes of these
bandits roamed through the countryside, and such were the
topsy-turvy conditions brought about by the new rulers that the
oppressed masses regarded them as heroes.

About a month after my resignation from the abbotship of
Kumbum, Shu, the chairman of the Tibet Commission, appeared
in my labrang with a proposal that I should go to Lhasa on behalf
of the communists to present their demands to the Dalai Lama.
If I accepted the proposal, he could promise me that my previous
obstinacy and my former relations with the Kuomintang and the
Western Powers in Lhasa would be overlooked. If on the other
hand I should pretend to accept their proposal and instead use
the opportunity to escape to India they would take good care to

see that I should never be allowed to set foot on Tibetan soil again. The proposal horrified me and I rejected it out of hand. I told Shu that he and his precious commission had a totally distorted picture of the situation in Lhasa, and that if I were foolish enough to go there as a communist messenger my life would be forfeit, because I should be regarded as a traitor.

But communists are not so easily put off. Shu certainly departed with his object unattained, but before long the secretary of the Governor arrived, and after him the Governor himself, and finally the new commanding general in Siling. And they each and all made the same proposal, although I had already firmly turned it down once. It was not long before it became clear to me that if I continued in my blunt refusal to do what they demanded I should find myself in great danger. Further, their insulting offer was obviously the last opportunity that would come my way of getting out of their clutches in the normal way and rejoining my family in Lhasa. In fact it struck me as highly likely that if I persisted in my refusal they would hold me as a hostage in order to blackmail Lhasa. With this the situation had become so critical that I had to reckon with the worst, and in the circumstances it seemed to me quite justifiable to pretend to accept their proposal and to use it as a means of making my escape.

An interview with the Tibetan Deputy-Governor helped me to make up my mind. As well as the Governor there were two Deputy-Governors in Siling, one for Mohammedan and the other for Tibetan affairs. The two men, who now served under the Red Chinese Governor, had accepted their posts more or less under duress; and one of them, Ma Dza-U, who was the leader of the Mohammedan ethnical group in the province, had been unable to prevent the arrest of his son by the new authorities. The Tibetan Deputy-Governor was a certain Geshi Sherab Rimpoche, an ambitious man whom I had known during my period of studies at Kumbum. As soon as I was alone with him I reproached him for having gone over to the side of the enemy, but this he denied, saying that it was a counsel of prudence to keep in with the new rulers as far as possible, particularly as they were so strong that it was impossible to resist them anyway. The right thing, in his view, was to collaborate with them lest worse befall.

His example showed me that the Red Chinese would always be able to find puppets willing, under this or that pretext, to do their bidding. In this case they had found a high Tibetan dignitary willing to collaborate with them. The situation looked hopeless to me and that made up my mind definitely: I decided to flee. However, in order to conceal my intentions from the authorities I told the chairman of the Tibetan Commission that I would like to go to Pekin to study and acquaint myself more thoroughly with the conditions of the country. I explained my decision to him by saying that I had come to the conclusion that I could be of more use to my country in Pekin than in Lhasa, where I should come under suspicion of being a traitor. They listened to my proposal with interest but came to no decision. But at least I obtained a valuable respite and at the same time I was able to begin preparations for a long journey without arousing their suspicion. However, it was not long before I was informed that my proposal that I should be allowed to go to Pekin had been rejected, and that, instead, I should prepare myself to leave for Lhasa as they had suggested.

I now told them that I would agree to their proposal, but on condition that I was allowed to take twenty high dignitaries of Kumbum with me as a retinue, since that would add weight to my mission when I arrived in Lhasa. The Tibet Commission declared itself in agreement with my proposal and asked me to present the list of the twenty people I wished to go with me. Unfortunately, this part of my plan to save the most influential and therefore the most endangered lamas from the clutches of the communists, did not succeed. After a short while I was handed back the list and told under various pretexts that my proposal was impossible: this man was too old; that man was too young; and so on. In the end only two names were accepted: those of Shar Kalden Gyamtso and Shalu Rimpoche.

Once again I was summoned to appear before the Tibet

Commission in Siling, and at this interview I was informed that I was to be accompanied on my journey by three Chinese; a married couple, and a wireless operator with a portable transmitter, as the authorities in Siling wished to remain in contact with my caravan throughout the journey and be kept constantly informed about its progress. This was, of course, very disagreeable but in the end there was nothing for it but to agree. During the further course of this interview the communists dropped the mask completely and bluntly made proposals which aroused my fierce indignation and resentment. What I had to listen to was so monstrous that I had difficulty in concealing my feelings. It was nothing less than a promise to make me Governor-General of Tibet if on my arrival in Lhasa I managed to persuade the Tibetan Government to welcome the entry of Chinese communist troops into Tibet as liberators, and to accept the Chinese People's Republic as an ally. As Governor-General, they pointed out, I should be in a position to assist and guide the great work of socialist construction in my country and to help replace antiquated religious beliefs with the new communist ideology. Should the Dalai Lama resist the march of progress, they indicated, ways and means would have to be found to get rid of him. At this point they even let me see quite clearly that if necessary they would regard fratricide as justifiable in the circumstances if there remained no other way of advancing the cause of communism. They even pointed out occasions on which people had actually committed such crimes "in the interests of the cause" and had subsequently been rewarded with high office.

It was only by dint of exercising the greatest self-control that I was able to conceal from my interlocutors the storm of indignation which their words loosed in me. What sort of a man did they think I was, for heaven's sake? Did they really suppose that I was capable of such abominations in return for the privileges of becoming their puppet? "If only I were already in Lhasa!" I thought desperately. "I would very quickly show them that they are mistaken in their estimate of me."

With great difficulty I forced myself to be calm and to answer them in a matter-of-fact way. In particular I asked them for further details concerning the long journey. They now provided me with a large-calibre pistol and twenty-five rounds of ammunition, three old Japanese rifles, three horses and three thousand gormos. I was then allowed to return to Kumbum with the instructions to make my way with my two companions to the usual caravan meeting-place at Tsaidam, where we would be joined by our Chinese companions for the journey.

All signs indicated that the summer caravans to Lhasa would not be very large this year. In view of the unsettled state of the country no one voluntarily undertook any long journey, since such journeys were, of course, much more dangerous than before. In the circumstances it was advisable that each of us should go armed, and I even began to welcome the idea of taking a wireless transmitter along with us, because then, if necessary, we might be able to summon the assistance of any patrols in our neighbourhood. When I got back to Kumbum I informed my two companions of the instructions the authorities had issued, and left it to Döndrub Gyantsen to see to the final preparations. I made no mention of the monstrous proposals and offers the Tibet Commission had made me.

The two human bloodhounds who had followed close on my heels for months were now withdrawn, and I was once again free to move around as I pleased. I regularly attended the general assembly in the monastery, performed my normal religious duties, and paid farewell visits to all my friends. The hours I spent with them were sorrowful, because I was well aware that there was very little likelihood that I should ever see any of them again. However, I put a good face on it and spoke to them cheerfully, because I was very anxious not to undermine the last vestiges of their hope and confidence. All the same, it was very difficult for me not to inform them of just how serious the situation was—as I had discovered only too clearly since my recent visit to the Tibet Commission. My farewell to the men whom I had thought to save by putting their names down as my travelling companions was particularly depressing. I now had to leave

On the occasion of the 2,500th anniversary of the birth of Buddha the
Dalai Lama came to India to take part in the great celebrations. He is
enthroned here under the "Tree of Knowledge" taking part in a religious
ceremony

After his flight from Tibet the Fourteenth Dalai Lama found a temporary residence in Birla House in Mussoorie, to the north of Delhi in the foothills of the Himalayas. This photograph was taken in the spring of 1960

Minyag Rimpoche, my old friend Lhagsam, and the many other intimate friends I had made in Kumbum, to an uncertain fate, together with the rest of the monks who made up the dwindling community. I hardly dared think of what the future would hold for them.

On the evening of my departure, feeling very sad at heart, I walked through the streets of the monastery. I visited the temples for the last time, running my hand over their ancient pillars, carefully placing my feet on their worn steps. My last visit was to the Serdong Temple, which contained our most precious treasures, and I stood, deeply moved, before the golden statue of Tsong Khapa, the Great Reformer, who, hundreds of years before, had opened up a new epoch in the history of Tibet; an epoch which now seemed to have reached its end. The holy-water stoup was freshly filled, but not one of the butter-lamps was alight now. Only the uncertain flame of a mustard-oil lamp showed up the over-life-size figure, which loomed up eerily in the gloom.

How quickly the change had come about! Less than a year ago this place had been lit up brilliantly by innumerable butter-lamps. My eyes roamed over the many books which lined the walls, the books which contained the truths of our religion. And I looked once more at the ceiling from which hung innumerable katas: the offerings of a pious monastic community and of a people happy in its beliefs. I bowed my head, prostrated myself for the last time before the statue of Tsong Khapa, and then left the holy place in profound distress of soul.

I left the monastery at the head of my small party on the last day of the sixth month of the Iron-Tiger year. A number of monks had obtained permission from the Tibetan Deputy-Governor in Siling to make a pilgrimage to Lhasa, and in all there were five small groups, each of which had a scout and a cook. I took advantage of the first stage of our journey to visit one or two friends. In Drakar Pedzong, where only nomads lived, I said farewell to Aru Rimpoche; and in a village by the Ko-Ko-Nor, Shalu Rimpoche joined my party. We made our way to

Tsaidam without trouble, and when we arrived there our papers were very carefully examined and we were closely questioned about ourselves and the reason for our journey, because the new authorities had established a frontier garrison of two hundred men across the caravan route. A detailed protocol was drawn up for each separate member of each caravan.

Everyone had to give his place of birth, the names and addresses of his next of kin, details of the arms he carried with him, the nature and content of each piece of luggage he was taking out, and the amount of money in his possession. Although the control was very strict we were not treated impolitely. Obviously they had received instructions not to subject us to any chicanery, but an incident which took place whilst we were in Tsaidam and caused us to protest indignantly, though in vain, indicated clearly enough that in the ordinary way a very different atmosphere prevailed at this frontier post. Two monks from Inner Mongolia were on their way to Lhasa as pilgrims, and they presented documents to this effect; but under some ridiculous pretext they were declared to be Kuomintang spies; whereupon they were bound and placed in a tent with a guard on the entrance.

When our three Chinese travelling companions had arrived and Shar Kalden Gyamtso had joined us, the caravan started on its way. There were now about thirty groups of us totalling in all about one hundred and seventy men, three thousand yaks, and five hundred horses and mules. The summer caravans had not been as small as this within living memory. However, the weather was favourable and we would have made good progress, but for the fact that the married couple who were accompanying us insisted on stopping for frequent rest days in between. For some reason of their own the two of them seemed to have determined to drag out the journey as long as possible. Every day they delayed the departure of our group, or invented some excuse or other to make us pitch camp before we intended to do so, and their behaviour held up the whole caravan. They were supposed not to understand Tibetan, but as a precaution we kept ourselves apart from them as much as possible. The Chinese wireless operator, on the other hand, was quite an agreeable fellow, and we often had long conversations with him.

Our journey dragged, and my spirits were not such as to allow me to enjoy the magnificent landscape. On the contrary its austerity and its immensity depressed me now, and rather scared me too. In addition, the constant delays which we were suffering made me nervous and irritable. I was impatient to be there and be able to present myself to the Dalai Lama and to pour out to him what I had been compelled to bottle up inside myself for many months.

But at last we reached the Tibetan frontier at Shagchukha, where the newly appointed Governor of the Northern Provinces of Tibet, a monk named Thubten Sangpo, was waiting to welcome me in the name of the Dalai Lama. It wasn't long before a violent altercation developed between the leader of our Chinese travelling companions and the Tibetan frontier guard, who refused to allow them to enter Tibetan territory. The furious retort of the Chinese that in that case I could not be allowed to go on either was received with astonished laughter. Had the man gone off his head? Didn't he realise that we were on Tibetan soil here and that the power of his superiors ended at the Tibetan frontier? His angry protest to the Governor was met with a polite but very firm refusal. Lhasa had been informed telegraphically of my coming, and the authorities there had quite rightly assumed that my Chinese travelling companions had been forced on to me and they were therefore refused entry.

When he realised that he was not going to be allowed to continue the journey to Lhasa with me the man completely lost his head and shouted that he had just received a wireless message to the effect that Red Chinese troops had already marched into Chamdo, the capital of the Tibetan eastern province of Kham. To make quite sure of convincing us he even told us the number of prisoners they had taken and the amounts of war material they had captured. With this he made himself highly unpopular and it was only with difficulty that the three Chinese were saved from being lynched by the indignant Tibetans, who felt themselves

betrayed. Had they not been told for months that the Chinese
Red Army was an army of liberation and freedom, and that
under no circumstances would it violate the Tibetan frontier?
And now communist troops had burst into Tibetan territory by
armed force. At least it would now be as clear as daylight to the
whole world that the "mission" for which they had tried to
misuse me in order to persuade the Dalai Lama to surrender
Tibet "peacefully" was a piece of treachery from beginning to
end.

The Governor, who had been given instructions from Lhasa
to avoid as far as possible any exacerbation of the situation, and
who was very willing to accept any reasonable compromise, now
did the only thing open to him: he had the three Chinese arrested
and taken southward under escort. The wireless transmitter was
confiscated.

We then went on to Nagchukha, which was the seat of the
provincial governor; and I used the days of rest we spent there
to write down everything I knew about the plans of the Chinese
communists. I then had this document carried posthaste to
Lhasa by special courier. Before I continued my journey the
news arrived in Nagchukha that in view of the seriousness of
the situation the National Assembly in Lhasa had decided to
declare the young Dalai Lama the supreme temporal ruler of
Tibet even before he obtained his majority, i.e., completed his
eighteenth year. The interregnum represented by the Regency
involved an administrative decentralisation which hampered
quick decisions, so it was to end on the tenth day of the tenth
month, when the Dalai Lama himself would take full power
into his hands; an occasion which was to be celebrated throughout the country with solemn religious services and rejoicing.

On my way to Lhasa I was met by messengers from the capital
bringing me a letter in which the Dalai Lama expressed his
delight at my safe arrival in Tibet. My mother had also sent a
message of greetings. About two hours' ride outside the capital
a large building had in the meantime been erected. It was to be
an electricity works under the supervision of our Austrian friend

Peter Aufschnaiter. When we arrived there we found many friends who congratulated me on my escape from the hands of the Chinese communists. I now put off my travelling clothes and put on the garments which had been sent out to me from Lhasa, and in this new guise I rode into the city with my party. The terrible times which lay behind me now seemed almost like a bad dream. I went straight to Changsaipshar where my mother welcomed me with a white good-luck scarf. I also handed her a kata and then we fell into each other's arms. Afterwards I went into the house with her, greeted all my relatives, and paid a short visit to the bedside of Lobsang Samten, who was seriously ill.

But I was too impatient to stay there for long, so I sent a messenger ahead to announce my coming to the Dalai Lama, and then hurried after him. My brother was very anxious to hear any further details which I was in a position to add to the dispatch I had already sent him from Nagchukha, and I now had to give him an exhaustive account of all my experiences in Kumbum and Siling. I was only too willing to talk and get it all off my chest, all the things which had depressed me for so many months, all the things which I had been compelled to keep bottled up inside me. The Dalai Lama listened with a serious face to what I had to tell him, occasionally interrupting my account with a question or two. When I came to the monstrous offer that the Red Chinese Tibetan Commission had made to me I hesitated. Dared I take such terrible and blasphemous words into my mouth in the presence of the Dalai Lama? But seeing my hesitation my brother ordered me to continue and hold back nothing. All the same, I had to do violence to my feelings in order to explain all the details of the devilish plans of the communists and of their base attempt to suborn me.

When I had at last finished my story the Dalai Lama remained silent for a long time, sunk in thought. And as for me, now that I had conjured up once again all the frightening things from which I had been fortunate enough to escape, I felt numbed with horror. I looked at my brother anxiously. What thoughts must be going through his mind! With a movement of the hand as though to dismiss an evil spectre he indicated that I should rise. We looked into each other's eyes for a moment or two, and behind those thick lenses I saw nothing but sympathy, love and concern for me. Was there much more to be said? We understood each other. My brother thanked me warmly and then I left.

I walked down the stone steps of the Potala with a great feeling of relief and content in my breast, and suddenly I felt so extremely tired that I could hardly remain upright. Now that at least a part of my burden had been taken from me I could have fallen into a dreamless sleep on the spot. I was grateful when attendants helped me to mount my horse, which then set off in the direction of Changsaipshar without further bidding. I turned my head and looked back at the Potala towards the window of the room in which the young ruler of my country now sat thinking over the new anxieties that I had been instrumental in bringing to him.

19. Farewell to Tibet

THE atmosphere in Lhasa was restless and unsettled. Many people were already making plans to flee the country. The Chinese communist troops had advanced deep into Tibetan territory, and any serious military resistance was unfortunately out of the question. The few heavily outnumbered troops which had offered some resistance had been compelled to withdraw, leaving many prisoners in the hands of the enemy. Would the Chinese Red Army now turn against Lhasa? And what would happen then? With horror people recalled the atrocious behaviour of the Chinese in Lhasa in 1910. The Dalai Lama had been compelled to flee then, and it was only after the Chinese Revolution of 1911 that he had been able to return to Lhasa. But were the Chinese communists likely to give up a position they had once captured? The Tibetan Government had already appealed to the United Nations, but its hands were tied. However, at the intervention of India the Chinese had declared themselves willing to negotiate, and a Tibetan delegation, of which my brother-in-law Püntso Trashi was a member, was already on its way to Pekin.

I felt quite certain that the utmost we should be able to obtain as a result of the negotiations was a postponement, even if an indefinite one, and therefore I determined to leave Lhasa; particularly as it would certainly not remain concealed from my mentors in Siling for long that I had, in fact, done everything to foil their plans. In the circumstances my continued presence in the capital would only be provocative and make the negotiations more difficult, so I decided that the best thing to do would be for me to move southwards towards the Indian border and there await the outcome. At the same time I begged my family to go with me. My mother agreed at once that the best thing in the circumstances was to leave Lhasa and she took my brothers and sisters (with the exception, of course, of the Dalai Lama) with her at once to Gyantse, where she proposed to wait for me. Unfortunately, Lobsang Samten was still too ill to travel, so he too had to stay behind.

When I had made all the necessary arrangements I took leave of the Dalai Lama and rode to my old monastery Drepung where I once again made the Chöjal, or formal sacrificial round, presented each monk with a sum of money, lit butter-lamps, and placed good-luck scarves on all the various altars. Then Döndrub Gyantsen appeared together with the other servants who were to accompany me, and I exchanged my monastic habit for travelling clothes and set out on the journey which was ultimately to take me to freedom—but also to exile.

We established ourselves in the Chumbi Valley near the Indian border. In the meantime the situation had so intensified that the Dalai Lama himself had also had to leave Lhasa, and his great caravan arrived shortly after we did. My brother took up his residence in Dungkar Monastery from where he remained in touch by courier with the rest of the government, which had stayed on in Lhasa. The high prelates of his retinue were also quartered in Dungkar Monastery, whilst the nobles and the officials who had accompanied him found quarters in the surrounding farmsteads.

Before long I was to be reminded that the Chinese communists had not forgotten me or given up hope of using me to serve their purposes. Various communications were sent to me demanding that I should use my influence with the Dalai Lama to prevent his leaving the country. The first letter in this strain came from an East Tibetan named Püntso Wangye, and I did not attach much importance to it. The man had been expelled from Lhasa in 1947 with the Kuomintang representatives and he had since gone over to the communists. What he now had to say coincided with what the Governor of Siling had already said. I was assured that if I were able to persuade the Dalai Lama to stay in Tibet there would be no reason why I should not return to Lhasa. The aim of the Chinese communists was obviously to persuade the world that they were on the best of terms not only with the Dalai Lama but also with all the members of his family. However, I desired to have nothing further to do with the Chinese communists, and I left no doubt in the minds of my relatives and of the retinue of the Dalai Lama that I had no intention of going back to Lhasa. The members of my family showed complete understanding for my decision, but the officials and nobles of the Dalai Lama's retinue sought to make me change my mind—no doubt because they feared difficulties.

But when my two travelling companions from Kumbum, Shalu Rimpoche and Shar Kalden Gyamtso, who had remained in Lhasa, also wrote me long letters in order to persuade me to return, I sent Döndrub Gyantsen back to Lhasa with messages in which I informed them in carefully phrased terms that for reasons of health I should have to stay in the Chumbi Valley until further notice. When he returned Döndrub Gyantsen brought back letters from them both, and the news that the Chinese married couple who had been told off to accompany me on my journey to Lhasa, and who had been arrested on the Tibetan frontier, had now been released and were living in Lhasa.

Shar Kalden Gyamtso merely sent me his best wishes for a speedy recovery and a quick return to the capital, but in his letter Shalu Rimpoche expressed himself quite openly, comparing himself to a long-established plant which was too old and deeply rooted to be transplanted, but saying that I was a still young and vigorous growth which could be moved with advantage to some more fruitful soil. That accorded completely with my own feelings, because I was now determined to seek that freedom abroad which I already knew from bitter experience was impossible under communist rule. But in view of the critical situation, and in order not to upset my family—my mother in particular was very unwilling to contemplate a separation—I laid my escape plans in secret.

In 1947 my friend Telopa Rimpoche, whom I had last seen in Pekin, had, through the mediation of an American business-man in Hongkong named Robert Drummond, obtained an invitation from the Johns Hopkins University which enabled him to go to the United States and thus escape from the clutches of the Chinese Reds. I now wrote a long and detailed letter to him in which I asked his advice as to the best means by which I could myself get to the United States as quickly as possible. He replied by return asking me to send him photographs of myself and Döndrub Gyantsen so that he could set his American friends to work to obtain permission for us both to enter the United States. By chance we both happened to have what was required and I sent the photographs off post-haste.

In the meantime the situation had become more and more difficult for me. We had received news that the Tibetan deputa-tion to Pekin had agreed to a seventeen-point treaty according to which the internal administration of the country was to be left in the hands of the Dalai Lama, and there was to be complete freedom of religious observance. As against this, the "Chinese People's Republic" would henceforth represent Tibet inter-nationally and undertake her "defence." The terms of this treaty confirmed many of my fears, because it meant that with this compromise we were entering into a period of complete depen-dence on Red China. In consequence I was more than ever deter-mined to leave the country. As it had been agreed that the Dalai Lama should wait in the Chumbi Valley for a Red Chinese General who would come from India to go back with him to Lhasa, there was obviously no time to lose. I must be safely on Indian soil before the Chinese communist delegation arrived. I therefore asked the Dalai Lama for permission to accompany my mother and the younger children on a pilgrimage to India, where I proposed to undergo a thorough medical examination.

I received the necessary permission in a formal audience with the Dalai Lama and then I made the prescribed sacrificial tour of Dungkar Monastery. When this was over I took leave of my two brothers in private. It was a sad moment for me when I stood in their presence; the Dalai Lama and Lobsang Samten, whose condition had in the meantime so much improved as to allow him to travel. They knew nothing of my ultimate plans, and I could not bring myself to add to their sorrow and distress by revealing them. Would I ever see either of them again? And if so, under what circumstances? No one seemed to have the slightest inkling of my intentions, and even the men in the immediate entourage of the Dalai Lama merely warned me to be very careful in my utterances whilst I was in India, particularly in reference to the seventeen-point treaty which had now been negotiated in Pekin.

With Döndrub Gyantsen and a few horses I crossed Natu Pass in light snowfall and made my way into Sikkim. Sorrowful thoughts were my companions too. I knew that I should in all probability never again set foot on Tibetan soil, that I should never again return to my home. Voluntarily I was now turning my back on my country for ever. I was fleeing from arbitrary violence and seeking freedom. I had personally experienced the frustrations of a free man when he is cast in chains, and I knew that I could not live without liberty. Others gave me a helping hand and smoothed my path. But I had never before quite realised that the price was to be my own country, and now I suffered all the tortures of the exile. I would never have believed it so difficult to say farewell for ever to my country. The idea of going abroad, where I should have to live with strangers and speak their tongue, seemed intolerable to me. But at the same time my understanding told me that it was impossible to go back now. Had I not already experienced what it was like to be a prisoner in my own country, helpless, and at the mercy of ruthless oppressors who hated and sought to destroy everything which was sacred to me and meant even more than life itself? No, the avenue of return was closed. Resolutely I urged on my horse and made my way through the increasingly heavy snowfall.

20. To and Fro in the World

I ARRIVED in Kalimpong to find a message waiting for me from Telopa Rimpoche to the effect that the American Committee for Free Asia was prepared to invite me and Döndrub Gyantsen to the United States for a year as its guests. With this certainty behind me I was now in a position to let my mother and Tsering Dröma know about my plans. They proposed to stay for some time in Kalimpong together with little Ngari Rimpoche. It was a great weight off my mind when I found that they agreed with me and showed complete understanding for my position, and when I left it was with my mother's blessing and good wishes. I now went by plane to Calcutta; and Pomdatsang, the Tibetan merchant who had already helped me and been my host on my pilgrimage to China, put me into touch with a Mr Patterson, a Scot who had been a missionary in Eastern Tibet, and whose knowledge of Tibetan was now of the greatest assistance to me, particularly in getting our travelling papers and our U.S. entry permits.

In Calcutta I once again had to hold the candle to the Devil. The Tibetan Delegation which had been in Pekin to negotiate the seventeen-point agreement was now in the city on its way back to Lhasa, together with the Red Chinese General Chang Chi-wu and his retinue. I went to see my brother-in-law Püntso Trashi, who, like all the other members of the Tibetan party, was staying in the Chinese Embassy. Whilst I was there I received a formal invitation from Chang Chi-wu to join his party and go back with them to Lhasa. Naturally, I could not turn down such an invitation offhand, and my situation was made even more difficult by Püntso Trashi himself, who urged me to accept it and return with the Tibetan delegation to Lhasa, where, as he assured me, I should have nothing to fear. Chang Chi-wu was very keen on my coming with them to Tibet, but I managed to take my leave without committing myself. Afterwards I sought an opportunity to speak to Püntso Trashi in private, and I then informed him that I was leaving by plane for the United States that very evening. The unexpected news shocked him and he did his utmost to persuade me to change my plans, even at the eleventh hour, but I shook my head and remained firm. When my brother-in-law saw that I was not to be moved, he promised to keep the information to himself, and we parted with mutual good wishes for our uncertain future.

Döndrub Gyantsen and I now flew to New York via London. My inadequate knowledge of foreign languages was not enough even for the most elementary matters and we had to rely on the friendly help of our fellow passangers, who certainly did everything they could to make things easier for us. All the same we were greatly relieved when in the great bustle and hubbub of Idlewild airport we heard ourselves addressed in the familiar Amdo dialect. The speaker was Robert Ekvall, who was the son of missionaries and had lived a long time in our country. He had come to welcome us on United States soil in the name of the American Committee for Free Asia. Under his wing I was better able to support the barrage of exploding flashlights as the photographers got to work, and the bombardment of questions from the assembled journalists. Mr Ekvall subsequently introduced us to everyday life in New York and did his best to acquaint us with the mentality of the average American; and it was in his company that we paid our first visits. Our reception by the American Committee for Free Asia made a happy impression on me, and in our honour there was yoghourt, mutton and strawberries.

After a few days in New York we went to stay with our generous mentor—who had become Bob Ekvall for us by this time—in his house in Fairfax, West Virginia, where Mrs Ekvall proved a very amiable and solicitous hostess. At last I had time to pay some attention to my health, which really was rather shaky. A thorough examination showed that my lungs were affected, though not very dangerously, and we were lent a small farmhouse in which we could live whilst I was undergoing medical treatment to restore me completely to health. Bob Ekvall visited us frequently, and the chauffeur who was placed at our disposal gave us our first lessons in English.

After a few weeks spent in the seclusion of West Virginia a telegram arrived from my brother Gaylo Döndrub informing me that he had succeeded in getting out of Red China in good time and was now living with his wife and child on Formosa in free Chinese territory. The telegram also announced his forthcoming visit to the United States. I was very glad to be able to invite him to stay with us at our farmhouse in Fairfax, and he and his small family did so for three months in all. They wanted to try to get back to Lhasa with my mother, who was finding the long separation from her family very difficult to bear. So long as my mother was in Kalimpong I had regular news of all my relatives, but then after a while no more letters arrived. First the wireless and then the newspapers brought short and very unsatisfactory reports of the happenings in Tibet, but before long even they ceased. It was as though the silence of the grave had descended on my country.

After a good six months treatment my doctor declared that I was completely cured. I should still have to take it easy for a while and observe certain precautions, but there was now no reason why I should not go to California and take a course in English at Berkeley University. At Berkeley I quickly made friends with Professor Lessing, a Tibetan scholar, and his wife; and I was able to be of assistance to him in the deciphering of Tibetan texts. The generous hospitality which was offered to me everywhere did something to help me over the difficult hours when I was overcome by homesickness. In general I found that the Californian climate suited me, and I made rapid progress with my studies.

One day in 1952 I received an invitation to attend the World Buddhist Congress in Tokio, and once again I set off on a journey with Döndrub Gyantsen, this time by ship. On the voyage across the Pacific I suffered a great deal from sea-sickness and I was heartily glad when I was at last able to set my feet on solid ground again on our arrival in Tokio. Amongst the group of people who were at the pier to welcome us were a number of my friends from the United States. The Abbot of the Buddhist monastery attached to the Honganji Temple invited us to be his guests during our stay and we went off with him to the monastery. I was able to make a number of valuable contacts at the World Congress, but my great wish—to visit the holy places in Ceylon —was not fulfilled.

The Indian identification papers I had used so far had now lapsed and there was no possibility of renewing them. Unfortunately this turned out to mean weeks of vain waiting, which soon lengthened into months, until finally I decided to use the enforced idleness to continue the study of Japanese I had started. And before long I had a small class of my own which I taught Tibetan. I made long journeys throughout the country, and I visited many temples and holy places, got to know many Japanese and made friends with members of the foreign colonies. Abbot Kitabatake was a generous and helpful host and I was able to turn to him in all my difficulties. My permission to stay in Japan was extended again and again, but permission to enter India and the United States was delayed beyond all measure. I suffered no privations during this time of waiting, but I certainly learned the bitterness, the frustrated hopes and the nagging anxieties of the emigrant who has to wage a seemingly hopeless nerve-racking struggle with a vast anonymous bureaucracy.

However, in the end a change in the U.S. immigration laws and the persistent help of many influential friends, and in particular of the World Church Services, finally secured permission for me to return to the United States. That was in 1955, and I chose the longer route over India and through Europe, because I wanted to meet Gyalo Döndrub in Calcutta. Four years previously, he had gone back to Lhasa with his family, together with my mother and the others, but after his long absence from Tibet he had found it difficult to get used to the new conditions prevailing there. He too found himself longing for freedom, so when the Reds offered him a diplomatic mission to Moscow on their behalf he accepted and then used the opportunity it afforded to escape to India. When we met he was able to tell me that all our relatives in Lhasa were well. Lobsang Samten had risen to high office and was now a Chikyab Khenpo and the High Chamberlain, whilst Püntso Trashi had been appointed commander of the Dalai Lama's bodyguard.

My sister Tsering Dröma had also come to Calcutta to meet me, but our joy at seeing her again was a little damped by her urgent attempts to persuade us both to return to Lhasa. The previous year she had accompanied the Dalai Lama on his visit to Pekin, and she admitted that whilst she was there she had been told that she must do her utmost to get the fugitive members of the Dalai Lama's family to return to Tibet. But apart from this, she found it sad that the family was now so broken up. She also told us that she was afraid that our obstinate refusal to go back would cause the Dalai Lama still further difficulties. With heavy hearts we both made it clear to her that so long as the Chinese communists were in power in Tibet there could be no return for us, as much as we longed to see our native land again. Because she urged us so persistently we did go to see the Chinese Consul in Calcutta, and he too did his utmost to persuade us to go back to Lhasa. But we remained firm and gave him a number of ostensibly good reasons which would prevent our return to Tibet for an indefinite period.

After a short stay in my brother's house in Darjeeling, where my younger sister Jetsün Pema, and the two children of Tsering Dröma, went to school, I flew to England. I spent a few days in the house of my old friend Mr Richardson in St Andrews. I had a number of long and highly interesting chats with him, and I never ceased to be astonished at the great knowledge of this prominent Tibet scholar. Not only did he know the history of each separate monastery in Tibet, but he also knew things about the history of my country which were new to me.

When I finally arrived back in New York again at last I was able to make arrangements for Döndrub Gyantsen to join me from Tokio, where he had been waiting; and he came via San Francisco. We were now both guests of the World Church Services. I began to study at Columbia University and I also gave lessons in Tibetan again, but Döndrub Gyantsen was anxious to do something or other with his hands, and he got himself a job in an aircraft factory. My old friends were once again at my side and I prepared myself to occupy some position in which, thanks to my new-won linguistic knowledge, I should be able to be of assistance to my fellow countrymen. Everywhere I had been throughout the world people had received me amiably and helped me gladly. I had made many friendships, and I had come to the conclusion that frontiers and language difficulties must not be allowed to stand between the peoples. I had already experienced for myself that the brotherhood of men of goodwill was able to overcome all difficulties.

One day I read in the newspapers that the Indian Buddhists had invited the Dalai Lama to come to India to be present at the celebration of the 2,500th anniversary of the birth of Buddha, and I immediately determined not to let this opportunity slip by of meeting my brother on neutral territory, so I began to pull every possible string to be able to go to India and join him there during his visit. Unfortunately I was soon disappointed to learn that the Dalai Lama had rejected the invitation—allegedly because he was overworked, and also on account of the climate, which would be detrimental to his health. I realised at once that these were not the real reasons for his refusal, and I began to be increasingly anxious about his fate and that of the other members of my family who had remained in Lhasa with him.

Despite this report that the Dalai Lama had been unable to accept the invitation of the Indian Buddhists, I continued the preparations for my journey, and in the autumn of 1956 I took the plane from New York. This time I made the journey in short

stages, because I wanted to see my old friends in Europe again
and at the same time to establish new contacts. I was warmly
welcomed in Britain, Holland, France, Italy and Switzerland,
where I made friends with many new people and got in touch
with a number of institutions whose assistance would prove invaluable in the future. I was particularly impressed by a motor
tour I made through Switzerland, whose mountains and mountain villages aroused melancholy recollections of my happy youth
in Tengtser.

I was met at the airport in Calcutta by Gyalo Döndrub's
wife, who gave me the good news that my mother was on her
way to India with Tsering Dröma and Püntso Trashi. My
brother had already gone off to meet them and escort them back
to Kalimpong. The very next day we set off northwards, and the
meeting with my mother after such a long parting was a great
joy to us both.

As they had travelled without any Chinese companions we
were able to talk to each other quite frankly. I learned that the
Chinese in Lhasa were behaving discreetly so far, but that conditions in Amdo had grown even worse. My mother had accompanied the Dalai Lama on a visit to Kumbum, and she had taken
advantage of her stay there to visit Tengtser and Balangtsa. Only
eight hundred monks were left in Kumbum, and they were living
a wretched and indigent life, not knowing what was going to
happen to them. Many of our relatives and friends in Tengtser
and Balangtsa had been deported or had lost their lives in the
disturbances of the past few years. And the only answer those
who were left would give to all inquiries as to their well-being
was: "Thanks to the great goodness of Mao Tse-tung we are
now living in peace." But their sad eyes, their sunken cheeks,
their dilapidated houses and the poor state of the cattle were
evidence enough that this was a lie learned by rote. My mother's
voice threatened to break down again and again as she told me
about her experiences in our old home.

Whilst we were enjoying our meeting and the happiness of
being together again, there were constant rumours that the

Dalai Lama would come to India after all. My mother and the others regarded it as very unlikely that he would be allowed to cross the frontier into India, but in the end it was reliably confirmed that he was actually coming, together with the Panchen Lama, to be present at the celebration of the great Buddhist anniversary. At that we were jubilant, and Gyalo Döndrub and I immediately organised a small caravan and set off to the frontier to meet him. We took up our quarters in a bungalow on Lake Tsongo beneath the Natu Pass, and there we waited for him with as much patience as we could muster. It was already late in the year and heavy falls of snow were making progress difficult.

At last, late one evening, we heard the bells of a large caravan coming down from the pass, and despite the heavy fall of snow we hurried up to meet it. Before long advance scouts loomed up out of the mist and informed us joyfully that the Dalai Lama was not far behind. We pressed on, passing pack animals and soldiers of the bodyguard on specially picked horses, and before long we met the larger group of the Dalai Lama's immediate retinue. The Dalai Lama ordered the others to halt and he rode forward to greet us. We prostrated ourselves three times before him and then handed our katas to the High Chamberlain, who had dismounted. He then placed katas round our necks in return. Smilingly the Dalai Lama watched the little ceremony, welcomed us with a few friendly words, and then gave the signal for the caravan to go forward again. Lobsang Samten and little Ngari Rimpoche, who was now ten years old, rode by our side, and the questions and the answers did not cease until we reached the bungalow where the Dalai Lama was to stay for the night.

After our brothers had recuperated from the fatigues of the journey, the High Chamberlain appeared and led us to the Dalai Lama, and for the first time in our lives we five brothers were assembled round the same table. It was a solemn moment, but then once again the questions and answers started up on all sides, for there was a tremendous amount to tell. A cheerful blaze burned in the fireplace, and the abbots whose task

it was to wait on the Dalai Lama kept us regularly supplied with
fresh tea and cakes. At the wish of the Dalai Lama we were
spending the whole evening together. The Chinese escort remained discreetly in the background, and we were left to enjoy
our meeting. For my part I was particularly happy to be able to
tell the Dalai Lama and my other brothers that the outside world
was deeply interested in the fate of Tibet, and that everywhere I
had encountered friendliness and been afforded willing help.
It was already midnight when the Dalai Lama rose, and the rest
of us retired. Gyalo Döndrub and I had a tent between us, and
neither of us found it easy to drop off, though we were certainly
tired—the flood of thoughts and memories this meeting had
aroused was too turbulent to allow us to go off to sleep easily.

After a cold night during which a great deal of snow fell we
went down into Gangtok where we found the whole town on its
feet to welcome the distinguished guest. The eager crowds held
katas in their hands, and as soon as the Dalai Lama came in
sight they threw themselves to the ground and prayed. The
monks of the small monastery in the neighbourhood blew
mightily on their instruments, and a police band played the
Tibetan and Indian national anthems. The Maharajah of Sikkim
and his whole family, and official representatives of the Indian
Government, escorted their guests to the great palace in which
we were given quarters, though the Dalai Lama himself stayed in
the guest quarters of a temple with the friendly and familiar name
of Tsuglagkhang, which is the same as that of the famous temple
in Lhasa.

Two days later we drove south in a column of motor-cars.
Whenever we passed through inhabited places the people turned
out in masses to line the streets to welcome the Dalai Lama. In
fact very often we found it difficult to thread our way through
the packed crowds in the streets of the villages and towns through
which we passed. Although the police were always there to keep
order they were very often unable to control the joyful enthusiasm
of the people, who were all in their best clothes. Innumerable
katas were tossed at the car of the Dalai Lama, who sat there

saluting left and right as he passed. Three planes were waiting on the airfield at Bagdogra to carry the Dalai Lama and his party to New Delhi, and accompanied by Ngari Rimpoche and Gyalo Döndrub I flew from Calcutta to the Indian capital by the normal air line.

The distinguished guest had a very full programme to carry out whilst he was in India, and he hurried from holy place to holy place and from reception to reception, visiting many factories and government institutions in between. Everywhere he appeared he was welcomed by great masses of enthusiastic people who had often waited hours for his coming.

Gyalo Döndrub and I attended almost all of the official receptions, and at one of them we met Chou En-lai. He had, it appeared, expressed a wish to the Dalai Lama to make our acquaintance, and although our brother left it entirely to us whether we should meet China's Foreign Minister or not, we decided that we could not very well refuse. Our meeting with one of the most powerful men in communist China made a deep impression on me, and the man's personality was outstanding even in the illustrious gathering which was present that day. Shortly before, the Indian Premier Nehru had engaged me in a friendly conversation, and I had an opportunity of telling him of my experiences during the past few years. Chou En-lai then came up to us with marked affability, and his whole bearing exuded the proverbial politeness of the highly cultured Chinese of the old school. He behaved himself in a very conciliatory fashion and his soft voice positively caressed the ear. Altogether his distinguished appearance and his very real charm were fascinating. As we expected, all he was interested in was to persuade Gyalo Döndrub and me to return to Lhasa; if we did this now we should thereby repair all the damage we had done in the past to the good relationship between Lhasa and Pekin, and at the same time we should be assured of his full support. When he noticed that he was not making much progress and that we showed no inclination to allow ourselves to be persuaded, he declared that a reception of this kind was not altogether the best atmosphere for discussing such important matters properly, and he therefore invited us to come and see him in the Chinese Embassy to continue the discussion.

We met him the next day in the presence of the Red General Ho Lün and Li Kotrang, the official interpreter, attached to the Dalai Lama's retinue. We put our case very frankly indeed. Chou En-lai wanted to know the reasons for our refusal to return, and so we gave them to him, one by one. We pointed out that communist China had not honoured the terms of the agreement which had been signed five years previously between Lhasa and Pekin; and we quoted examples of Chinese behaviour obviously directed towards bringing about the final dissolution of Tibet as an independent State. We blamed the Chinese invaders for the shortage of foodstuffs, the rising prices, and the expropriation without compensation of land to build the strategic roads. We also complained that the powers of the Dalai Lama had been restricted and that our religion had been persecuted; and in support of this latter contention I described my own disagreeable experiences as Abbot of Kumbum. In conclusion we declared that we could only conclude from all this that the Chinese communists were deliberately out to destroy everything that was holy and dear to us.

When I had finished what I had to say and looked around at the silent circle of long faces I was a little shocked at my own temerity, but when Chou En-lai began to answer me his face was all smiles again, and his voice was as unctuous as ever. In fact there was no sign at all that my brutally frank words had upset him in the least. He began by saying that we should not allow the mistakes and misunderstandings which were unavoidable at the beginning of any great new undertaking to prevent us from appreciating China's good intentions. It was the sincerest wish of the Chinese People's Republic to improve the conditions of life in Tibet, and to bring its people to share fully in the ceaseless tide of progress. Without any change in his voice he then declared that the Dalai Lama had a most important part to play in the fulfilment of these great plans, and that therefore his speedy return to Lhasa was essential. All we could say in reply to this was that we had no knowledge of the intentions of the Dalai Lama, but that as far as we were concerned we had chosen to live in freedom. We parted from Chou En-lai on terms of the greatest politeness, and the same day he flew back to China.

When his official obligations had been fulfilled the Dalai Lama invited us all to stay with him for a few days in a hotel in Calcutta, so that once again the family was united for a while. When my mother made tea for her assembled brood in the old familiar way it seemed to me almost that the rather dull and typical hotel room began to look like our old kitchen in Tengtser. We older ones reminisced, and told the younger ones, the little brothers and sister, and the nephews and nieces and cousins, of the happy days we had spent in the uplands of Amdo as children. And later on in the evening, when they had gone to bed, we talked with the Dalai Lama and my mother of the future outlook, and I did not conceal my opinion that their days in Tibet were numbered too. But I could see quite clearly that in the existing circumstances there was no question of his not returning to Lhasa, for my brother could not and would not leave his country and his people in the lurch, and he still felt that his presence there might help to prevent the worst.

The time for us to part came all too quickly. Gyalo Döndrub and I found it very difficult to reconcile ourselves to our brother's departure, particularly as our worst fears had been given substance during the past few weeks. In our hearts we wondered whether we should ever see him again. It seemed quite on the cards that he had been permitted to cross the Tibetan frontier for the last time before the final blows were launched to destroy the ancient Tibetan State. When in February 1957 the weather worsened so suddenly that the return journey had to be postponed for a whole ten days we were inclined to see the hand of Providence in it. However, the Dalai Lama himself gave no indication that he had changed his mind, and in order not to spoil the harmony of our last hours together we took good care to say nothing either. At least it was decided that on account of his weakened state after an operation Lobsang Samten should stay on in my mother's house in Kalimpong, to undertake the long journey to Lhasa with other members of the family only when the warmer weather came. After a while the weather did improve and then the Dalai Lama began the long journey home. Gyalo Döndrub and I accompanied him as far as the frontier, where his retinue, which had gone on ahead, was waiting for him. Once again, as at the time of his arrival months previously, there were heavy falls of snow. We made our final farewells at the foot of the Natu Pass, prostrated ourselves before him, and handed over our katas.

Sadly we returned to Kalimpong, where Lobsang Samten greatly surprised us by saying that he no longer felt himself capable of carrying the heavy burden of his office as Chikyab Khenpo, and that he therefore did not intend to return to Lhasa. For a long time he had played the role of mediator between the Dalai Lama and the Chinese, and this had required all his diplomatic skill and exhausted his strength. In this very thankless task he had succeeded in retaining the confidence of both sides, but now after his recent operation he felt himself too exhausted to continue in his burdensome office.

After considering the matter carefully from every angle he wrote a request to the Dalai Lama and the Tibetan Government to relieve him of his office. Our mother heard his decision with mixed feelings. On the one hand she had the deepest sympathy with him in his difficult position, and she quite realised that he must give up a burden he could no longer carry effectively, but on the other she was deeply worried at the idea that the Dalai Lama must now lose one of his most reliable collaborators. And, in addition, of course, she feared that Lobsang Samten's refusal to return to Lhasa would mean further unpleasantness and difficulties for the Dalai Lama with the Chinese. She bade a sad farewell to us all when Gyalo Döndrub and Lobsang Samten left to accompany me to Calcutta where I was to take the plane for New York.

I had promised Lobsang Samten that as soon as I was in the

United States again I would do everything possible to obtain permission for him to come there too; and, in fact, it was not long before I succeeded in securing an invitation for him from Georgetown University in Washington. It was at about this time too that I managed to fulfil a long-felt wish on my own behalf. For years I had wanted to visit the holy places in Thailand, Burma and Ceylon, and in 1958 an invitation to attend the World Buddhist Congress in Bangkok at last gave me the opportunity. On the way back I broke the journey in Calcutta and went off to Kalimpong to meet members of my family again. Gyalo Döndrub now told me of the increasing destitution and misery of the Tibetan fugitives who were now crossing the Himalayas in increasing numbers in order to find that freedom which was impossible under communist rule. Their numbers were becoming so great that they were beginning to represent not only a very real economic problem, but also a political embarrassment to India. Private charity was no longer sufficient to meet even the barest needs of the fugitives, whilst at the same time the Indian Government, though sympathetic, feared, and understandably so, to do anything which would lead to international complications and Chinese diplomatic protests. In the circumstances therefore the urgently necessary assistance must come from elsewhere.

On hearing this I decided at once what I must do. It looked to me as though all those years in which I had travelled about the world so much and made so many valuable contacts were now to find their true significance and usefulness as a means of organising the assistance required by my unfortunate fellow Tibetans who had been driven from their homes and their country by communist oppression. I now flew back to New York, stopping on the way in Europe; and in both continents I approached various powerful institutions and welfare organisations and got them to make a start with the provision of organised assistance for the Tibetan refugees. It was not long after that before I received the news that the first consignments of tents, blankets and tinned foodstuffs sent off by the World Church Services had arrived in India and were being distributed among the refugees. From Seattle, where I had accepted the offer of a position in the Far Eastern Institute, I now organised further relief measures. I found willing helpers almost everywhere, and it was a source of great satisfaction to me that I was in a position to further the great cause with both advice and practical action.

21. The Price of Liberty

ONE Friday evening in March 1959 I was in the small kitchen of my New York apartment just preparing myself a soup according to a typical Tibetan recipe, and at the same time listening to the news on the wireless when the announcer reported that an insurrection had broken out in Tibet. I forgot my soup now and listened eagerly to the calm and unhurried voice of the news reader as it told of violent disturbances in Lhasa. A vast concourse of people had surrounded the Summer Palace in order to prevent the Chinese communists from seizing the Dalai Lama. Another great crowd, consisting chiefly of women, had marched to the Indian Embassy to ask for help for the Dalai Lama. I stood there with my mind in a whirl. What I had most feared for many years had come about at last. I knew already that during the past few weeks the situation in Tibet had become critical. The Chinese communists had demanded that the Dalai Lama should go to Pekin, and the Tibetan National Assembly had rejected the demand. Had the Chinese communists now tried to kidnap the secular ruler of Tibet and the spiritual head of Tibetan Buddhism?

I rang up Lobsang Samten, who was in Washington. He too was tremendously exercised at the news and he promised to come to New York at once, that very evening. I then telephoned various friends but I hardly knew what to say in reply to their consoling words. Some of them invited me to stay the night with them, but I refused. I preferred to be on my own and sit by the wireless in order not to miss a single bulletin. At about midnight the newsboys began to shout special editions of the newspapers in the streets, and I rushed out and bought every newspaper I could get hold of in the hope of obtaining further news, but although I studied them from cover to cover they contained no more than I had already heard on the wireless.

What was going to happen now? The lives of my relatives were obviously in the greatest danger. Would they be able to escape? The Dalai Lama, I knew, was young, vigorous and in good health, he would be quite capable of the fatigues of any journey. On the other hand, the Chinese would clearly move heaven and earth to prevent his escape. Was he even still at liberty? My mother was already sixty years old, and Ngari Rimpoche, who was studying in Drebung now, was still a child. All in all, I was worried by the most disagreeable imaginings and there was no question of sleep for me that night.

Lobsang Samten arrived at last, and we did our best to console each other, but I think we merely succeeded in communicating our particular fears to each other. The following morning we were at the offices of the World Church Services waiting impatiently for the staff to arrive. Here, too, we met with encouraging words, coupled with exhortations to be patient; and we were asked for detailed information about conditions in Tibet, and in particular about the topography of Lhasa, for the use of the Press.

For days we were swayed this way and that by hopes and fears, but even worse than the tormenting uncertainty was the feeling of helplessness, the inability to do anything at all to influence events. Döndrub Gyantsen had got leave from the aircraft works in which he was employed in order to join me in New York, and the son of a Tibetan official Shakapa was also with us, so we took it in turns to listen to the wireless bulletins. Unfortunately the news was sparse, vague and sometimes even contradictory. We could not make out for certain whether the Dalai Lama had fled or not. The Chinese were reported to be using parachute troops. But where, and what for? Had our brother fled to the mountains, and were they pursuing him there? A report from Chinese sources declared that the Dalai Lama had been captured by his own people. That was, of course, rubbish on the face of it, because no Tibetan would dare to lay hands on the sacred person of the Dalai Lama. Another report declared that he had fled on horseback but that he had fallen from the saddle and seriously injured himself. Did that mean that he was unable to continue his flight, or was the whole report false? But at last the great news came—and from a Chinese source too! The Dalai Lama had succeeded in making his way over the frontier into Indian territory. However, if that were so, how did it come about that the Indian stations were silent on the point?

One morning when I arrived at one of the many wireless broadcasting stations to be interviewed a reliable report came through that the Dalai Lama was safe on Indian soil with the members of his family and a retinue of ninety-five Tibetans. Radiant with joy I hurried home with the great news, and we drafted a telegram of congratulations and at the same time promised to come ourselves as soon as we were able, and this we sent off via Gyalo Döndrub. However, it didn't prove all that easy for us to go, and in the end I had to fly alone. I arrived in Tokio at the end of May, and immediately got in touch with those circles which were trying to organise international support for the Tibetan cause. The Japanese Buddhists were the first to demand assistance and independence for Tibet, and to organise a Tibet Convention.

A few days later Gyalo Döndrub met me at the airfield in New Delhi, and from there we set off immediately in a motorcar for Mussoorie. We arrived there at three o'clock in the morning, but found ourselves unable to enter the town because of a road block which the Indian authorities had erected to keep out undesirable elements. The instructions of the guards were so strict on the point that despite everything we could do and say we were kept there kicking our heels for over four hours before permission at last came through to allow us to pass. Once in the town we went straight to the Savoy Hotel, where we were informed that on this day, as on every Thursday, the Dalai Lama would be holding an audience.

On the way to Birla House, which was his temporary residence in Mussoorie we overtook many pilgrims in their best clothes all making their way to the audience; and the closer we came to Birla House the bigger the crowds grew until in the end they were so dense that we had to leave the car and make our way forward on foot. We were met in the garden of Birla House by Ngari Rimpoche who ran up to us excitedly and embraced us warmly. He then accompanied us indoors where the Dalai Lama was waiting for us on the staircase to take us straight into his private apartments. I was about to prostrate myself before him, as I had always been accustomed to do, and to present the usual kata, when with a gesture of the hand he indicated that I should not do so here. Wordlessly he pointed to a thanka with the picture of Sangye Chömdende Buddha; and deeply moved I lay my good-luck scarf over it. Henceforth our reverential greetings were to honour the gods alone; from now on the Dalai Lama regarded himself only as the first fugitive amongst his oppressed people.

We sat down, butter-tea was brought in, and my brother began to tell us about his flight. A highly suspicious demand on the part of the Chinese had provoked the insurrection. Against all protocol the Dalai Lama had been asked to present himself at the head-quarters of the Chinese forces, without an escort and as incon-spicuously as possible. The members of the Cabinet had strongly advised the Dalai Lama not to go and he had remained in the Norbu Lingka. Young Ngari Rimpoche, who was still studying in Drebung Monastery, had received a somewhat similar invita-tion. The lad had been told that he was to meet his brother the Dalai Lama there so he had hurried off from Drebung. For-tunately, after a few hours' vain wait, they had released him and he had then gone to his mother's house.

The news of this strange invitation to the Dalai Lama had spread throughout the town like wildfire, and before long thou-sands of anxious and indignant people had gathered round the summer residence, the Norbu Lingka. The crowds were above all anxious to prevent the Dalai Lama from leaving the protection of its fortress-like walls. In the meantime the Dalai Lama had

sent for my mother and Ngari Rimpoche to join him in the
Norbu Lingka. They just managed to do so before the Chinese
closed all means of ingress. As the crowds refused to disperse
and remained patiently waiting, the Chinese opened fire. My
relatives escaped through a side door disguised as servants and
made their way along a path leading to Kyichu. After an adven-
turous flight they finally managed to reach safety over the
Indian border.

I would gladly have learned more, but the time for the audience
had now arrived, and the High Chamberlain came in and asked
the Dalai Lama to show himself to the crowds which were
gathered in front of the house. We parted now and I went to my
mother's room. She was standing at the window and looking out
at the crowds which had gathered down below to pay their
respects to her son, the Dalai Lama. Silently I went to her side
and she took my hand. Looking out above the heads of the crowds
across the beautiful landscape I saw the snow-capped peaks of
the Himalayas in the distance. Beyond them lay my unfortunate
country. My mother was the first to break the silence:

"Jigmela," she said, in a low voice, using my childhood name
for the first time for many years. "Jigmela, from now on we are
refugees too."

I led her back into the room and sat down beside her. The
consoling words I wanted to say did not come so easily. Yes, of
course, we were all in safety; and we could rely on a certain
amount of assistance, but we had lost our country. The enemies
of our religion and our way of life had the upper hand there now,
and they were intent on destroying everything that we held dear.
Our people were forced to bow their backs to the oppressors, and
those who refused to do so, lost their lives, or were carried off to
forced labour. How many of our friends had already suffered so
harsh a fate! Many of them had been killed, and others had
disappeared never to be heard of again. And those few of whom
we had received news during the past few months were living
in great distress and under terrible conditions. For example,
my old and revered teacher Minyag Rimpoche had been carried

off with many others to break stones for the new roads our oppressors were building.

Before long I was called for by my brother again. He had heard with great joy that I had made it my business to organise help for the Tibetan refugees, and now he questioned me in detail concerning the measures which had been taken abroad to alleviate the sad lot of these unfortunates. When he had listened to what I had to say he expressed his gratitude to all those many unknown people all over the world who had come forward to help us in our misfortunes.

In the following weeks, at the instructions of the Dalai Lama, I visited the refugee camps in Northern India. Many thousands of our fellow countrymen were being looked after there. I made a detailed report when I returned, and then we worked out further measures to secure assistance. With the official approval of the Dalai Lama I was now to continue the work I had begun, and call upon the world to afford us continued support. The situation was urgent. There was unfortunately every reason to suppose that the stream of fugitives would increase; and, in particular, it was to be feared that in consequence the Indian Government would find itself in political difficulties.

So once again I set out on my travels, but this time it was not so painful to part from my nearest and dearest because I knew that they were all in safety and that I should soon see them all again. As my plane winged its way towards the West I looked back for a long time at the peaks of the Himalayas, the throne of our gods, the gods of my lost country Tibet.